New Ways of Using Computers in Language Teaching

Tim Boswood, Editor

New Ways in TESOL Series II
Innovative Classroom Techniques
Jack C. Richards, Series Editor

Teachers of English to Speakers of Other Languages, Inc.

Typeset in Garamond Book, Tiffany Demi and Rockwell
by Capitol Communication Systems, Inc., Crofton, Maryland USA
and printed by
Pantagraph Printing, Bloomington, Illinois USA

Teachers of English to Speakers of Other Languages, Inc. (TESOL)
1600 Cameron Street, Suite 300
Alexandria, VA 22314 USA
Tel 703-836-0774 • Fax 703-836-7864 • e-mail: publ@tesol.edu • http://www.tesol.edu

Director of Communications and Marketing: Helen Kornblum
Managing Editor: Marilyn Kupetz
Copy Editor: Ellen F. Garshick
Cover Design: Ann Kammerer

TESOL thanks Inaam Mansoor, Daniel Norton, the staff, and the students of the Arlington Education and Employment Program (REEP), in Arlington, Virginia, for their participation and assistance.

ISBN 0-939-791-69-2
Library of Congress Catalogue No. 96-061904

Contents

Acknowledgments

This book could not have been written without the technology that it espouses. E-mail links with authors and editors, access to ESL World Wide Web sites, and text and graphics processors have all played their part. My thanks are due to all the teachers whose enthusiasm about the new media spurred them to find the time to share their ideas and expertise in this book. Special appreciation is due to the authors of the Getting Started pieces and Contributor's Notes. I also thank the organizers and members of *TESLCA-L* for the wealth of practical and theoretical ideas shared in that forum. To the editing staff at TESOL, especially Managing Editor Marilyn Kupetz and copy editor Ellen Garshick, my admiration for their professionalism and understanding.

Introduction

It is a truism in the language teaching field that people learn a language by using it. People learn to communicate by communicating, and this collection reflects how teachers are currently exploiting the potential of new channels of communication to help others develop their language and communication skills.

One thing, however, is certain. By the time this book reaches you, the so-called cutting edge of computer technology will certainly have moved beyond the scenes described by the contributors to these pages. Equally certain is the fact that 99% of language teachers do not have access to cutting-edge technology. Worldwide, the number of language teaching institutions with very basic computer installations or none at all considerably exceeds the number with sophisticated multimedia computer labs.

These two facts raise a problem for anyone writing (or reading) about new technology and its educational uses. If the ideas presented rely on use of the latest technical developments, they risk being beyond the reach of most teachers. Yet the purpose of this volume is to illustrate the full potential of the new media in our field. I have adopted four strategies to deal with this problem:

1. Teachers who are working in all kinds of situations have contributed activities that involve computers in language development. Some of these activities require sophisticated installations, but the majority do not. They can be implemented with quite minimal setups, some even with a single, slow computer with a monochrome monitor.

2. The focus is on pedagogy, not technology. The activities included here were chosen because they implement sound learning strategies, not just because they use the latest technology. The basic purpose of this collection is to present good teaching plans—practical, productive ideas for using the tools available—that will outlast specific technical configurations.

3. The activities will not generally require you to go out and buy specific, teaching-oriented software packages. Instead, they present ways of making use of the software that you are likely to find on any workplace computer system: word-processing, Web browser, database, spreadsheet, and page-layout programs. This is not, therefore, a book about computer-assisted language learning (CALL) in the classic sense of using purpose-written CALL software. It is a book about how to use generic software packages for teaching purposes.

4. The book includes Getting Started activities and Contributor's Notes written by experienced practitioners in the field. These are specially devised to help newcomers orient themselves to the basic concepts in an area and get productive quickly. The Getting Started activities will help make this collection accessible to the many teachers for whom working with computers is a novel, exciting, but in some respects challenging development of their professional skills.

The rest of this introduction gives a brief survey of the kinds of activities that teachers are using and that can be found in this book.

The Activities

The range of computer applications is staggering, from the straightforward use of word-processing software for writing assignments through international e-mail projects, World Wide Web research assignments, class Web sites and on-line magazines, game playing with CDROMs, concordancing, and audiosignal processing for ear training and pronunciation practice. The activities in this volume are organized into sections according to the major software used and, within the sections, from simple to complex.

Part I, Word Processing and Desktop Publishing, contains activities that make use of the features of word-processing and desktop publishing programs to help students develop their skills in conceptualizing, drafting, and editing written work.

Part II, Getting Connected: E-Mail and MOOs, explains how to use the medium of electronic communication to engage students and teachers in collaborative learning activities both within and outside their institutions.

Part III, Working With the Web, covers what is without a doubt the big growth industry in CALL. The activities tap Web sites as sources of facts for data definition, search, gathering, and organization, and opinions for argument. In other activities students act as information providers by setting up Web sites and contributing their work to on-line collections.

The activities in Part IV, The Multimedia Machine, make use of two very different kinds of software that take advantage of the sound and video technology incorporated into most personal computers. The first group of activities shows how to incorporate "edutainment" and reference software into teaching activities, and the second explores the use of sound technology to teach pronunciation.

Part V, Concordancing, shows how to use concordancers, the programs that analyze text corpora, to inform the design of worksheets, provide comparative data about students' writing and target models, and even hand over to students.

All in all, it would be hard to think of a computer application that cannot be turned to the use of language teaching. Part VI, Other Applications, contains activities using database software, spreadsheets as data sources for writing about statistics and interpreting graphic data representations, HyperCard in game activities, and other creative uses of software for language learning.

On-Line Resources

Teachers have not been slow in establishing resources on-line to support others moving into these areas and to aid in networking among professionals with similar interests. An Internet search on the term *ESL* generates hundreds of sites, including on-line databases, individual Web sites containing materials, and discussion lists.

One of the best and longest established ESL databases is the *Computer Enhanced Language Instruction Archive* (*CELIA*), maintained at La Trobe University in Australia. This site contains shareware and freeware for IBM-compatible computers running DOS and Windows and for Macintosh computers, mostly collected by TESOL's software librarians. The site is subdivided into directories holding programs for games, listening, grammar, and other subject areas. The easiest way to access *CELIA* is through your Web browser at ftp://ftp.latrobe.edu.au or http://www.latrobe.edu.au/

www/celia/celia.html. Further language-related sites can be accessed from the excellent collection at the University of Sussex (UK) Language Centre's Web site (http://www.sussex.ac.uk/langc/welcome.html).

Finally, any teacher interested in computer applications in ESL should join one or more on-line discussion groups, such as *TESLCA-L* or *NETEACH-L* (see Getting Started on the World Wide Web for instructions on joining these lists).

Clearly, the wave of digital information processing is at last reaching critical mass in the educational professions. Stevens (1995), who has contributed to this collection, writes that this revolution affects "not only teachers but professionals of any stripe seeking to maintain their skills and competitive edge in a world that is coming more and more to exploit the potential inherent in digital technologies." Concerning the decision to jump on board the computer bandwagon, he goes on to say, "I don't think the question for most serious professionals is whether, but when and how to go about it."

I agree that it's not whether but when, and when is preferably now. This book will help make that leap an easier one.

A Warning

Web sites come and go with frightening speed. All the addresses mentioned in these pages were checked soon before this book went to press, but some will certainly have changed or disappeared by the time you try to reach them. I apologize for this inevitable consequence of the rapid development of the virtual world.

References

Computer Enhanced Language Instruction Archive (CELIA) [On-line]. Available: ftp://ftp.archive.latrobe.edu.au/pub/CELIA; http://www.latrobe.edu.au/www/celia/celia.html; gopher://gopher.latrobe.edu/Information Technology Services/La Trobe Archive/pub/CELIA

Stevens, V. (Usecpi@aol.com). (1995, November 30). Opinions wanted. *TESLCA-L* [On-line]. Available E-mail: teslca-l@cunyvm.cuny.edu

Welcome to the University of Sussex Language Center [On-line]. (1997). Available: http://www.sussex.ac.uk/langc/welcome.html

Users' Guide to Activities

Part II: Getting Connected: E-Mail and MOOs

Conferencing

Partner Classes and Keypals

MOOs

Part III: Working With the Web

Part IV: The Multimedia Machine

CD-ROM "Edutainment" and Reference Software

Abbreviations

ASCII	American Standard for Computer Information Interchange
CALL	computer-assisted language learning
CD-ROM	compact disk read-only memory
DOS	disk operating system
DTP	desktop publishing
e-zine	electronic magazine
FAQ	frequently asked question
FTP	file transfer protocol
HTML	hypertext markup language
keypal	e-mail pen pal
KWIC	key word in context
LAN	local area network
MOO	MUDs, object-oriented
MS-DOS	Microsoft Disk Operating System
MUD	multiuser dimension, multiuser domain, multiuser dungeon
RTF	rich text format
URL	uniform resource locator
WWW	World Wide Web

Part I: Word Processing and Desktop Publishing

Thuy Tien (Tina) Cash at the Arlington Education and Employment Program (REEP), Arlington, Virginia USA.

Editor's Note

The activities in Part I make use of word-processing and desktop publishing (DTP) software. These programs are far more than a digital substitute for paper and pen. Their impact on the conceptualization, drafting, and editing processes in writing is profound and has been researched in some detail (Pennington, 1996).

Composing and Editing

The activities in the first section familiarize students with word-processing programs and help students develop their writing and editing skills in various genres. Word-processing programs, just as they have given writers unprecedented flexibility in editing their work, give teachers a valuable tool in taking students through the writing process and teaching them how to edit. Activities focus on the use of word-processing features (such as cut-and-paste and find-and-replace) and the ability to save multiple drafts of a text to teach text reconstruction, encourage peer correction, develop vocabulary, and develop organizational skills in writing. The bundled add-ons of supporting software, such as thesauruses, spelling checkers, and grammar checkers, enhance students' flexibility in creating text and lend themselves to specific uses for language development.

Desktop Publishing

Dedicated DTP and page layout programs, such as PageMaker or Publisher, and the growing DTP capability of mainstream word-processing programs open up a new potential for low-cost print production integrating graphics with text. These programs allow students to produce sophisticated documents such as class magazines, leaflets, tourist guides, and other forms of institutional and corporate communication.

The Poem Processor

Word-processing programs have a special ability to encourage users to play with text, both in the choice of words and in the design of the text itself, the typography, and the layout. These capabilities are illustrated in The Poem Processor, a suite of activities that encourage students to write, arrange, and share different types of poetry with their teachers, classmates, and keypals.

References

Pagemaker (Version 6.0) [Computer software]. (1996). Seattle, WA: Adobe Systems.

Pennington, M. C. (1996). The way of the computer: Developing writing skills in an electronic environment. In S. Fotos (Ed.), *Multimedia language teaching* (pp. 93–113). San Francisco: Logos.

Publisher (Version 2.0) [Computer software]. (1995). Redmond, WA: Microsoft.

◆ Composing and Editing Word-Processing Mastery

Levels
High beginning +

Aims
Master word-processing skills

Class Time
One class period

Preparation Time
5–20 minutes

Resources
Computer for every one to two students
Word-processing software
Printer

This activity is designed to help students at all levels develop proficiency in word processing. In addition to manipulating text, students follow directions, make grammatical changes, and produce spontaneous writing. On the successful completion of this activity, most students will have acquired adequate word-processing skills for independent use.

Procedure

1. Before class, choose or prepare a text suited to the students' level of English. Prepare a set of instructions for typing in and working with the text in a word-processing program (see the Appendix).
2. Briefly review the word-processing skills addressed in this activity. Stress to the students the necessity of saving what they type.
3. Explain the directions for the activity.
4. Have the students type in the entire text in the word-processing program and make the indicated changes. Circulate among the students to offer help when necessary. Ask students who are already proficient in word processing to help beginners.

Caveats and Options

1. Show the students the essentials of word processing before embarking on this hands-on activity.
2. Choose the text and the changes to be made to reflect current classroom activities in content, grammar, and writing skills.

Appendix: Sample Text and Directions

(1) Tom Davis leads a very busy life. (2) His job as a computer consultant keeps him in his office from early in the morning to late at night. (3) It also takes him an hour to drive to work in his car and another hour to drive home again. (4) All day long, he meets clients, talks on the telephone, and works at his computer. (5) By the end of the day, he is exhausted and usually falls asleep in his chair while watching television. (6) However, when Saturday comes, Tom is a different man. (7) He gets up early, jogs around the lake near his apartment, then has a leisurely breakfast with his friend, Sam. (8) They usually go shopping in the afternoon, then go out to visit friends or eat in a restaurant. (9) On Sunday, Tom goes to visit his parents in a nearby town and goes for a walk in the country if the weather is good. (10) However, one day Tom doesn't come back from his walk . . . .

Directions:

1. Type in the text above using 12-point New York font. Save the text.
2. Give a title to the text. Center the title. Make it bold and in 14-point type.
3. Double space the text.
4. Change *Tom* to *Susan* throughout the text. Change pronouns if necessary.
5. Delete Sentence 5.
6. Put Sentence 4 before Sentence 3.
7. Make Sentence 6 the beginning of a new paragraph.
8. Write two sentences of your own after Sentence 10 to continue the story.
9. Add your name to the top right corner.
10. Use the spelling checker to check for any spelling errors.
11. Save your text.
12. Print out your text.

Contributor

Helen Huntley teaches ESL courses in the Department of Foreign Languages at West Virginia University, in the United States (e-mail: huntley@greene.pgh.net).

How Do You Use It?

Levels
Intermediate +

Aims
Present written
instructions clearly and
precisely
Identify the main points
of a specialized text
Learn software-related
lexical items

Class Time
2–3 hours over three
sessions

Preparation Time
About 45 minutes

Resources
Computer for every two
to three students
Two software programs
unfamiliar to some
students
Printer(s)

Many of the instructions for software packages are written in English. The instructions can present two major problems: They are not always very clearly written, and they use computer-related metalanguage. By the end of the three sessions of this activity, the students will have been introduced to and manipulated some basic computer metalanguage in the form of instructions for the use of a computer software package. At the same time, they practice their reading and writing skills while producing their instruction sheets and practice their listening and speaking skills during the group discussions.

Procedure

Before Class

1. Prepare an instruction sheet for each of the two software packages to serve as models for the students. The models should be simple and clear but sufficiently detailed for the students to be able to use the packages (see Appendix A for an example).

Session 1

1. Introduce the activity, perhaps by presenting and critiquing a poorly written instruction sheet.
2. Divide the students into two groups. Have the students in twos or threes within these groups use the model instruction sheet to learn to use one of the new software packages. Have computer-literate peers deal with any technical or computer-related language problems the students encounter (if possible), or do so yourself.

3. Ask the students to discuss guidelines for writing a clear instruction sheet. Focus the students' attention on
   ● the importance of clear, to-the-point instructions
   ● accuracy of grammar, spelling, and punctuation
   ● the structure of the text in terms of coherence and cohesion

Session 2

1. Referring to the guidelines discussed in Session 1 but without reference to the model instruction sheets, ask the students (in groups as above) to prepare an instruction sheet for their software package for the students who have been studying the other package (see Appendix B).
2. Have the students exchange computers and use the instruction sheet prepared by the other group to learn how to use the other software package.

Session 3

1. Ask the students to edit the instruction sheets, using the criteria from Session 1, and return them to the producers.
2. In two large groups (one for each package), have the students select the best version of their instructions from the drafts produced by the small groups.

Caveats and Options

1. The students need only basic word-processing skills for this activity. If they are more advanced, ask them to produce a "professional" instruction manual with visuals and other elements as part of the project.
2. Have the students exchange drafts in either disk or hard-copy format.
3. Because of the exploratory nature of the tasks, these sessions can provide the students with an introduction to the systems in a computer-based learning facility.
4. Do not choose software packages that are so complex that the students are unable either to understand what they are supposed to do or to express themselves clearly. Be sure that there is support to

help the students focus on the key program features to include in the instructions.

5. To increase motivation, use the completed instruction sheets for students who use the programs in the future.
6. Have the students take home the selected drafts from Session 3 to check and further improve them in preparation for final plenary feedback in Session 4.
7. If time is limited, ask the students to edit and change a poorly drafted sheet instead of writing instructions from scratch with the aid of the guidelines.
8. Because the sessions are very learner focused, limit your input to giving advice on language and computer problems and ensuring that the students are fully engaged in the activities.

References and Further Reading

Gapmaster [Computer software]. (n.d.). London: Wida Software/Euro-centres.

Storyboard [Computer software]. (n.d.). London: Wida Software/Euro-centres.

Appendix A: Sample Model Instruction Sheet

Using Storyboard

1. Type *SB* and press the <enter> key.
2. At the *Open a file* menu, choose one text by double-clicking the mouse on one text title.
3. Read the instruction screen and use the mouse to select one of the options at the bottom of the screen: *Hide all words* or *Show given words*.
4. On the next screen, you will see the text with black boxes in place of letters for each word. Look at the text and try to guess one of the words. Type your idea in the blue box at the bottom of the screen. If you have problems guessing, use the mouse to click on one of the options on the right of your screen: *Letter* will show you the first letter of the word, *Word* will give you the whole word, and *Hint* will sometimes give you some clues. Finally, when you have finished, click on *Text* to see the complete text and compare it with your ideas. To

exit from these options, click on the green square in the top left corner of the screen.

5. To exit from the program, select *Quit* from the *File* menu at the top of the screen.

Appendix B: Sample Instructions Written by Students

(uncorrected; low-intermediate level)

Using Gapmaster

1. Type "gm" and push the "enter" key.
2. At the "open a file" menu, choose one of the text by click the mouse.
3. Read the instruction carefully to use this program. Push the "explore mode" button below if you want immediate answer or push "exam mode" button if you want the answers at the end.
4. On the next screen, you will see the sentence with space and you have to type a correct word in the empty space—if you are not sure the word you can pres the "shape" button on the right hand side it gives you the numbers of the word. Or you can press "hint" it will let you know the first letter of the word. "answers" will tell you the complete word. Above these buttons, it has a square which will tell you a gap number and the word you type is correct or wrong.
5. When you have finished click the green button on the top corner of the left hands side. It comes out "Do you really want to stop?" then click on "Yes" to exit. Otherwise click NO to continue.

Contributor

Bruce Morrison is a lecturer and coordinates the Centre for Independent Language Learning at Hong Kong Polytechnic University.

Correct My Work, Please

Levels
Intermediate +

Aims
Learn to correct peers'
work
Learn independently

Class Time
30 minutes

Preparation Time
About 15 minutes

Resources
Computer for each
group of students
Word-processing
software
Printer(s)

Many teachers correct students' work by employing a correction code system or correcting the mistakes themselves. Getting students to reflect on these mistakes once the work is returned is still an area that needs to be addressed. This activity presents the concept of correction in an enjoyable and interesting way and focuses students on peer correction, a technique that is often difficult to promote.

Procedure

1. Decide which area of language to focus on (see Caveats and Options). Prepare a copy of an appropriate text on disk for each group of students. Give the groups the same text or different texts. Have each group copy their text onto the hard disk of the computer to ensure that the original text is not lost.
2. Ask the students to alter the text by making specific areas of language incorrect. For example, if you wish to focus on punctuation, ask the students to erase or alter the punctuation in the text.
3. Ask the students to save the altered text on the hard disk. Have them change places with another group of students and correct that group's altered text as much as possible.
4. Have the students return to their own computer to check the corrected version of their text. If there are any mistakes, have them print the text, and give it to the correcting group of students to check again.
5. Have the students decide on a method for showing the group where the mistakes are. You may find that their method reflects yours.

Caveats and Options

1. Have the students replace certain words or phrases with nonsense words as a way of focusing on vocabulary and the structure of words within a sentence (e.g., *Where do you google from?*).
2. To focus on the logical ordering of ideas in a text, have the students rearrange the format or organization of the text.
3. Encourage the students to enter their own text through a pretask activity (e.g., using visuals, discussion, or reconstruction of a text).

Contributor

Sue Fitzgerald is a lecturer in the English Language Study-Centre at Hong Kong Polytechnic University (e-mail: egsusan@hkpucc.polyu.edu.hk).

Introducing Text

Levels
Intermediate +

Aims
Learn the relationship
between a text and its
introduction

Class Time
45 minutes

Preparation Time
20 minutes

Resources
Computer for every
three students
Word-processing
software
Good piece of student
writing on disk
Printer

Introductions to student writing should preview the content and the organization of the text for the reader. Perhaps one reason some student writers are not good at writing introductions is that they are too familiar with their text. In this activity students reorganize and write introductions for pieces of text with which they are not familiar. This will encourage them to search the text for its organizational features and main points and prepare a good introduction. The reorganization and the collaborative drafting would be difficult to undertake without the use of word-processing software.

Procedure

1. Prepare the student text by
   - deleting the writer's name
   - deleting the introduction
   - moving all the section headings to a single list
   - jumbling the paragraphs

   Leave the conclusion clearly marked as such.
2. Talk to the class about the organizational features of a text and the way they should be reflected in the introduction.
3. Distribute the text to your class as a disk file. Ask the students to work in groups of three around a computer with word-processing software to reconstruct the text. They must
   - reorganize the paragraphs into the correct sections
   - write a new introduction
4. Encourage the students to experiment by reorganizing and redrafting as much as they want.
5. Remind the students to use the spelling checker if there is one.

6. When the task is completed, ask the students to print out their work.
7. In the next lesson ask the groups to swap printouts and comment on the accuracy of the reorganization and the quality of the introduction in each other's work.
8. Collect the printouts and the peer reviews so that you can assess the students' work and evaluate the success of this exercise.

Contributor

David Gardner is a senior language instructor in the English Centre of the University of Hong Kong (e-mail: dgardner@hkucc.hku.hk).

Find and Replace

Levels
Intermediate +

Aims
Develop vocabulary
Distinguish apparent
synonyms

Class Time
1 hour

Preparation Time
1 hour

Resources
Computer for each
student
Word-processing
software
Printer(s)
Scanner (optional)

True synonyms are rare in any language, and students in the course of learning new vocabulary find it difficult to decide between two apparent synonyms. This activity gives students a chance to feel the effect of changing one word into another in a text, to say for themselves which substitutions work and which do not, and possibly to learn why. Students can see the effects of the changes right on the computer screen with no messy rubbing or crossing out.

Procedure

1. Select or compose a text that contains pairs of words (Words A and B) that are synonymous and, in your experience, difficult for the students to choose between. The more often these words appear in the text, the better the text will serve the purpose.
2. Type the text into a word-processing program, or scan it into a word-processed file with the help of an optical character recognition program.
3. Distribute a hard copy of the text to each student, and have the students read the text to get a general understanding of it.
4. Give each student a disk copy of the word-processed file, or put the file on the network in advance so that the students can retrieve the file for use on their own machine.
5. Instruct the students to use the *find* or *find and replace* command of the word-processing software to replace Word A with Word B. Ask the students to take a little time to think about the substitution each time the software finds a word.
6. Ask the students to read the text again and decide which substitutions work well and which do not.
7. Divide the students into groups. Ask them to compare judgments.

8. Discuss with the whole class which substitutions work, which do not, and why. Explain as you go.
9. Repeat Steps 5–8 by substituting Word B with Word A.

Caveats and Options

1. If you feel it necessary, explain the two words briefly before asking the students to do the find-and-replace operation.
2. The students will usually be able to say which substitutions sound natural and which do not, though they may not be able to say why. Helping the students to know why actually means helping the students to draw their own conclusions about language patterns and grammar.
3. Carry out the activity as a game. A correct judgment made about the substitution scores a point, and the student with the most points wins the game.
4. If printing facilities are available, ask the students to print out the revised copies and read them on paper.

Contributor

Bruce Ka-Cheung Ma is a lecturer in English in the Division of Language Studies at the City University of Hong Kong (e-mail: lsbrusma@cityu.edu.hk).

Checking the Spelling Checker

Levels
Intermediate +

Aims
Learn the limits of a
computerized spelling
checker

Class Time
45 minutes

Preparation Time
30 minutes

Resources
Computer for every
three students
Word-processing
software with spelling
checker
Printer

Students who are familiar with word-processing software tend to rely heavily on built-in spelling checkers, leaving teachers to spend more profitably the time they would have spent on correcting typographical errors. However, spelling checkers are not really intelligent; they attempt to provide the correct word based on the pattern of the erroneous word. To overcome this failing, most spelling checkers offer a list of possible solutions. Student writers tend to accept the first word that spelling checkers offer without checking it for meaning, resulting in writing that is littered with perfectly spelled but erroneous words. This activity encourages the students to take a more critical look at what the spelling checker is doing to their texts.

Procedure

1. Write a short text in a word-processed file. Include in it words that the spelling checker will get wrong. A good way to start is by identifying out-of-place words in your students' writing. (See Appendix A for an example of how texts can be corrupted by bad spell checking.)
2. Distribute the file to groups of students, and ask them to run a spelling check and list in a table the words the spelling checker stops at, the first solution offered, and the solution they eventually select (see Appendix B).
3. When the groups have completed the task, ask them to swap lists with another group and evaluate each other's efforts.
4. Conduct a feedback session with the class to discover the full list of errors and solutions. Ask the class to suggest ways of avoiding the problem of "wrong" corrections.

Appendix A: How Texts Can Be Corrupted by Spelling Checkers

Original text with typing errors (to be given to students)

> While making the presentation we found that we had to sto using the comuter with the vesual display overlay. The cable we had brought with us was too sort, so we had to pjt the computer too close to the screen. This put an an impisable dimand on the audience because the text was too small to rad.

Text after the spelling checker has made its suggestions

> While making the presentation we found that we had to sot using the commuter whit the vessel display overlay. The cable we had brought with us was too sort, so we had to Pat the computer too close to the screen. This put an impassable diamond on the audience because the text was too small to ad.

What the writer actually wants the text to say [used as an answer sheet]

> While making the presentation we found that we had to stop using the computer with the visual display overlay. The cable we had brought with us was too short, so we had to put the computer too close to the screen. This put an impossible demand on the audience because the text was too small to read.

Appendix B: Table for Recording Findings

Checking the Spelling Checker		
Word the spelling checker stopped at	First solution offered	Solution you chose

Contributor

David Gardner is a senior language instructor in the English Centre of the University of Hong Kong (e-mail: dgardner@hkucc.hku.hk).

Thesaurus Testing

Levels
Intermediate +

Aims
Learn the limits of a
computerized thesaurus

Class Time
45 minutes

Preparation Time
20 minutes

Resources
Computer for every
three students
Word-processing
software with thesaurus
Printed dictionaries

Caveats and Options

S tudents who use a thesaurus in word-processing software are often not critical of its suggestions, perhaps because they believe that the machine must be right. This activity encourages students to test the quality of the responses they get from their thesaurus.

Procedure

1. Write a short text in a word-processed file. Underline about 10 words for which you would like the students to discover alternatives.
2. Add a table at the end of the file in which the students will record their findings (see the Appendix).
3. Distribute the file to the students and ask them to work in groups of three to do the following:
    ● list alternative words that they already know
    ● list alternative words suggested by the thesaurus (up to six words)
    ● check the dictionary to see whether these words are suitable for the context
4. Conduct a feedback session with the class to discuss the suitability of the thesaurus's suggestions.
5. Ask the class to decide whether they trust the thesaurus or not.

1. If you particularly want this activity to encourage the students to make more use of a thesaurus, choose words that will show its usefulness and accuracy.
2. If you particularly want to caution the students against trusting the thesaurus unquestioningly, choose words that show its failings.
3. If you want the students to give the thesaurus a fair trial, choose a fair variety of words.

Appendix

Thesaurus Testing				
Word	Alternatives you know	Suitable in this context? (Check the dictionary.)	Alternatives suggested by the thesaurus	Suitable in this context? (Check the dictionary.)

Contributor

David Gardner is a senior language instructor in the English Centre of the University of Hong Kong (e-mail: dgardner@bkucc.bku.bk).

Adjective Power Booster: Using the Thesaurus to Spice Up Writing

Levels
Low intermediate +

Aims
Avoid bland adjectives

Class Time
One class session

Preparation Time
20 minutes

Resources
Computer for every one
to two students
Word-processing
software with thesaurus
Paper thesaurus

In this activity students learn how to use the thesaurus in word-processing software. They apply it to their own writing to make it more interesting and descriptive and to extend their active and passive vocabulary.

Procedure

1. Before class, choose a text that contains many adjectives describing people or places and that could be improved in descriptive power. The text may be teacher written, student written, or textbook based. Highlight or underline the adjectives to be changed. Load the text into the computer to avoid taking up class time with typing.
2. In class, discuss the meaning of a thesaurus and demonstrate its use with a paper copy. Explain the advantages of using a thesaurus.
3. Demonstrate how the thesaurus on a computer works, and allow the students to practice by typing in several key words or phrases.
4. Instruct the students to open up the text file (or type it in) and use the thesaurus to replace each highlighted or underlined adjective with an appropriate synonym. Remind them that they may need to check the meaning and usage of the adjective before applying it.
5. Have the students print out the finished copy, and allow them to compare their adjectives with those chosen by their peers.
6. Ask the students to open up one of their own pieces of writing and improve it by using the thesaurus to vary their use of adjectives.

Caveats and Options

1. Make sure the students know the basics of word processing before attempting this activity.
2. Have the students replace adjectives with antonyms to change the meaning of the text.
3. Have the students use the thesaurus to find synonyms for other parts of speech in the text.

Appendix: Sample Text

(low intermediate)

It was a good day to go to the beach; the sky was clear and the temperature was reasonable. The Smiths decided to take advantage of this nice weather and packed up their beach gear before heading out for the ocean. The trip was long and boring for the three active children, but they finally arrived just as a bad wind started to blow. Fred Smith, the father, was annoyed at the unexpected change in the weather, but his pleasant wife, Alice, said that everything would be fine. The excited youngsters jumped out of the car and immediately wanted to swim in the blue water of the ocean. They put on their attractive new swimsuits and went down to the perfect sandy beach. Before long, it started to rain, and the bad weather forced everyone off the beach. The Smiths were so upset that they turned around and made the long trip back home again. Instead, they watched a great film together in the comfort of their own home.

Contributor

Helen Huntley teaches ESL courses in the Department of Foreign Languages at West Virginia University, in the United States (e-mail: huntley@greene.pgh.net).

Getting to Know You!

Levels
Low intermediate +

Aims
Break the ice at the start
of new classes
Write personal
information

Class Time
1–2 hours over two
sessions

Preparation Time
15 minutes before
Session 1
45 minutes between
Sessions 1 and 2

Resources
Computer for every two
to three students
Word-processing
software
Printer(s)
Scanner (optional)

Many teachers employ ice-breaking activities at the start of a new class. This activity adapts a classic introductory writing activity to computers. By the end of the sessions, each student will have a class album containing information about each class member, optionally with scanned photos as well. The students get an opportunity to meet their colleagues and to work together on a simple project while sharing some information about themselves. The teacher also gains a writing sample from each student.

Procedure

1. Compose a short (100- to 200-word) introductory statement about yourself, print it out, and prepare one hard copy for each student. This text will serve as a starting point for the students in preparing statements about themselves.
2. In Session 1, introduce the activity and present the information about yourself.
3. Group the students into pairs or threes, with each group having access to a computer.
4. Direct the students to compose (on the keyboard) an introductory statement for each group member and to save it on a disk. Instruct them to write not about themselves but about one other member of their group, which will require them to interview each other. Circulate, comment, and advise on the writing. Collect the students' disks.
5. Before Session 2, compile the statements into a single document, print it, and make one hard copy for each student in the class and for yourself. Information for a class of 20 fits easily on four sheets of paper.
6. Distribute the information in Session 2.

Caveats and Options

1. Because the students need only basic word-processing ability for this activity, it can serve as an introduction to the systems in a computer-based writing lab. If the students have more advanced ability (e.g., desktop publishing skills), have them assemble the document themselves and enhance the quality of the final product.
2. If you have access to a scanner, include a scanned photo on your own information sheet. Ask the students to bring in their own photos (for Session 1 if possible). Scan them and add them to the introductions.
3. Make sure no names or photos are included in the statements, and use them for an oral information-gap exercise in Session 2. Circulate the sheets, instruct the students to mix and, through introductions and conversation, to identify which statements describe which students. If appropriate, give a small prize to whoever finds the names of all the students first.
4. After reading the statements from their classmates, the students may want to revise or develop their own introductions. Incorporate the revised versions into a final document distributed at the next class.
5. Combine the variations above as follows:
   - Preparation: Compose your statement.
   - Session 1: Have the students draft their initial statements (with no names).
   - Preparation: Compile the statements into a single document.
   - Session 2: Conduct the information-gap oral exercise, have the students revise their statements, and collect the photos.
   - Preparation: Scan the photos and compile them with the revised statements into the final album.
   - Session 3: Distribute the album to the students.
6. Be aware that cultural values may restrict the willingness of some students to reveal personal information or to provide photographs to strangers.

Contributor

Tim Boswood works on the BA in English for Professional Communication at the City University of Hong Kong (e-mail: entim@cityu.edu.hk).

Refining Report Writing

Levels
Intermediate +

Aims
Organize, plan, and
write reports
Adopt a process
approach to writing
Develop autonomy in
learning

Class Time
45 minutes

Preparation Time
30 minutes

Resources
Computer for every two
students
Word-processing
software
Recommendation report
Feedback sheet

Students often find revising and editing their work a laborious process, especially if the written exercise is done with pen and paper. Even if the work is word processed, the feedback loses some of its impact as there is often a time lag between the first draft and subsequent revision. Students may benefit more from the process approach to writing if redrafting immediately follows the feedback. Pairing up the students stimulates communication not only with but around information systems (Little, 1996; Stevens, 1992). Little refers to interaction around computer-assisted language learning as learning conversations in which the processes of analysis, planning, and synthesis are made explicit.

Procedure

1. Divide the class in half. Give one half a recommendation report with the introduction section missing. Give the other half the same report with the conclusion and recommendation sections missing.
2. Put the students in pairs to complete either the introduction or conclusion and recommendation sections of the report.
3. When each pair of students has written their section of the report using context clues from the body of the report, have them change computers with another pair of students who have written a different section.
4. Ask each pair to compare the other pair's word-processed output on the screen with their model version of either the introduction or the conclusion and recommendation. Have each pair fill in the first column (Draft 1) of a feedback sheet that gives some pointers for editing (see the Appendix).
5. Have each pair redraft their section in light of the other pair's comments.

6. Have the students repeat Step 4, filling the column for Draft 2.
7. Repeat Step 4 to allow for further refinement of the report's introduction or conclusion and recommendation sections.
8. Ask each pair to compare their final version with that suggested in the report.
9. In the final roundup session, comment on acceptable and unacceptable alternatives to the model version.

Caveats and Options

1. Although the students are provided with a model report, warn them against being prescriptive and encourage them to use their judgment as to whether an alternative organizational pattern or item of vocabulary is acceptable or not. Circulate among the different pairs to deal with any queries the students bring up.
2. Make the activity more difficult by asking the students to come up with their own comments instead of giving them a guided feedback checklist.
3. For another reconstruction activity, give the students a job advertisement and the résumé of an applicant and ask them to compose the body of the letter.

References and Further Reading

Little, D. (1996). Freedom to learn and compulsion to interact: Promoting learner autonomy through the use of information systems and information technologies. In R. Pemberton, E. S. L. Li, W. W. F. Orr, & H. Pierson (Eds.), *Control: Autonomy in language learning* (pp. 203-218). Hong Kong: Hong Kong University Press.

Stevens, V. (1992). Humanism and CALL: A coming of age? In M. C. Pennington & V. Stevens (Eds.), *Computers in applied linguistics* (pp. 11-38). Clevedon, England: Multilingual Matters.

Appendix: Sample Feedback Sheet

Pointers	Draft 1 comments	Draft 2 comments
Content: Background information Terms of reference Purpose Procedure Scope		
Organization: Are the above points ordered in a logical, coherent manner?		
Language: Tenses (past for procedure) Formality (e.g., *discuss* vs. *talk about*) Collocation (e.g., *conduct a survey*, not *make a survey*)		

Contributors

Lynne Flowerdew is coordinator of a technical communication skills course at the Hong Kong University of Science and Technology (e-mail: lclynne@usthk.ust.hk). Pansy Lam teaches technical communication skills and business communication skills courses at the Hong Kong University of Science and Technology.

Flexible Text: Exploring Alternatives and Meaning

Levels
Low intermediate +

Aims
Perceive text as mutable
Explore alternative
renderings of text
View revisions as natural
and desirable

Class Time
2–3 hours over three
sessions

Preparation Time
None

Resources
Computer for each
student
Word-processing
software
Printer

Teachers recognize that good writing demands rewriting, but students tend to see the written word as final and unchangeable. This exercise presents an opportunity for students to realize that text is mutable by considering alternative ways of rendering text. In the process, they see how revisions shape and refine meaning, resulting in clearer and more effective writing.

Procedure

1. Before Session 1, ask the students to write a short essay (100–150 words) on any topic. This will serve as the text that each one will revise.

Session 1

1. Have the students type their essays, using the word-processing software. Ask them to divide the essay into constituent elements and to leave a double space between them. (Depending on the level of the students and the aspect of writing under focus, the elements could be sentences, clauses, or phrases.) At the end of class, have the students print two copies of this essay (one to hand in and one to take home).
2. Ask the students to write an alternative version for each element before the next class. The alternative version does not necessarily have to be better, just somewhat different.

Session 2

1. Have the students type in each alternative element beneath the original. To ease distinguishing between the two, ask them to indent the alternative version slightly from the original. Have the students

print two copies of this dual-version essay (one to hand in and one to take home).

2. Tell the students to choose between the alternatives, cutting one version of each element and saving the other. At the end of class, have the students print two copies of this final version of the essay (one to hand in and one to take home).

Session 3

1. Ask the students to write about the original version and the final, revised version, explaining why they think each selected alternative is the better of the two. At the end of class, have the students print this essay and hand it in.

Caveats and Options

1. The homework in this exercise is a concession to students who are slow at either typing or revising. With higher level students, do the entire activity in class (perhaps making the printing of a student copy at each stage unnecessary).

2. For a more focused exercise, select a text for revising—even to the extent of dividing it into its constituent elements for the students—and provide the text to the students on the computers. This option involves 1–3 hours of preparation.

3. Although many different aspects of writing suggest themselves for focus (conjunctions, modifiers, voice, register, or even punctuation, mechanics, and highlighting), focus on one aspect at a time for the sake of efficiency. Base your decision on the course's subject matter, the lesson's objectives, and the students' proficiencies.

4. Though an essay might lend itself to a variety of aspects for revision, be careful not to spend too much time on any one essay; the students' interest is likely to flag. The main goal is to encourage the concept of alternative renderings as an integral part of the writing process.

Contributor

Jay Lundelius is the area coordinator of English for professional communication in the English Language Teaching Unit at the Chinese University of Hong Kong (e-mail: jaylundelius@cuhk.edu.hk).

On-Screen Outlining for Reading Comprehension

Levels
Intermediate +

Aims
See the sequence and hierarchy of ideas in a text
Learn the benefits of discovering its organization

Class Time
45 minutes

Preparation Time
30 minutes

Resources
Computer for every two students
Word-processing software
Printer(s)
PC viewer (optional)

In this activity students practice outlining a text they have read using any word-processing software that allows a variety of font sizes. The computer activity has clear advantages over a similar paper-and-pencil exercise: ease of shuffling and reshuffling, of using different fonts and sizes for the different levels of the outline, of changing the outline after feedback from peers or teacher, and of printing and reprinting the outline.

Procedure

Before Class

1. Choose two texts. One will serve as an example in Step 6; the students will work with the other.
2. Prepare an outline of each text. Type the outlines into the word-processing program, scrambling the points within the outlines if you wish. Write an answer key for each outline.
3. Prepare disk copies of the outlines if necessary, or copy them onto the network server so they will be accessible to all students.

Session 1

1. Assign one of the texts for homework. Tell the students that they will be outlining the text and that they should therefore pay attention to the text's organization and main points.

Session 2

1. Have the students work in pairs.
2. Explain the activity and demonstrate how to unscramble the outline of the second text, using a PC viewer if one is available.

3. Ask the students to organize the outline for the homework text and to assign a heading or subheading category to each item.
4. Have the students compare their outline to the full text and discuss it with their partner.
5. Ask the students to revise their outline by promoting or demoting items (moving items up or down).
6. When they are satisfied with the outlines, let the students print them.

Follow-up

1. Have the students compare their outlines with those of other pairs.
2. Ask them to hand in their outlines or compare them with the answer key.

Caveats and Options

1. This activity was written to be used with Word but can be used with any word-processing software that has an outlining feature.
2. In a more advanced class, ask the students to prepare the outline of the text from scratch instead of providing the list yourself. Have them either write the items as a list and then proceed as in Session 2 above, or organize their list hierarchically from the beginning. Allow them to proceed according to their preferences.
3. Adapt the activity for a writing class:
   - To encourage the students to make an outline before they write a paper, show them a sample paper you have written, show them the outline, and explain how the outline helped you organize your thoughts and influenced the final product.
   - Ask them to type the main points they would like to deal with in their paper or composition, as well as any secondary points or details they would like to include. Explain that the sequence is not important at this point.
   - Once they have finished their list, tell them to organize it.
   - Have the students proceed as in Session 2 above.
   - Have the students use their outlines as titles and subtitles to guide them when they write.

References and Further Reading

Word (Version 6.0) [Computer software]. (1994). Redmond, WA: Microsoft.

Appendix: Sample Outline (Unscrambled)

I. Introduction: What are robots?

II. The history of robots
    important breakthroughs

III. Advantages and use of robots
    in medicine
    in industry
    in the police force
        to help the bomb squad
        to spy on people

IV. Problems

V. Conclusion: It seems that robots will become more sophisticated and yet cheaper. Housewives will use them to help them with their housework. More enterprises will purchase robots.

Contributor

Miriam Schcolnik is the director of the Language Learning Center and ESL course coordinator at Tel Aviv University, Israel. She has published books, course materials, and multimedia software (e-mail: smiriam @post.tau.ac.il).

WriteOn.hlp

Levels
High intermediate +

Aims
Write letters of
invitation
Learn how to accept
and decline an invitation

Class Time
1–2 hours

Preparation Time
30 minutes

Resources
Computer for every two
to three students
Windows word-
processing software
Printer(s)
Scanner (optional)

Writing a letter is a very complicated task that requires the students to demonstrate many previously learned language skills and related knowledge. When asked to write a letter, many students do not know how to begin. WriteOn.hlp is a teacher-created Windows help file that can reduce this immense load by providing the students with enough cues to write a good letter. It remains on-line with the students throughout the task, offering the students a quick way to find information. Like the topics in a Windows Help file, the topics in the WriteOn.hlp contain one or more jumps that the students can click (or select and press <enter>) to display a related topic. They can move, resize, maximize, or minimize the WriteOn.hlp window, just as they can any other window. At the end of the lesson, the students produce a professional-looking letter.

Procedure

1. Use word-processing software that can save a file in rich text format (*.rtf*). Many Windows programs can do this, including the Write program shipped with Windows 3.x.
2. Write a data file, just as you would an ordinary text file, that is a template containing relevant English patterns, key words and expressions, and a format for a letter of invitation.
3. Select the topics (e.g., layouts, salutations, openers) and certain lines of text. Add hidden codes to them that will enable these topics and text lines to become hypertext, in which a mouse click activates a link between the searched topic and its full details. (See the Windows 3.x help file and the books in References and Further Reading.)

4. Create a map file that tells the compiler what the topics in the *.rtf* file are and whether it contains pictures. Save it in text-only format with the extension *.prj*. If you are new to Windows help file construction, some time reading the relevant literature will show you how to write your own program with no difficulty (see References and Further Reading).

5. When the *.rtf* and *.prj* files are completed, compile them by using HC30.EXE or HC31.EXE, which can be found in the Windows directory. These two copyright-free compilers ship with Microsoft Windows 3.x and DOS 5.x and 6.x. Name the compiled file *WriteOn*. HC31.EXE will automatically give it the extension *.hlp*. Use the Windows File Manager to copy WriteOn.hlp to every system.

6. Group the students into twos or threes, with each group having access to a system. Run the Windows program. Use the File Manager to find WriteOn.hlp. Double-click on it, and start the word-processing software, too. The students will be able to move back and forth between the two programs and easily transfer all information in WriteOn.hlp to the word-processing software for editing.

7. Direct the students to compose a letter of invitation (on the keyboard). Ask them to
   - study the various topics available in WriteOn.hlp
   - copy the letter template from the program to their word-processing software
   - write their address and the date
   - select an appropriate salutation and paste it in their letter
   - make changes to names and specify the correct time and places
   - select other relevant patterns and expressions
   - compile all these statements into a proper letter
   - check the spelling and grammar
   - save the letter to a disk

8. Collect the disks. Back up the students' files and correct their work. Make one hard copy of the corrected work for each student in the class and for yourself. Ask the students to compare their original work in the backup file with the corrected one.

9. Ask the students to write a letter accepting or declining an invitation, following the same procedure.
10. Distribute the hard copies of the letters to the students for them to keep in their workbooks for future reference.

Caveats and Options

1. The students only need basic word-processing ability for this activity, and they usually find most Windows word-processing software easy to use. Teachers at Chulalongkorn University Language Institute in Thailand use CW for Windows, a shareware program created by the Engineering Faculty.
2. Conduct this activity in the self-access learning center or in a computer-based lab. Have students with more advanced ability (e.g., desktop publishing skills) help teach the inexperienced ones.
3. If you have access to a scanner, include some scanned pictures of letters and envelopes in WriteOn.hlp, or include a picture of the class in the program and allow the students to keep it to use whenever they want to write a letter of this type. Doing this ensures that the program will not be circulated in the computer software market.
4. Use a commercial compiler to help create WriteOn.hlp. Two are Doc-To-Help and RoboHelp (see References and Further Reading). A compiler automatically does the coding in the background as you create a text file and creates other files, such as the map file and the *.rtf* file.
5. If you wish, ask the students to read other students' work, make comments, and improve it.

References and Further Reading

Cameron, C. (1989). *Computer assisted language learning.* Worcester, England: Billing & Sons.

Doc-To-Help (Version 2.0) [Computer software]. (1996). New York: WexTech Systems.

Jennings, R. (1994). Creating help files for database applications. In *Database developer's guide with Visual Basic 3* (pp. 909–946). Indianapolis, IN: Sams.

Jones, C. (1987). *Using computers in the language classroom.* Essex, England: Longman.

RoboHelp 95 for WinHelp 4 (Revision A) [Computer software]. (1995). La Jolla, CA: Blue Sky Software.

Windows Write (Version 3.11) [Computer software]. (1993). Redmond, WA: Microsoft.

Contributor

Thiraboon (Terry) Somboontakerng is an English for science and technology lecturer at Chulalongkorn University Language Institute, Thailand (e-mail: fflntsb@chulkn.car.chula.ac.th).

◆ Desktop Publishing
Rebus Writing—Really!

Levels
High beginning +

Aims
Familiarize students
with simple graphics-
editing tools
Practice using two
applications
simultaneously
Have fun using English

Class Time
45–60 minutes

Preparation Time
15–20 minutes

Resources
Computers capable of
running two
applications
simultaneously
Word-processing and
graphics software
Clip-art files
Printer

The basic "Dear-Mom-and-Dad" (or "Dear-John") letter is much more lively when students substitute pictures for words. This activity is an enjoyable way for students to use their English language and computer skills creatively.

Procedure

1. Introduce the students to the basic graphics-editing tools that are available with your software.

   ● To do this quickly, lead the students through the tools one by one, demonstrating and allowing practice time on a sample image with each one.

   ● To go slightly more slowly but use a more interactive method, arrange the students in pairs and give them a handout containing a captured photo of the tool menu, with instructions to explore and identify the functions of each of the tools. Include or follow up with a matching list of the tools' exact names. Demonstrate how to "harvest" an image of choice and import it into the word-processing document. Have the students label their handout with notes as their discoveries unfold. This method works well with the students in pairs.

2. Suggest topic(s) to write about. Examples are *the summer of 19XX: A Letter Home*, *Dear John*, a description of a recent class event or field trip, and a "twisted" version of a fictitious or true tale.

3. Have the students open the word-processing and graphics applications. Show them how best to manipulate the two screens on their monitor so that they can easily switch back and forth between them

(the ease of doing so will vary with screen sizes and computer systems).

4. Have the students work either from a template or sample letter or in a completely original word-processing document to compose, print, and, if possible, mail a letter using partly text and partly imported images as substitutes for words.

Caveats and Options

1. To find clip art and graphics:

   - Look in multimedia and graphics software files that you already have (in ClarisWorks, Digital Chisel, HyperCard, Kid Pix, and other software programs) for clip art, art stacks, borders, templates, stamps, and other graphics that you can copy.

   - Obtain disks of inexpensive shareware clip art, which are inexpensive and easily available through retailers, catalogs, and shareware archives on the Internet.

   - Run a search on the Internet and download current freeware and shareware files from such sources as the alt.binaries.clip-art newsgroup archive; World Wide Web sites such as *Brad's Favorite Clip Art* (Stone, 1992), *Best of BCS Art* (Durst, n.d.), *CMU English Server* (Sauer, 1993), *Color Expressions* (Sterling, 1994), *Funet Collection* (1992), *Sandra's Clip Art Server* (Loosemore, n.d.), *Sunshine Sampler* (Durst, 1992), and *TAEX Clip Art Collection* (Texas Agricultural Extension, 1992); and file transfer protocol (FTP) sites such as the U.S. National Aeronautics and Space Administration space-related logos (Jenks, 1994) (see References and Further Reading).

   - To minimize confusion, especially for less advanced students, put all the art into one file on a hard drive or server for the students to access.

2. Set up a class mailbox through which the students send paper mail to each other. Include these letters as part of their correspondence.

3. Have the students create other types of documents (e.g., thank-you notes, birthday cards, Valentine cards, and holiday cards).

4. Create a class bulletin board to display the finished documents, or copy and bind them in a class anthology.

5. Incorporate other computer skills:
   - writing text inside borders and larger clip-art templates
   - copying and pasting Internet graphics into documents (with attention to copyright)
   - for the artistically advanced, original artwork

References and Further Reading

ClarisWorks (Version 4.0) [Computer software]. (1996). Santa Clara, CA: Claris.

[Clip art newsgroup]. Available Usenet: alt.binaries.clip-art archive

Digital Chisel (Version 2.0) [Computer software]. (1995). Portland, OR: Pierian Spring Software.

Durst, C. (1992). *Sunshine sampler* [On-line]. Available: http://www.ist.net/clipart/sunshine-sampler.html

Durst, C. (n.d.). *Best of BCS art* [On-line]. Available: http://www.ist.net/clipart/best-of-bcs-art.html

Funet collection [On-line]. (1992). Available: http://www.ist.net/clipart/funet.html

HyperCard (Version 2.3) [Computer software]. (1995). Cupertino, CA: Apple Computer.

Jenks, K. (1994). [U.S. National Aeronautics and Space Administration logos]. Available FTP: Hostname: explorer.arc.nasa.gov Directory: pub/SPACE/LOGOS

Kid Pix (Version 2) [Computer software]. (1995). Novato, CA: Brøderbund Software.

Loosemore, S. (n.d.). *Sandra's clip art server* [On-line]. Available: http://www.meche.rpi.edu/web/clipart.html

Sauer, G. (1993). *CMU English server clip art* [On-line]. Available: http://www.ist.net/clipart/cmu-english-server.html

Sterling, M. (1994). *Color expressions* [On-line]. Available: http://www.ist.net/clipart/color-expressions.html

Stone, B. (1992). *Brad's favorite clip art* [On-line]. Available: http://www. ist.net/clipart/brads-clipart-II/html

Texas Agricultural Extension. (1996). *TAEX clip art collection* [On-line]. Available: http://leviathan.tamu.edu:70/ls/clipart

Contributor

Leslie Opp-Beckman is an ESL instructor at the University of Oregon's American English Institute, in the United States (e-mail: leslieob@oregon .uoregon.edu; http://darkwing.uoregon.edu/~leslieob/index.html).

Job Hunting

Levels
Intermediate +

Aims
Practice writing a
résumé and letter of
application

Class Time
1–2 hours

Preparation Time
10 minutes

Resources
Computer for every two
to three students
Word-processing
software
Printer
Job advertisements
Skeleton application
letter
Sample résumés and
format

When students learn how to write a résumé and letter of application in their writing class, less emphasis seems to be placed on presentation than on content. This activity not only encourages students to discuss content and layout but also allows students to manipulate the text on the computer to produce a professionally formatted document. The samples of work can be kept in a file for future reference or displayed in the classroom.

Procedure

1. Divide the students into pairs or triads.
2. Display a number of job advertisements in a prominent place. Have each group of students choose one. If you wish, hold a 10- to 15-minute discussion about the most inviting job on offer.
3. Ask the students to design their own résumé including information they consider important (see Caveats and Options). At the end of the activity, have the students look at the samples and compare them with a standard résumé format.
4. Give each group a skeleton application letter (see the Appendix). Ask the students to prepare a letter of application appropriate for the job they chose in Step 2.
5. Print a copy of the group's résumé and letter for each student in that group.
6. Ask the groups to comment on their résumé design.
7. Collect and file the samples of work or display them on a class notice board.

Caveats and Options

1. Give lower level students a sample résumé and letter of application in Step 3, or supply a skeleton layout on disk.

2. As a follow-up, have some groups take on the role of the employer, discuss whether another applicant group is suitable for the job, and compose a letter offering the job or rejecting the applicant. If you wish, have the other group reply with a letter of acceptance.
3. Before the activity, ask the students to look in local newspapers or magazines for a suitable job advertisement. This personalizes the activity and makes it seem more realistic.
4. Before the activity (preferably in an earlier class), show the students examples of badly designed résumés and poorly written letters of application. Discuss why they are not reasonable examples of text.
5. As a follow-up, have the students prepare a role play of a job interview.

Appendix: Skeleton Application Letter

Depending on the level of the students, give more or less guidance on the layout of the letter.

Your address

Potential employer's address

Dear _____:

[Refer to the advertisement.]

With reference to your advertisement in the _____,
I would like to apply for the position of
_____.

[Summarize your experience.]

As you can see from the enclosed résumé, I have had _____
experience in _____.

[Describe what you did.]

[Tell why the new job interests you.]

I am suitable for this position because
_____.

Yours _____

Contributor

Sue Fitzgerald is a lecturer in the English Department at Hong Kong Polytechnic University (e-mail: egsusan@hkpucc.polyu.edu.hk).

Let's Sell It!

Levels
Intermediate +

Aims
Practice writing creative
sales letters
Improve keyboarding
Cooperate in small
groups

Class Time
2-4 class sessions

Preparation Time
10 minutes

Resources
Computer for every two
to three students
Simple text-editing
software
Printer
Unusual object
Overhead projector or
networked classroom

Numerous classes teach students skills such as typing or keyboarding, English, business, and marketing. Soon after graduation, however, students must merge these skills. In this activity, students use their creativity, their writing skills, and their keyboarding skills as they simulate the creation of a sales or promotion letter. The ability to use the text editor to make changes to the letter and print it out more than once can lead to some interesting variations.

Procedure

1. Find an object that can be used as a simulated product. A real product is all right, but the students may be heavily influenced by existing promotions for it. For example, use your favorite coffee mug, an old pair of socks (well cleaned, of course), or an interesting paperweight.
2. Form small groups of two to three students for each computer.
3. Explain the goal of creating sales letters or promotion letters for a product, but do not let the students see the product yet.
4. To add some time pressure to the simulation, set a time limit for when the letter must be finished.
5. Set out the product for everyone to see. Have each group send one or two students to examine the product while the others work at the computer on writing the letter. Have the students print their letters.
6. Collect the printouts. Save the disk files for the letters on a hard or floppy disk.
7. Copy the printouts onto overhead transparencies, or use a networked classroom to review the results in the next class session.

Caveats and Options

1. Expand the activity to fit the hardware and software available in your lab. If desktop publishing software is available, replace the sales letter with a flashy promotion letter that includes special formatting such as bullets, different fonts, and multiple columns.
2. Use a scanner or video/electronic camera to capture images of the product being sold. Have the students place them in the promotion letter.
3. After the letters are done, move the groups to different computers so that they can view the work of other groups.
4. After Step 7,
   - Allow each group to open a copy of another group's letter.
   - Ask the groups to make changes to the product, print it, and turn it in.
   - Copy the modified printouts to overhead transparencies.
   - In class, allow each group to display their letter and explain the reasons for their design, wording, and graphics.
   - Allow the group that made changes to display its version and explain the changes.

Contributor

Clyde A. Warden is a business English instructor at the Overseas Chinese College of Commerce in Taichung, Taiwan.

Visit Our City

Levels
Intermediate +

Aims
Develop summarizing
skills
Practice writing
descriptions
Learn about cultural
aspects of a city

Class Time
50 minutes

Preparation Time
30 minutes

Resources
Computer for every two
to three students
Word-processing
software
Desktop publishing
software on at least one
system
Printer(s)
Tourist brochures

Summarizing requires a great deal of practice for L2 learners. This activity requires students to summarize in order to produce a class brochure promoting the cultural attractions of the city in which they are living.

Procedure

1. Show the students brochures on places of interest in your city (e.g., the zoo, a museum, a historical site, a recreational facility).
2. Establish a purpose for producing a single brochure that consolidates information from an assortment of brochures. Students studying abroad, for instance, will create one brochure to send home in order to acquaint friends and family with their new city. Students studying English as a foreign language in their native country will create a brochure promoting their hometown to send to a sister city in another country.
3. Group the students into pairs or triads. Give each group a brochure featuring a particular place of interest or entertainment attraction of your city that is different from that given to any other group.
4. Direct the groups to read their brochures, discuss their attractions, and decide on the three most important things they want to say about their assigned attraction.
5. Instruct each group to compose on the computer one paragraph of no more than four sentences that describes the three most important features of their cultural/entertainment attraction. Circulate and advise the students on selecting pertinent information and writing it in a concise manner.
6. Direct the students to save the paragraphs onto their disks. Collect the disks.

7. Ask each group to select, cut out, and label the one picture from its brochure that best illustrates the group's paragraph. Collect the pictures.
8. Print the students' paragraphs and assemble the paragraphs and pictures into a brochure. Distribute it to the students.

Caveats and Options

1. Allow students with desktop publishing skills to assemble and publish the document themselves. Assign the other students to final editing tasks.
2. If you have access to a scanner, scan in the pictures selected by each group and use them to illustrate the brochure.
3. Brochures are commonly available through hotels, chambers of commerce, and tourist organizations. If you live in an area where brochures are not available, obtain brochures on attractions in your state or national capital ("Visit Our Capital") or large cities of other countries.
4. An interesting variation in theme is "Our Class's Dream Trip," in which each group contributes information on one city to visit on a class trip around the world. The students receive additional composing practice by writing to chambers of commerce to request brochures on places of interest in their cities.

Contributor

Mary Ellen Butler-Pascoe is an associate professor of TESOL and chair of the Department of Education at United States International University, San Diego, California, in the United States.

◆ The Poem Processor
Scintillating Cinquaines: Poems Even Nonpoets Can Write

Levels
High beginning +

Aims
Use language creatively
Review basic parts of
speech
Practice capitalization
and punctuation

Class Time
30–45 minutes

Preparation Time
5–10 minutes

Resources
Computer for each
student
Word-processing
software
Sample cinquaines and
templates
Handout, blackboard, or
overhead projector

Cinquaines
by Leslie Opp-Beckman

Cinquaines
Eloquent, emotive
Pondering, probing, producing
Poems from the heart never fade.
Creations

This activity is a simple, dynamic way for students to individually create poems. Writing cinquaines, or five-line poems, is fast and enjoyable and yields a variety of interesting results. (Lines 2 and 3 in this example coincidentally contain alliteration—not at all a requirement!)

Procedure

1. Divide the students into small groups of three to five. Give the groups one sample poem each (see Appendix A) and ask them to prepare to report orally and informally to the rest of the class as follows:
    - What are the structure and form of the poem (e.g., the parts of speech in each line, the use of synonyms)?
    - What is the emotional tone of the poem?
    - What is the relationship between the first and last lines?

    Allow the students to use dictionaries, as necessary, to figure out unfamiliar words.

2. Have the students report on their assigned poems. Discuss and outline clearly with the students their observations regarding the topics in Step 1. Write the analysis on the blackboard or overhead projector screen, present it on a handout, or both. For example,

Line	Analysis
1: Cinquaines	one NOUN-A
2: Eloquent, emotive	two related ADJECTIVES
3: Pondering, probing, producing	three descriptive GERUNDS (verb + *-ing*)
4: Poems from the heart never fade.	one complete SENTENCE
5: Creations	one NOUN-B (a synonym of NOUN-A)

3. Ask the groups to brainstorm as many pairs of synonyms as they can (e.g., *vacation-holidays, artist-creator, Paris-paradise, life-journey, war-hell*). Write the pairs on the blackboard or overhead screen as suggestions. Allow the students to use a dictionary, a thesaurus, or both.
4. With the students, choose one of the brainstormed pairs and write a cinquaine poem about it on the blackboard or overhead screen.
5. Give the students each a template (see Appendix B). Have them write one or more cinquaines on the subject(s) of their choice.

Caveats and Options

1. In Step 2, have the students practice with you and then read their assigned poem to the class.
2. Add artwork, captured video images, or student photos to the poems.
3. Gather the poems into a printed class anthology.
4. Have the students submit the poems to e-zines on the World Wide Web (e.g., *WINGS*).

References and Further Reading

WINGS Electronic Magazine [On-line serial]. Available: http://weber.u .washington.edu/~wings; E-mail: wings@u.washington.edu

Appendix A: Sample Cinquaines

Eel
Long, greasy
Winding, swimming, swirling
An eel is both elegant and ugly.
Sushi

Water
Sweet, clear
Shimmering, sliding, sloshing
Take a breath and jump
Splash

The sky
Wonderful, beautiful
Raining, shining, snowing
The sky is alive.
The universe

Shakespeare
Boring, difficult
Lecturing, acting, translating
Some people think Shakespeare is great.
Writer

Appendix B: Cinquaine Template

Title of Poem
Author's Name

_____

_____, _____

_____, _____, _____

_____.

_____

Contributor

Leslie Opp-Beckman is an ESL instructor at the University of Oregon's American English Institute, in the United States (e-mail: leslieob@oregon .uoregon.edu; http://darkwing.uoregon.edu/~leslieob/index.html).

Diamantes: For Poets Who Are "Diamonds in the Rough"

Levels
High beginning +

Aims
Use language creatively
Review basic parts of
speech, with a focus on
gerunds
Practice capitalization
and punctuation

Class Time
30–45 minutes

Preparation Time
5–10 minutes

Resources
Computer for each
student
Word-processing
software
Sample diamantes and
templates
Handout, blackboard, or
overhead projector

This is a simple, dynamic way for students to create poems individually. Writing diamantes (diamond-shaped poems) is fast and enjoyable and yields a variety of interesting results.

Procedure

1. Divide the students into small groups of three to five. Give the groups one sample poem each (see Appendix A) and ask them to prepare to report orally and informally to the rest of the class on the following questions:
    - What are the structure and form of the poem (e.g., the parts of speech in each line, the use of synonyms).
    - What is the emotional tone of the poem?
    - What is the relationship between the first and last lines?
    - Where is the exact middle of the poem? What happens there?
    Allow the students to use dictionaries, as necessary, to figure out unfamiliar words.

2. Have the students report on their assigned poems. Discuss and outline clearly with the students their observations regarding the tasks in Step 1. Write the analysis on the blackboard or overhead projector screen, present it on a handout, or both. For example,

Line	Analysis
1: Winter	one NOUN-A
2: Rainy, cold	two ADJECTIVES-A
3: Skiing, skating, sledding	three GERUNDS-A (verb + *-ing*)
4: Mountains, wind, breeze, ocean	two more NOUNS-A + two more NOUNS-B
5: Swimming, surfing, scuba diving	three GERUNDS-B (verb + *-ing*)
6: Sunny, hot	two ADJECTIVES -B
7: Summer	one NOUN-B

Also discuss and outline the students' observations regarding opposites, the bidirectional flow of the poem, the middle meeting point, and the overall form.

3. Ask the groups to brainstorm as many pairs of opposites as possible (e.g., *school days–holidays, woman-man, love-hatred, peace-war, divorce-marriage*). Write the pairs on the blackboard or overhead projector screen.

4. With the students, choose one of the brainstormed pairs and write a diamante about it on the blackboard or overhead projector screen.

5. Give the students each a template (see Appendix B). Have them write one or more diamantes on the subject(s) of their choice.

Caveats and Options

1. In Step 2, have the students practice with you and then read their assigned poem to the class.

2. Add artwork, captured video images, or student photos to the poems.

3. Gather the poems into a printed class anthology.

4. Have the students submit the poems to e-zines on the World Wide Web (e.g., *WINGS*; see References and Further Reading).

References and Further Reading

WINGS Electronic Magazine [On-line serial]. Available: http://weber.u.washington.edu/~wings; E-mail: wings@u.washington.edu

Appendix A: Sample Diamantes

Winter
Rainy, cold
Skiing, skating, sledding
Mountains, wind, breeze, ocean
Swimming, surfing, scuba diving
Sunny, hot
Summer

Studies
Unhappy, difficult
Boring, succeeding, sleeping
Library, pencil, bicycle, outside
Interesting, exciting, failing
Happy, easy
Play

Love
Wonderful, beautiful
Caring, liking, thinking
Innocence, smile, tear, guilt
Fighting, violating, disgusting
Terrible, scary
Hatred

Mountain
High, rocky
Flying, looking, killing
Eagle, power, fear, rabbit
Living, moving, breathing
Deep, beautiful
Valley

Appendix B: Diamante Template

Title of Poem
Author's Name

_____

_____, _____

_____, _____, _____

_____, _____, _____, _____

_____, _____, _____

_____, _____

_____

Contributor

Leslie Opp-Beckman is an ESL instructor at the University of Oregon's American English Institute in Eugene, in the United States (e-mail: leslieob@oregon.uoregon.edu; http://darkwing.uoregon.edu/~leslieob/index.html).

The Haiku Novel

Levels
Intermediate +

Aims
Learn the ideas behind
haiku
Become interested in
forms of poetry
Practice summarizing
and desktop publishing
skills
Negotiate meaning with
classmates

Class Time
2-3 hours

Preparation Time
30-60 minutes

Resources
Computer for every two
students
Word-processing or
desktop publishing
software
Local area network
(optional)
Printer (optional)

Students often have difficulty absorbing an entire novel when the teaching of it stretches over a series of weekly lessons. The following method of summarizing the novel allows students to negotiate their own plot summaries and convert the summaries into a form that stresses the novel's emotional and thematic impact. Organizing the text along with appendixes and footnotes in an attractive page layout further taps the students' editorial skills.

Procedure

1. If the students are unfamiliar with haiku, introduce the form as in Digital Concrete Poetry, Steps 1-4.
2. Divide a novel that the class has read into sections, and assign each section to a pair of students. This is most conveniently done by chapters, but smaller sections can be used just as easily.
3. Ask each pair to prepare a three- to five-line summary of their section. Have the students share their section summaries on the computer lab's local area network, if it has one. If not, have the students print out the section summaries and share them with their classmates.
4. Have the students negotiate the style and voice of their section summaries to make them consistent, ensure that there are smooth transitions among the various sections, and ensure that no section is of a length disproportionate to its importance in the novel. Have the students print the summaries.
5. Collect the summaries. Distribute one section summary to each pair of students, ensuring that no pair receives their own piece; this will encourage further collaborative learning as poets check back with

the summary writers. Have each pair write the section summary into a haiku.

6. Have the class edit and approve the draft haiku using faithfulness to the summaries as one measure of success.

7. Collect the final drafts and collate them into a group poetic summary of the whole novel.

8. Ask the students whether any of the poetic summaries might be unfamiliar to a person not familiar with the novel. If so, encourage them to add appropriate footnotes and other annotations. If the novel contains unusual vocabulary, ask the students to write a glossary or make illustrations.

9. Have the students use a desktop publishing program to publish the results, negotiating the best layout to emphasize the importance of the ideas in the text and properly including annotations and footnotes.

10. Print or electronically publish a copy of the final product for each student.

Caveats and Options

1. To use the activity before the class reads the novel, prepare the summary yourself (see the Appendix for an example). Then divide the summary into passages, distribute them to pairs of students, and proceed as in Steps 5 and 6. Once the haiku are finished and collaboratively approved, ask the students to assemble them into one summary.

2. If computer access is limited, have the students do some of the steps as homework.

3. Encourage the students to try the same exercise with another poetic form, such as the sonnet, rhyming couplet, limerick (especially for humorous novels), and other short poetic forms. Try, for example, putting the day's news into a sonnet.

4. As a follow-up, scramble the completed haiku and have the students in the same or a different class rearrange them into a sensible order.

5. If you teach younger students, have them use haiku or other poetic forms to describe such activities as a day trip to the zoo.

6. Extend the activity with Digital Concrete Poetry (in this volume).

References and Further Reading

Shelley, M. (1978). *Frankenstein: Or, the modern Prometheus*. New York: New American Library. (Original work published 1831)

Appendix: A Novel Summarized Into Key Passages

Modern ideas of Frankenstein's monster are mostly influenced by the 1931 movie and movie posters featuring Boris Karloff as an inarticulate green-skinned giant with bolts in his neck. The passages in italics following the summaries are the actual descriptions of the monster from Shelley's *Frankenstein* (1831/1978).

Victor Frankenstein dreams of defeating death. He studies medicine at university and attempts to create life. When Victor Frankenstein first looks over his completed work, he is amazed:
I saw the dull yellow eye of the creature open; it breathed hard, and a convulsive motion agitated its limbs. (p. 56)

But in a moment, he becomes horrified.
His limbs were in proportion, and I had selected his features as beautiful. Beautiful!—Great God! His yellow skin scarcely covered the work of muscles and arteries beneath, but these luxuriances only formed a more horrid contrast with his watery eyes that seemed almost of the same colour as the dun-white sockets in which they were set, his shrivelled complexion and straight black lips. (p. 56)

Victor leaves and throws himself exhausted onto his bed. His nightmares are interrupted by the more horrible appearance of the monster.
I beheld the wretch—the miserable monster whom I had created. He held up the curtain of the bed; and his eyes, if eyes they may be called, were fixed on me. His jaws opened, and he muttered some inarticulate sounds, while a grin wrinkled his cheeks. He might have spoken, but I did not hear; one hand was stretched out, seemingly to detain me, but I escaped and rushed downstairs. (p. 57)

After the monster has killed Victor Frankenstein's young brother and caused the murder to be blamed on an innocent servant girl, Victor and the monster meet in the misty mountains.

He approached; his countenance bespoke bitter anguish, combined with disdain and malignity, while its unearthly ugliness rendered it almost too horrible for human eyes. (p. 95)

The monster is lonely and wants a bride. He asks Victor to create a female monster, promising to leave afterward for the vast wilds of South America.

A fiendish rage animated him as he said this; his face was wrinkled into contortions too horrible for human eyes to behold; but presently he calmed himself and proceeded. (p. 141)

As Victor begins the work he finds the monster has followed him and is watching his work.

A ghastly grin wrinkled his lips as he gazed on me, where I sat fulfilling the task which he had allotted to me. (p. 161)

But Victor regrets his decision to create a second monster and worries that the monster and his bride will in turn give birth to new creatures. Victor decides to destroy the monster's bride.

As I looked on him, his countenance expressed the utmost extent of malice and treachery. I thought with a sensation of madness on my promise of creating another like him, and trembling with passion, tore to pieces the thing on which I was engaged. The wretch saw me destroy the creature on whose future existence he depended for his happiness, and, with a howl of devilish despair and revenge, withdrew. (p. 161)

The monster soon takes revenge on Victor by killing his best friend and then fulfilling a promise to be with Victor on his wedding night. But it is not to kill Victor; instead he kills Victor's bride, Elizabeth. Too late to save her, Victor bursts into the room and finds blood everywhere. He looks through the open window.

The shutters had been thrown back; and, with a sensation of horror not to be described, I saw at the open window a figure most hideous and abhorred. A grin was on the face of the monster; he seemed to jeer, as with his fiendish finger he pointed towards the corpse of my wife. (pp. 189–190)

Victor pursues the monster across Europe and Russia towards the North Pole. On the point of death, Victor meets a ship locked in the ice and tells his story to the captain, whose letters and diaries are the format of this novel. After Victor dies, the monster appears. The captain describes their meeting.

I entered the cabin where lay the remains of my ill-fated and admirable friend. Over him hung a form which I cannot find words to describe: gigantic in stature, yet uncouth and distorted in its proportions. As he hung over the coffin, his face was concealed by long locks of ragged hair; but one vast hand was extended, in colour and apparent texture like that of a mummy. When he heard the sound of my approach, he ceased to utter exclamations of grief and horror, and sprung towards the window. Never did I behold a vision so horrible as his face, of such loathsome, yet appalling hideousness. I shut my eyes, involuntarily, and endeavoured to recollect what were my duties with regard to this destroyer. I called on him to stay. (p. 207)

Contributor

Ken Keobke is a lecturer in the Division of Language Studies at the City University of Hong Kong and a PhD candidate in the area of computer-assisted language learning (e-mail: keobke@cityu.edu.hk).

Digital Concrete Poetry

Levels
Intermediate +

Aims
Learn ideas behind
concrete poetry
Practice style options in
word processing
Explore meanings of
words
Learn about haiku and
other short poetic forms

Class Time
1–2 hours

Preparation Time
30 minutes

Resources
Computer for every two
to three students
Word-processing
software
Haiku
Blackboard or overhead
projector
Desktop publishing or
paint software, clip art
(optional)

Concrete poetry uses the shapes of letters and words to create visual representations of the ideas behind the text. Since the time of the ancient Greeks, people have enjoyed shaping letters, words, and sentences into images. One famous example is Apollinaire's (1980) poem about rain, in which the numbers descend like raindrops. In other concrete poems the letters form the outline of the object being described, such as a fruit. The computer presents a wonderful opportunity for the learner to explore the meaning of words and create concrete poetry by manipulating the font style and size and experimenting with placement, particularly within a painting or page-layout program.

Procedure

1. If the students are not already familiar with the form, introduce the haiku.
   - It is a short Japanese poem that focuses on emotion and the moment, often with conflicting visual images.
   - It does not have to rhyme.
   - It usually has three lines that sometimes follow a five-seven-five syllable structure. Although this structure is flexible, it helps some students narrow their focus.
2. After giving a couple of categories, such as a season and an emotion, ask the students to suggest some strong images. Write them on the blackboard or an overhead transparency.
3. Using the images as raw material, ask the students in pairs to write a few haiku in which they combine an image with a reference to the time, place, or season.

4. Show the students some classical haiku (available in most libraries). Ask the students how the layout of the haiku could influence their meaning. Some common ways are spacing, letter size, choice of font, tracking and leading, and the arrangement of letters. If you wish, show examples of font sizes and styles in headlines from popular magazines.
5. Enter the students' favorite haiku into the software program being used. Ask the students to work with the font size and style and the page layout to reflect and enhance the haiku's meaning.
6. Encourage collaboration and group critiques.

Caveats and Options

1. This activity is useful in introducing students to the word-processing, page-layout, and painting capabilities of computer software.
2. If your software's capabilities are limited, to encourage future learning be sure to acquaint the students with what more sophisticated software can do.
3. Especially with younger students, provide more structure (e.g., by giving the students a template of the outline of an apple—or any other object—in which they can write the text of a poem).

References and Further Reading

Apollinaire, G. (1980). It's raining. In *Calligrammes* (A. H. Greet, Trans.). Berkeley: University of California Press.
Word (Version 6.0) [Computer software]. (1994). Redmond, WA: Microsoft.

Appendix: Two Concrete Haiku

The following two haiku were created using the character and border options in Microsoft Word for Windows.

This haiku respects the five-seven-five structure and uses different point sizes, a character for the sun from the standard Wingding typeface, boldface, italics, superscript and subscript characters, a box (with the border style set to *none*) and 10% grey shading.

H ☼ T baby cry*ingggggggggggggggg*
mum *b*o u *n* c e *s* him up *and* down
SOOOOOOOOOOOOOOOOOOOOn he falls asleep.

This haiku uses different point sizes, small capitals, italics, boldface, and strike-through text.

The batter stands *UP.*

FAST! THE WORLD MOVES TOO **FAST!**

Three ~~strikes and you're out~~.

Contributor

Ken Keobke is a lecturer in the Division of Language Studies at the City University of Hong Kong and a PhD candidate in the area of computer-assisted language learning (e-mail: keobke@cityu.edu.hk).

Concept Pattern Poems

Levels
Any

Aims
Use poetry to share multicultural backgrounds and traditions
Create anthologies of student poetry

Class Time
Variable

Preparation Time
5 minutes

Resources
Computer for every two to three students
Word-processing software
E-mail partner
Printer
Scanner (optional)

Concept pattern poems, which describe the characteristics of a single concept, word, or phrase, are commonly about people, places, objects, or events. They are a great way to share cultural traditions and customs with your e-mail partner, and they challenge students with creative writing forms. By the end of the lesson, the students will have compiled an illustrated album of poetry that focuses on cultural traditions, customs, and activities.

Procedure

1. Do the activity with your class concurrently with your e-mail partner.
2. Show the students the examples of concept pattern poetry in the Appendix.
3. On the blackboard, write the names of the cultural groups represented in your class (e.g., Chinese, Puerto Rican, East Indian). Brainstorm with the students a list of customs, traditions, holidays, festivals, foods, and beliefs that are unique to each group.
4. Ask groups of two to five students from the same cultural group to select one topic from the list that corresponds to their own backgrounds. For example, a group of Malay students might select the holiday of Ramadan, Thaipussom, going to mosque, or a traditional food or game.
5. Have the students each compose their own concept pattern poems.
6. Arrange the students in clusters of two or three per computer. Have one student type his or her poem while the others read it aloud, edit, and make suggestions regarding content, language usage, and spelling. Ask the students to take turns until all the poems are typed.
7. Send the poems to your e-mail partner. Collect the poems from your partner's class and your own. Compile them into a draft anthology

and print copies for your students to distribute and read at the next class session. Use this step either as an exercise in peer editing or simply as reading and listening practice. At this stage, any further revisions can be made. Make sure both your class and your partner's participate in the editing and revision process.

8. Print a final copy of the anthology, including pictures or photos, either scanned or sent as hard copies. Share the anthology with your partner electronically or via surface mail.

Caveats and Options

1. Contribute your poems to the anthology as well to allow the students to get to know you better.
2. Use the poems for a guessing game: Hand them out at random. Have the students read them aloud and see if they can guess the authors.
3. Share the poems with other classes or display them in a prominent place at school.
4. If your partner school does not have access to a good printer or photocopy machine, volunteer to compile the anthology, and mail your partner a copy.

Appendix: Concept Pattern Poems

Chinese Noodles

Let me tell you about Chinese noodles.
We eat lots of noodles for lunch and dinner.
There are wide noodles and thin noodles.
Some people like bean noodles, but I prefer rice noodles.
There are also wheat noodles but they are not so popular in Hong Kong.
We eat our noodles with chopsticks, never with forks.
We mix them with vegetables, beans, fish balls and meats.
We also eat noodles in hot soup.
There is a famous noodle restaurant near my house called Choy Lee.
They serve my favorite fishball noodle soup there!

Chinese New Year

Chinese New Year is . . .
Lucky money
shining through my eyes.
Flower markets with peach blossoms,
narcissus and orange trees.
Chinese New Year is ...
Red paper with lucky words,
new red clothes and red envelopes filled with lucky money
Chinese New Year is . . .
Crowds on the streets,
in the flower market and in the dining room.
It is the click click noise from mah jong tables.
Chinese New Year is . . .
vocabulary tests—
"Kung Hei Fat Choi," "Lung Ma Jing Sun," and
"Nien Nien Yao Yu."
Chinese New Year is . . .
Performances like
lion and dragon dances and firework shows.
It is sour muscles from legs running
to the east to visit uncle, to the south to visit auntie
to the west to visit grandma and to the north to my friends.
Chinese New Year is . . .
the murmuring from temples
wishing for protection, riches, wealth and luck.
Chinese New Year is . . .
joy and excitement for children and adults.

(Johnson Wong, Year 9)

Contributor

Roseanne Greenfield has taught for the past 12 years in the United States, Taiwan, Guatemala, and Hong Kong. She currently works at the Chinese International School in Hong Kong and is pursuing a joint EdD program in TESOL and learning and technology in the United States (e-mail: 100314.1246@compuserve.com).

Part II: Getting Connected: E-Mail and MOOs

Saba Gebremedhin at the Arlington Education and Employment Program (REEP), Arlington, Virginia USA.

Editor's Note

Teachers have experimented for years with electronic submission of and feedback on written work, and the integration of word-processing and communication tools has opened up new possibilities. Part II includes activities involving e-mail and MOOs, which allow students to engage in collaborative learning activities within and outside their own institutions and countries (for other ideas on e-mail and networking projects, see Warschauer, 1995a, 1995b).

Conferencing

Conferencing via e-mail, or communicating with classmates and teachers through networked computers, offers many opportunities for language learning. The activities in this section involve solving information-gap tasks, writing a "chained" mystery, writing questions and answers, and writing news stories. In all of these tasks, the easy, immediate, and relatively informal means of communication provided by e-mail motivates the students and ensures that they receive meaningful feedback from their classmates and teacher.

Partner Classes and Keypals

Writing to a pen pals via e-mail (keypals) is usually an exciting prospect for students. The exchanges, whether student-to-student or class-to-class, exemplify writing for communicative purposes, especially when the keypals are from different cultures. The activities here introduce e-mail-based partner activities and explain how to access and use such resources as the *International E-Mail Tandem Network*, which matches up students learning the same language in different parts of the world, and *EVENT-SL*, an electronic forum in which ESL students around the world discuss current events. (For a World Wide Web–related keypal project, see Getting to Know You Better From Across the Globe in Part III.)

MOOs

MOOs (MUDs, object oriented), or real-time, on-line chat domains, are a related technology. These multiuser environments provide a language-rich setting for game playing, discussion, problem solving, and socializing among teachers and students. Getting Started With MOOs: MOO and YOO—What to DOO explains the basics of MOOs, and two other activities show how to apply the MOO environment to student-teacher conferencing and on-line chatting.

References

Warschauer, M. (1995a). *E-mail for English teaching: Bringing the Internet and computer learning networks into the language classroom.* Alexandria, VA: TESOL.

Warschauer, M. (Ed.). (1995b). *Virtual connections: Online activities and projects for networking language learners.* Honolulu: University of Hawaii Press.

◆ Conferencing
Can You Tell Me . . . ?

Levels
Low intermediate +

Aims
Practice question forms
Practice using e-mail

Class Time
90 minutes

Preparation Time
1 hour

Resources
Computer and e-mail
access for each student
Word-processing
software
Network

In a world where electronic communication is becoming more and more common, students need opportunities to learn about and use this medium for getting and giving information. In this activity, students practice using e-mail by communicating with their partner to gather information for an information-gap task.

Procedure

1. Prepare an information-gap activity for two people. Any kind of information gap is possible. Make copies for each student.
2. Assign partners to the students.
3. Teach the students how to connect with their partners via electronic communication software. The procedure will vary slightly depending upon your software and system.
4. Direct the students to ask questions by e-mail to get the information they need to do the information-gap activity and to supply information in response to their partner's questions.
5. Either collect and grade the finished worksheets, or have the partners present their information to the class.

Caveats and Options

1. Adapt the activity for mixed-level classes by designing several information-gap activities at various levels.
2. Give each partner a different picture. Have the partners write and e-mail sentences or questions to find the similarities and differences between two pictures. If you wish, have the partners use word-processing software to compile a list or write a paragraph.
3. Examples of electronic communication applications software include Windows for Workgroups–Chat, ClassWriter (for Macintosh), and Daedalus Integrated Writing Environment.

References and Further Reading

Daedalus Integrated Writing Environment (Version 4.0) [Computer software]. (1990). Austin, TX: Daedalus Group.

Freeman, H., & Simmons, M. (1995). Chat through Windows for Workgroups. *Modern English Teacher 4*(3), 32–35.

Kirschner, S. (n.d.). ClassWriter (Version 2.0) [Computer software]. Santa Barbara, CA: Intellimation.

Windows for Workgroups (Version 3.11) [Computer software]. (1995). Redmond, WA: Microsoft.

Contributor

Patricia Thornton is an associate professor of English at Kinjo Gakuin University in Nagoya, Japan (e-mail: thornton@kinjo-u.ac.jp).

It Takes My Speech Away

Levels
High intermediate +

Aims
Practice creative writing
Improve negotiation
skills

Class Time
2 hours over two to
three sessions

Preparation Time
20 minutes

Resources
Computer and e-mail
access for each student
Network

Conferencing with classmates through a computer, instead of simply talking to one another, adds to students' enjoyment of this creative writing activity. Students work together to write a simple vignette and critique each other's work.

Procedure

1. Before class, divide the students into groups of three or four. Name the groups *A, B, C,* and so on, and assign e-mail addresses to each student as well as each group. Compile and make copies of a list of the names and e-mail addresses.
2. Make sure the students know how to compose messages in the e-mail program.
3. In class, explain to the students that they will work in groups by e-mail to write a scene with themselves as the cast. Emphasize the necessity of maintaining silence during the task.
4. Hand out a printed list of the names and e-mail addresses of everybody in the class, including yourself and the assigned groups.
5. Seat the group members away from each other so that they cannot communicate orally. Tell the students that they are not allowed to talk and that, if a problem arises, they should mail a message to you and wait for your answer.
6. Have the group members contact each other, introduce themselves, and choose a group leader, all by e-mail.
7. Have each group think of a topic or situation and collaboratively write a short scene about it with themselves as the cast.
8. After lengthy written negotiations among the authors/actors across the computer lab, have the group leaders send a "job-done" message to you followed by the text of their scene.

9. Examine the scenes. Send a message to the group leaders directing them to send the group's scene to another group.
10. Have the groups read and criticize each other's plays and send their written critique back to the authoring group.
11. Repeat Steps 1–10 with different groups.

Caveats and Options

1. This activity may look difficult, but it works well if you encourage the students to maintain the spirit of group work.
2. If the e-mail software you use does not automatically save the document on the screen at regular intervals, instruct the students to save their writing every 2 minutes or so as a precaution against system failure.

Contributor

Wisam Mansour is an assistant professor of English at the Applied Science University in Amman, Jordan.

Sharing Words via E-Mail

Levels
Low intermediate +

Aims
Understand and use
new vocabulary
Write conversationally
and formally

Class Time
Session 1: 5–10 minutes
Session 2: 15–20
minutes

Preparation Time
2 minutes per student

Resources
E-mail access for each
student

ESL teachers frequently ask students to keep personal vocabulary lists and share their words with their classmates in class. This common practice is sometimes sabotaged by the length of time spent writing information on the blackboard, poor definitions, or incorrect sample sentences. Having students use e-mail to share words, definitions, and sentences makes this procedure run much more smoothly. The activity helps students understand the words, find ways to use them in their own writing, and develop their writing skills as they communicate with their classmates and teachers.

Procedure

Before Session 1

1. Have the students keep personal vocabulary lists and share their words in class for several weeks.

Session 1

1. Move the exercise to the medium of e-mail: Describe the activity as a whole to the students in class and tell them that e-mail is a more effective and faster way to present information about their word than having one student write it on the blackboard while the others copy it. Suggest that they start keeping a computerized vocabulary list instead of, or in addition to, their handwritten one.
2. Tell the students to e-mail a word to their classmates and teacher by a certain day or time, along with the part of speech, the definition, and a sentence using the word (see the Appendix).

Session 2

1. Direct the students to read the messages from their classmates and add the information they contain to their personal vocabulary list. For example, intermediate students added *fiasco, tangible, scour, nefarious, priggish, bigot, upbringing, buzz* (as in high), *trivial,* and *chaos* to their lists.
2. Read the students' messages and correct their sample sentences as necessary by sending individual messages. For example, to correct the sentence *The students scoured their classmate for hours*, which omits the object and *for* that make clear the meaning of *scour* used, send a message to that student, who will send a revised sentence to his or her classmates.
3. Instruct the students to bring their personal vocabulary lists, with the added words, to class.

Session 3

1. Tell the students to write sentences using a certain number of the shared words (e.g., 5 words out of 10). Help the students as necessary. A sample sentence with the words listed above is *The nefarious bigot overcame his priggish upbringing and got a buzz.*
2. Ask the students to share their sentences orally.

Caveats and Options

1. Have the students write a sentence using the shared words at home and share the sentences in class.
2. Have the students write their sentences on the blackboard or on an overhead transparency for all the students to copy.
3. Have the students e-mail the sentences using the shared words to you. Cut and paste the sentences onto one page and distribute them, either electronically or as a handout.
4. For lower level students, choose words for the activity that are related to a certain topic or that come from a common reading assignment.
5. Have the students work in pairs or groups to write one sentence.
6. Instead of doing Step 2 in Session 2, have the students rewrite the other students' original sentences. For Yukari's word in the Appendix,

another sentence could be *Princess Di needs tangible evidence before she can divorce Prince Charles.*

7. Make sure a large number of students send their words on time for Session 1, or it will be difficult to hold an effective Session 2.

8. You may need to remind the students to choose words that are appropriate for them to learn right now rather than words that are particularly difficult to use. For example, a low-intermediate student should not choose words such as *edacious* (gluttonous), *recumbent* (prostrate), or *jejune* (tedious) just because they are in the dictionary.

Appendix: Vocabulary Word Messages

(high intermediate)

Subject: new word

Hi, my new word is really curious because I think it's not a usual word and have the same spelling and mean in Portuguese:

fiasco – noun – the complete failure of something planned.

Ex. The party was a total fiasco.

Bye, see you in class.

(M. Lima, October 11, 1995)

Subject: Yukari's Word!!

Hello, my friends. How are you doing? I'm sick . . . .

Here is my word

TANGIBLE (adj.) touchable or real

EX: Yukari insisted on some tangible evidence from her friend before she would . believe her husband was cheating on her.

Have fun with my word, okay?

SEE YOU LATER, have a good night!!

(Y. Sato, Oct. 18, 1995)

Contributor

Ellen Butki teaches for ESL Services at the University of Texas at Austin, in the United States. She is co-monitor of EVENT-SL (e-mail: ebutki@mail. utexas.edu).

Mysteries That Rattle Your Chains

Levels
High beginning +

Aims
Develop writing fluency
and depth
Write communicatively
in English
Produce a polished
collection of writing
quickly

Class Time
2–3 hours

Preparation Time
10–15 minutes

Resources
Computer and e-mail
access for each student
Word-processing
software
Printer
Keypals inside or
outside class
Large or small basket(s)

In this activity, students compose a mystery story in a three-part exchange, or chain, in which a different student writes the beginning, middle, and end. Using the Crazy Basket will spark creative juices and overcome writer's block.

Procedure

Before Class

1. Compile a list of the students' e-mail addresses. (Obtain signed consent forms for the exchange of addresses as needed.) Divide the students into groups of three.
2. If you are using an outside keypal class, communicate with the other instructor well in advance to agree on the groupings and the timing and direction of the exchanges.
3. Write unusual or even bizarre words and phrases on pieces of paper and fold them up to put in the Crazy Baskets. Include characters, objects, places, actions, and events. Small objects or folded-up magazines pictures work well, too. Optionally, allow the students to contribute words and phrases.

In Class

1. As a warm-up activity, have the students in their groups brainstorm as many words and phrases they can to start a mystery (e.g., *It was a dark and stormy night* ...; *Once on a night with no moon* ...; *Long, long ago on a lonely road* ...). Do the same for the different ways to end mysteries (... *and nobody knows where they are today;* ... *you can still see her ghost in the tower.*). Discuss or review transition words and phrases such as *first, then, after that, suddenly,* and *you'll never guess what happened next.* Post the results of the brainstorm-

ing on a file, on the blackboard, or on a handout for the students to refer to during the writing process.

2. Place the folded-up pieces of paper in the Crazy Basket(s).

3. To avoid confusion, tell the students to use the same time or tense (past or present). Tell Partner 1 to write the introductory part of the mystery and e-mail it to Partner 2. Have Partner 2 form a reply consisting of Partner 1's introduction and a middle part written by Partner 2, and send it on to Partner 3. Tell Partner 3 to finish the story, embellish it with a title, and send copies of the entire story to the other two partners and to the instructor. Students who are stumped during the process may pull something out of the Crazy Basket, but they may not exchange what they receive: They must use whatever comes out of the basket.

4. Use whatever editing process has been established in class to refine the stories.

5. Compile the stories into an anthology. Enhance it with illustrations or collages as desired.

Caveats and Options

1. The length of the story will vary according to the students' abilities and interests.

2. With outside keypals, have your students write the introduction and ending; send the stories out to the other class only for the middle section. In this way you are sure to end up with your students' original story-starters.

3. Have the students use a spelling checker on their story segments if possible.

4. This activity works especially well near a "spooky" holiday or occasion (e.g., Halloween, a full moon, other mysterious events from the cultures represented in the class).

5. For an alternate warm-up activity,
   - Type up and copy a list of typical mystery beginnings, transitions, and endings. Cut the list into strips.
   - Have the students work in small groups of three to five. Give each group of students a set of strips and ask them to separate the strips into beginnings, transitions, and endings. Discuss and expand on the results.

6. For another warm-up activity,
   - Visit an old cemetery and make some tombstone rubbings.
   - Encourage the students to guess the story behind the rubbing: How old was the deceased? Did he or she have any special attributes? Was the person related to those represented by the other rubbings? What were the circumstances of the person's death? (Note: Use this warm-up only with students from cultures that bury their dead in cemeteries and are comfortable wandering around in them.)
7. Encourage the students to use an alias or pen name. This kind of anonymity sometimes frees students of their writing inhibitions.
8. Use a different story format (e.g., fantasy, fable, fairy tale, modern "twisted" fairy tale, science fiction, horror).
9. For more advanced groups, consider raising the number of exchanges to four or five.

Contributor

Leslie Opp-Beckman is an ESL instructor at the University of Oregon's American English Institute, in the United States (e-mail: leslieob@oregon. uoregon.edu; http://darkwing.uoregon.edu/~leslieob/index.html).

Questions for Novels, or
Novel Questions ;-)

Levels
Low intermediate +

Aims
Develop active reading
skills

Class Time
20–30 minutes

Preparation Time
30–40 minutes

Resources
Computer and e-mail
access for each student
Word-processing
software
Printer
Novel

In classes where students read and discuss a novel, this activity will help students become active readers as they write questions for other students to answer each week. As they compose, e-mail, and answer questions, they pay attention to and become involved with the plot and characters in the novel.

Procedure

1. Before class, write questions for the material you will cover during the first 2 weeks the novel is discussed in class. Model the types of questions you want the students to write: those requiring a specific answer, those asking for opinions, or those requiring a combination of the two.

2. In class, organize the students into Team A and Team B, and designate a leader for each team. Team A will write questions for Team B to answer and vice versa.

3. Ask the students to e-mail to you two questions about a specific part of the book before the next discussion session. Specify that they must know the answers to the questions; they should not write questions they have about the book. Use some of your own questions to illustrate the task. Tell them to specify in their message whether they are on Team A or Team B.

4. Choose the best or most interesting question from each student's message.

5. Cut and paste the questions into a word-processed document, separating the questions for Team A and Team B to form one question sheet for each team. Do not include the author's name with the question.

6. Spell-check the final product. Edit the questions if needed or appropriate.

7. Print out the question sheets.

8. In class, give one question sheet to each team. Have each team work together to answer the questions; allow the students to use their books. Put the team leader in charge of making sure everyone participates.

9. When all of the students have finished answering the questions, have Team A read their questions and answers to the class, passing the sheet around so each member participates. Appoint the authors of each question (on Team B) as the ultimate arbitrators of whether an answer is correct and appropriate. Allow the authors to add their answers or explain why they wrote the question.

10. Repeat Step 9, reversing the teams.

11. Repeat this activity for each weekly discussion of the novel, changing team members for variety.

Caveats and Options

1. Have the team leaders collect the questions from their classmates via e-mail and then e-mail them all to you.

2. Require the students to e-mail answers with their questions.

3. To make the activity more difficult, do not allow the students to look at their books while answering the questions.

4. Have the students write questions for their own team members to answer.

5. The entire activity can take place electronically and outside of class as follows:

- Instead of giving the question sheets to the students, e-mail them.
- Have the team members either collectively or individually answer the questions.
- Have Team A e-mail their answers to Team B and vice versa, sending copies to you as well. This option changes the nature of the activity: The team members use their reading and writing skills instead of their listening and speaking skills to interact.

6. It may take a while for students to learn how to write "good" questions. Lower level students may feel more comfortable composing and answering questions that have a specific answer rather than those that ask for an opinion.

7. If the students don't send you their questions in time, the questions are too easy, or the same question is asked repeatedly, add some of your own questions.

Contributor

Ellen Butki teaches for ESL Services at the University of Texas at Austin, in the United States. She is co-monitor of EVENT-SL *(e-mail: ebutki@mail. utexas.edu).*

The Virtual Newsroom

Levels
Intermediate +

Aims
Write news stories

Class Time
2–4 hours

Preparation Time
2 hours

Resources
Computer and e-mail
access for each student
Word-processing
software
Printer

A big part of the news-writing process is quickly deciding on the priority of information as it flows into the newsroom. This activity aims to expose students to the pressures and deadlines involved in that process and train them to make the same quick decisions about their writing strategies. It encourages students to develop a more disciplined approach to their writing by building on their awareness of limitations of time and space. Students also learn that information for news writing is never fixed but changes constantly with the evolution of news events and that news writers need to constantly change and update their stories to keep pace with the changing situations they write about. This exercise uses the students' e-mail accounts to replicate the transfer of information to modern newsrooms via e-mail, the Internet, or direct modem.

Procedure

1. Before class, prepare several short dispatches or unstructured sequences in a running news story (see the Appendix).
2. In class, give the students the following instructions:
   - Write a news story based on information sent by e-mail that will be updated over an unspecified number of stages during class.
   - Open your e-mail at regular intervals during class to receive these updates. At the end of the class, your stories should contain the most salient facts from the latest updates—in other words, the best information available on the issue by the time you have to stop writing.
   - Structure your story according to conventional news-writing style: Place facts in an inverted pyramid structure according to a hierarchy of value.

Impose a word length on the students' final story (in the example in the Appendix, 200 words) to force the students to select and discard facts according to their news value.

3. Send out the episodic dispatches via e-mail to the students at irregular intervals, but do not tell the students when you are going to send a dispatch. Have the students download the messages into active word-processing files.

4. Have the students work in the active files to compose news stories from the raw material of the source information (in news jargon, they *work up a running story*).

5. Have the students print out their stories and hand them in for assessment.

Caveats and Options

1. For advanced students, provide dispatches for two running stories at the same time.

2. Introduce contradictory statements into the dispatches to make the students aware that they should not accept all the information they receive at face value and that they need to be cautious in selecting facts, particularly those from unofficial sources, to include in their story.

3. Use the activity to reinforce earlier lessons on accuracy, clarity, and brevity in news writing. Students have to not only keep up with the flow of new information but also reshape it into better news copy.

4. In an interesting elaboration of this model, introduce nontext information sources, such as a tape recording of an eyewitness describing a scene related to an incident.

Appendix: Sample Dispatches

The following running story dispatches were used for a class in Hong Kong. Note that the story has a strong local flavor. The class started at 2:00 p.m., and the items were sent out via e-mail at the times specified.

Item 1 (sent at 2:05)

> Reports from police headquarters say there has been a shooting incident at a Kowloon school during a visit by Governor Chris Patten.
>
> Several police vehicles have rushed to the school in Beacon Hill. Ambulances are also at the scene. There is no word yet on any casualties. Governor Patten arrived at the school at 10 this morning to open a new wing.

Item 2 (sent at 2:09)

> Police have detained a man after a shooting incident at the English Foundation School in Beacon Hill. Governor Patten was officially opening the school's new art and craft block. Several shots were heard shortly after 10 o'clock.
>
> A witness at the scene said he saw several police officers manhandling a man and pushing him into a police van. The van then sped off with its siren wailing.

Item 3 (sent at 2:13)

> Governor Patten was injured in an apparent assassination attempt earlier today. A statement issued by Baptist Hospital at 3:35 this afternoon said Mr. Patten was out of danger after surgeons successfully removed a bullet from his chest. A second bullet had passed through his thigh. A police spokesman said the gun used was a Chinese-made automatic pistol. The shots were fired from about 10 meters away as Mr. Patten was cutting a ribbon to open a new wing of the Beacon Hill international school. Witnesses said at least six shots were fired. One hit a glass door that shattered in a shower of fragments. Cleaners were still sweeping up the glass late this afternoon.

Item 4 (sent at 2:28)

> The principal of a Beacon Hill international school died shortly after being admitted to hospital from wounds he received in an assassination attempt against the Governor Chris Patten. School staff have been instructed not to talk to the media about the incident, and all statements are to come from the official school spokesman. The Beacon Hill English Foundation School is attended by the children of many expatriates working in Hong Kong as well as those of residents who have returned to the territory after living abroad.

Item 5 (sent at 2:48)

> Mrs. Gwendolin Smythe, a senior teacher at the school, said everyone was in a deep state of shock.
>
> "John was admired and respected by everyone at the school," she said. "I can't tell you how much we will all miss him."
>
> The school will stay closed for the remainder of this week. Staff and students are expected to attend Mr. Nicholson's funeral in large numbers.

Item 6 (sent at 3:05)

> The British Prime Minister, Mr. John Major, sent a message of condolence to Mr. Nicholson's family. He described the attack as a heinous crime that would not go unpunished. Mr. Patten is expected to remain in hospital for several days. There is to be a full inquiry into whether there was a lapse in security that allowed the gunman to get so close to the Governor. Yesterday's attack was the first assassination attempt against a Hong Kong governor.

Item 7 (sent at 3:17)

> The British army garrison responsible for Hong Kong's external security has been placed on full alert with all leave postponed. It is not yet known if the gunman was acting alone or whether he had an accomplice.

Item 8 (sent at 3:21)

> The third person injured in the attack was a member of the school board, Mr. Sunil Patel, who received a bullet wound to the elbow. Mr. Patten was opening the school's new craft block as part of a busy day of official duties. He was due to open a new radiography facility at Baptist Hospital one hour after the attack took place.

Item 9 (sent at 3:33)

> Radio TV Hong Kong (RTHK) received a call 30 minutes after the attack saying Mr Patten had been shot to revenge the crimes he had committed against the Hong Kong people. The caller, who spoke Cantonese with a Mandarin accent, identified himself as a member of the Hong Kong Liberation Society. He said more attacks against British targets were planned.

Item 10 (sent at 3:48)

> The governor's wife was reportedly rushing back from a trip in Britain. She had gone there to nurse her ailing mother.

Contributor

Barry Lowe is a former journalist who teaches media theory and journalism in the City University of Hong Kong's English for Professional Communication program (e-mail: enbarry@cityu.edu.hk).

◆ Partner Classes and Keypals
E-Mail Keypalling for Writing Fluency

Levels
Intermediate +

Aims
Increase writing fluency
Write for an authentic
audience

Class Time
1 hour

Preparation Time
30 minutes

Resources
Computer and e-mail
access for each student
Word-processing
software (optional)

Most students have the experience of writing only to and for their teacher. The opportunity to write to an e-mail pen pal (keypal), especially an overseas keypal, generally interests and excites them. They also learn to write for communicative purposes, particularly when they are writing to someone from a different culture.

Procedure

1. Before the semester begins, join an international e-mail list such as *Intercultural E-Mail Classroom Connections* (see References and Further Reading). Decide on the objectives of your e-mail project, and post a message to the list stating them and requesting a partner class. State clearly the type of class you want, including the grade level.
2. After you are assigned a partner classroom, send a list of your students' names and e-mail addresses to your partner teacher so that he or she can match up student keypals. (Or ask your partner teacher to send you his or her list so that you can match them up.) Type up the list before class.
3. In class, introduce the activity. Explain the e-mail system to students new to e-mail. Have them write their introductory message, send it to their partner, and save it to a floppy disk for future reference.
4. Make it clear that you expect the students to communicate with their keypals at least once a week. After the first exchange, encourage the students to explore various topics for future discussion with keypals. If possible, have them incorporate their discussion into their course essays.

Caveats and Options

1. Make sure the students know that they can retrieve the mail messages they have saved using any word-processing software or the e-mail program itself.
2. Encourage the students to prepare mail messages off-line, particularly if you assign more than one keypal to each student. But remind them to save word-processing files in ASCII (DOS text) format for easy uploading and easy retrieval by their keypals.
3. If the students prepare mail messages off-line, encourage them to use spelling checkers and the thesaurus that come with most word-processing software. If they have access to a UNIX account, encourage them to use Pine, because it is user friendly and comes with a spelling checker.
4. Whenever possible, incorporate the e-mail project into your course rather than treating it as an add-on. Give the students class time to check and send mail.
5. Be available to advise students new to e-mail and computers. Enlist the help of students who are good with computers.
6. This type of intercultural e-mail project works best if the focus is on expressing ideas fluently rather than on using the target language accurately. However, you can point out typographical errors and easy-to-fix grammar problems more easily when the students are composing on the upright screen than when they are writing with pen and paper. The ease of editing and the transient nature of on-screen writing lessens the embarrassment students feel when you point out their mistakes.

References and Further Reading

Intercultural E-Mail Classroom Connections [On-line]. Available E-mail: iecc-request@stolaf.edu (for K–12); iecc-he-request@stolaf.edu (college/university) Message: subscribe

Pine (Version 3.91) [Computer software]. (1994). Seattle: University of Washington.

Contributor

John Wong is a lecturer in the English Section of the Language Institute at the City University of Hong Kong (e-mail: lijohnw@cpccux0.cityu. edu.hk).

E-Mail Tandem Network I: Discussion Forum

Levels
High beginning +

Aims
Communicate with
native speakers via
written texts

Class Time
Variable

Preparation Time
Variable

Resources
E-mail access for each
student

The *International E-Mail Tandem Network* was founded in 1993 and has been supported since 1994 by the Commission of the European Communities (Lingua Project 94-03/1507/D-VB). It contains different subnets, each consisting of two groups of learners with different mother tongues (e.g., German-Danish, German-Spanish, German-English, English-French, German-Japanese, and many more). Each group is learning the language and learning about the culture of the other in bilingual discussion forums and tandem work. A central dating agency matches up partners, and a database contains tandem- and network-related material (e.g., learning and technical support, tasks for tandem work).

In each subnet's forum, the participants freely discuss various themes, especially those concerning the culture and language of the respective countries. Contributions are usually bilingual but need not be; the levels of the participants range from beginner (e.g., "My name is . . . , my hobbies are . . .") to expert (often teachers participating in the subnet). The idea behind this is that even participants communicating in their mother tongue can learn about the foreign language. The aim of the network is authentic communication. Language is an aid for communication and not an end in itself. The participants are learning autonomously, as they, not their teachers, are responsible for their learning.

This activity explains how to participate in the network's forums. E-Mail Tandem Network II: Partners shows how to work with a partner.

Procedure

These instructions are directed to the participants.

1. Preparation: Choose the subnet you wish to participate in and subscribe to it by sending e-mail to majordomo@tandem.uni-trier.de. In the body of the message write *subscribe [forum-name]* (e.g., *subscribe deu-nih*) (see References and Further Reading).

2. Feedback and introduction: You will receive the welcome message of the corresponding forum. Send an e-mail message to the forum at [forum-name]@tandem.uni-trier.de (e.g., deu-nih@tandem.uni-trier.de) to introduce yourself, preferably in your language and in the language of the forum.
3. Everyday activities: Read and write messages to communicate with the other forum participants.

Caveats and Options

1. No teacher is necessary for participation in the discussion forums.
2. Because the discussion forums use Internet-based e-mail, they are publicly accessible and free of charge at least for university-based users.

References and Further Reading

Contact the coordinator of the *International E-Mail Tandem Network*, Helmut Brammerts, by e-mail at brammerh@slf.ruhr-uni-bochum.de or by post at Seminar für Sprachlehrforschung, Ruhr-Universität Bochum, D-44780 Bochum, Germany.

International E-Mail Tandem Network [On-line; subnets]. Available: http://marvin.uni-trier.de/; ftp.slf.ruhr-uni-bochum.de; E-mail: majordomo @tandem.uni-trier.de Message: subscribe [forum-name]

Contributors

Martina Gunske von Kölln has an MA in research on foreign language acquisition and the use of the Internet in foreign language acquisition and in teaching German as a foreign language. Markus Gunske von Kölln is a computer engineer. They are the coordinators of the subnet Deu-Nih of the International E-Mail Tandem Network (e-mail: gunske @hss.shizuoka.ac.jp; http://cc.matsuyama-u.ac.jp/~markusvk).

E-Mail Tandem Network II: Partners

Levels
High beginning +

Aims
Communicate with native speakers via written texts

Class Time
Variable

Preparation Time
Variable

Resources
E-mail access for each student

The *International E-Mail Tandem Network* (*IECC*) was founded in 1993 and has been supported since 1994 by the Commission of the European Communities (Lingua Project 94-03/1507/D-VB). It contains different subnets consisting of two groups of learners, each with a different mother tongue (e.g., German-Danish, German-Spanish, German-English, English-French, German-Japanese, and many more). Each group learns the language and learns about the culture of the other via bilingual discussion forums and tandem work. A central dating agency matches up partners, and a database contains tandem- and network-related material (e.g., learning and technical support, tasks for tandem work).

Pairs of participants do the tandem work in either free tandems or moderated tandems. In the latter the supervisor is responsible for scheduling activities; in the former the partners can decide by themselves what to do and when.

This activity explains how to participate in free or moderated tandems. E-Mail Tandem Network I: Discussion Forum shows how to contribute to the network's forums.

Procedure

These instructions are directed to the participants.

1. Preparation: Contact the dating agency by sending an e-mail message to tandem@slf.ruhr-uni-bochum.de. In the body of the message, state your native language and the language you want to learn through tandem work.
2. When you receive the e-mail address of your partner along with information about him or her, contact your partner and introduce yourself.
3. Everyday activities: Communicate with your partner. If you are participating in moderated tandem work, complete the exercises you get from your teacher with the help of your partner.

Caveats and Options

1. For tandem work (except for the moderated tandem), no teacher is necessary.
2. Teachers can integrate the moderated tandem in class work by assigning the students to work on tasks for cultural communication with their partner. Some tasks are available on the *IECC*'s World Wide Web site (http://marvin.uni-trier.de) or by file transfer protocol (FTP) (ftp.slf.ruhr-uni-bochum.de).
3. Unlike the classic tandem, the E-Mail Tandem includes only writing and reading skills. But the advantages are that grammar, vocabulary, and ideas can be set up properly and that the tandem is not time- or location-bound.

References and Further Reading

Contact the coordinator of the *International E-Mail Tandem Network*, Helmut Brammerts, by e-mail at brammerh@slf.ruhr-uni-bochum.de or by post at Seminar für Sprachlehrforschung, Ruhr-Universität Bochum, D-44780 Bochum, Germany.

International E-Mail Tandem Network [On-line; tandems]. Available: http://marvin.uni-trier.de/; ftp.slf.ruhr-uni-bochum.de; E-mail: tandem@slf .ruhr-uni-bochum.de Message: [native language and language you want to learn]

Contributors

Martina Gunske von Kölln has an MA in research on foreign language acquisition and the use of Internet in foreign language acquisition and in teaching German as a foreign language. Markus Gunske von Kölln is a computer engineer. They are the coordinators of the subnet Deu-Nib of the International E-Mail Tandem Network (e-mail: gunske@hss.shizuoka .ac.jp; http://cc.matsuyama-u.ac.jp/~markusvk).

Partner Puzzles With Cloze Paragraphs

Levels
Any

Aims
Exchange school and
community information
Use context clues
Write descriptive
paragraphs

Class Time
Variable

Preparation Time
5 minutes

Resources
Computer for every two
to three students
Word-processing
software
E-mail access (teacher)
Partner class
Encoder box and
scanner (optional)

This game uses cloze paragraphs to introduce information about new e-mail partners and share background information about the partners' school and community. It can complement classroom activities on descriptive writing and inferences.

Procedure

1. Before class, make a list of the types of information that you would like to convey to your partner class. Categories might include school curriculum, local geography, scenery, customs and traditions, school grounds, community languages, ethnic groups, and school sports.

2. In class, either have cooperative student groups select individual topics, or select one for the whole class.

3. Have groups of two to three students brainstorm to compile a list of 20–30 words related to each topic. For example, the topic *climate* might elicit words such as *icy, thaw, extreme, moderate, rainfall, plow, humidity, four seasons, landslides,* and *flooding*.

4. Ask the students to use the word list and the word-processing software to write their own descriptive paragraphs about their topic.

5. When the paragraphs are complete, remove key vocabulary words as well as occasional verbs, adjectives, adverbs, and prepositions to form a cloze passage (see the Appendix).

6. For easy reference, number each blank of the puzzle.

7. E-mail the cloze puzzles to your partner class, and ask the students and teacher to reciprocate.

8. After receiving your partners' puzzles, have the students work in cooperative groups to figure out the answers. Brainstorm as a class on

synonyms and alternative answers as well. E-mail your answers to your partner class.

9. When you receive your students' puzzles back from your partners, check their guesses and let them know the intended answers either by sending an answer key or by pointing out discrepancies on particular answers.

Caveats and Options

1. For cooperative writing, have the students take turns writing one sentence at a time until the paragraph is complete. For a whole-class activity, ask the students to volunteer sentences while you write them on the blackboard.

2. If you have an encoder box, hook up your computer to a television to create whole-class cloze paragraphs so the students can see the paragraph as it is being written.

3. There may be many suitable responses for each blank space. For example, answers to Item 2 in the Appendix might include the words *small, compact, cramped,* or even *hilly.* If you wish, discuss synonyms and alternative answers before sending the key to your partner class, or include synonyms and alternative answers in your key.

4. Use the activity to complement a unit on descriptive writing.

5. If you have a scanner, have the student groups collect photos and drawings to illustrate their individual topics.

Appendix: Sample Cloze Passage

Hong Kong __1__ a very __2__ place. You can almost walk from one __3__ to the other. There is very little __4__ land, so people have to __5__ their homes on hillsides. Shops and houses are __6__ very close together to make the best __7__ of limited space. Most of our homes are in high- __8__ apartments. Therefore, many of us have to take an __9__ up many stories before we reach our __10__ . At my flat we have a great __11__ of Victoria Harbor from the kitchen window.

Because land is __12__ , we usually don't have __13__ outside. However, there are many public __14__ where we can play sports and get a bit of __15__ air. There are also many hiking __16__ in the nearby mountains. Hiking is a good __17__ to get out of the __18__ and enjoy the __19__ outdoors.

Contributor

Roseanne Greenfield has taught for the past 12 years in the United States, Taiwan, Guatemala, and Hong Kong. She currently works at the Chinese International School in Hong Kong and is pursuing a joint EdD program in TESOL and learning and technology in the United States (e-mail: 100314.1246@compuserve.com).

Poetic E-Mail Introductions

Levels
Any

Aims
Write a poetic
self-introduction
Create anthologies of
poetry and biographical
sketches

Class Time
Three class sessions +

Preparation Time
5 minutes

Resources
Computer for every two
to three students
Word-processing
software
E-mail access (teacher)
E-mail partner for each
student
Poetic form and formula
Encoder box and
scanner (optional)

The first impression we give new e-mail partners is a lasting one. However, many times students' self-introductions to new e-mail partners can be superficial and lack imagination. The use of acrostic or biographical poems as introductions challenges students with creative writing forms and allows them to share feelings, goals, and background information about school and family life. By the end of the session, the students will have compiled an album of their new partners' poems as well as their own.

Procedure

1. Present examples of poetic introductions and the formula for creating them (see the Appendix).
2. Arrange the students in clusters of two or three per computer. Have the students compose acrostic or biographical poems, either by handwriting them first or by typing directly into the word-processing software. As the students type their poems, have the partners read them aloud, edit, and make suggestions regarding content, usage, and spelling. Have the students save their poems on a disk when they are finished composing.
3. Collect the disks, and compile the poems into a single document on your e-mail program. (Or show the students how to do this.) Print the document.
4. In the next class session, distribute copies of the document to use as an exercise in peer editing or simply as reading/listening practice.
5. E-mail the document to your partner school. Ask your partners for comments, critiques, or responses, or have them contribute to the peer editing.

6. When you receive your partners' poems, assist with the editing process.
7. Produce a final album of poems either by combining pieces from both classes or by publishing two separate anthologies.

Caveats and Options:

1. If you do not have e-mail access, use this exercise as an icebreaker at the beginning of the term. Print out the poems and publish them as an anthology as a way of learning about new students.
2. Contribute your own poems to allow the students to get to know you.
3. If you have access to a scanner, send pictures or drawings to your partner school(s) to illustrate your poems.
4. Use the biographical poems (published without the first and last lines) as a guessing game. Hand out the poems at random, and have the students read them out loud. See if they can guess the authors.
5. Use other poetic forms, such as rhyming poems, haiku, and limericks.
6. As whole-class oral activity, have the students write introductory acrostic poems with the name of their school, community, or state. Write the class-generated poem on the chalkboard, and select two or three students to transfer it into your e-mail anthology.
7. If you have an encoder box, hook up your computer to a television to create whole-class acrostic poems so that the students can see the poem as it is being written.

Appendix: Poetic Forms for Introductions

Acrostic: Use the letters of your first name (and last name if desired).

Philip is my name.
Hiking is one of my favorite hobbies, and so is
Ice Skating.
Learning Mandarin is what I like to do best at school, but
I'm not very good at Math.
Practicing Kung Fu is how I spend my Saturdays.

(Philip Kwok, Year 7)

Biographical: Use the formula below or create your own.

Tell your first name—Use three adjectives to describe yourself—Identify your family—Tell about your hobbies—Tell about your school life—Tell about something that you are pleased with or that makes you happy—Tell about something you are wary about or dislike—List four nouns that tell about you—Name your school, community, or city—Tell your last name

Linda
Creative, Friendly, Social
Sister of Tony and Michael the "Beast"
Who loves to oil paint and sing Vanessa Williams' songs
Who enjoys Choir, English and Drama
But not Spanish or Soccer
Who has just gotten a part in the school play called "Mame"
But who also has a bit of stage fright
And is worried because she has the Chicken Pox!
Dreamer, Artist, Record Collector, Roller Skater
Who loves the Massachusetts countryside in the fall
Olvetti

Contributor

Roseanne Greenfield has taught for the past 12 years in the United States, Taiwan, Guatemala, and Hong Kong. She currently works at the Chinese International School in Hong Kong and is pursuing a joint EdD program in TESOL and learning and technology in the United States (e-mail: 100314.1246@compuserve.com).

Armchair Travelers on the Information Highway

Levels
Any

Aims
Improve writing clarity
and fluency, reading
skills, and vocabulary
Practice oral skills
Learn about another
culture

Class Time
Computer: 2–5 hours
inside or outside class
Classroom: 4–6 hours

Preparation Time
1–2 hours

Resources
Computer and e-mail
access for every three
students
Word-processing
software
Printer

The technology of e-mail can be used in the foreign language classroom to improve students' writing skills. In this structured activity, students of English share information about their city with students of English in another city via e-mail. As they share this information, they develop their ability to write clearly and more fluently in English. They also participate in small-group discussions and give oral presentations about the other city. This activity promotes cross-cultural awareness as well.

Procedure

Before the Term Starts

1. Locate an ESL/EFL teacher in a city in another country willing to collaborate with you on this project. (For the purposes of illustration, the two cities cited in this explanation are Washington, DC, and Paris, France.)
2. Clarify at the outset exactly what you will expect the students to do, and make up a schedule that both teachers will follow as faithfully as possible. This e-mail project may be the heart of the course or only a part of it.

In Class

1. If necessary, teach the students how to use e-mail.
2. Divide the students in each class into small groups (three per group is ideal). Combine each small group in Washington with a small group in Paris to form a "net group."
3. Ask each student in Washington to write a self-introduction and send it to the students in his or her net group in Paris via e-mail. The students in Paris will do likewise.

4. Ask each net group to decide on a cultural aspect of the cities on which to focus and to reach that decision by means of negotiations via e-mail. Possible aspects are fashion, food, politics, art treasures, tourist attractions, historical monuments, ethnic groups, and universities.

5. Direct each small group in Washington to prepare a list of 10 questions about Paris related to the net group's topic. Each small group in Paris will make up questions about Washington, DC. Ask the students to e-mail the questions on the date decided on by the teachers.

6. Have each small group print out a copy of the questions they receive for consideration. Have the members of each small group collectively answer the questions. If they are unable to answer all of the questions, tell them to ask you or to do some additional research to find the answers.

7. Ask the students to e-mail their responses to the questions on the date decided on.

8. Let the students look over the responses and see if they have any additional questions. If so, have the students e-mail these questions to their net group along with a request to provide any other information of interest on the topic.

9. Direct each small group to write an essay based on the information that it has received from its net friends. Combine all the student essays from both cities into one final written product.

10. In addition to the collection of essays, ask each small group to plan a group oral presentation on its topic to present to the entire class.

Caveats and Options

1. Make sure the students in the two classes have approximately the same proficiency level in English.

2. Make sure the two teachers are equally committed to the project and give it an important place in the course syllabus.

3. Arrange the project so that its purpose in both classes is the same. It will not work well if one teacher wants to emphasize written assignments and the other oral.

4. Schedule the starting and ending dates and the vacation breaks of the classes as closely as possible.

5. The two cities do not have to be in two different countries.
6. Require either a written product or an oral presentation at the end of the project instead of both.
7. Ask the students to send photos of themselves along with the self-introductions in Step 3.
8. Have each small group prepare a "culture package" to send to its net friends. These packages could include items related to the group topic (e.g., fashion magazines if the topic is fashion) and items of general interest, such as city maps and postcards of important places. The students could also include audio cassette tapes with recordings of their voices and music—traditional or popular. These items would greatly enhance the students' oral presentations.
9. For an enjoyable supplemental activity, have the students produce a videotape of people or places related to their topics in order to bring their city alive to their net friends.
10. Although doing the activity with two cities is probably ideal, this project could be expanded to include students from more than two cities. The volume of e-mail and the planning involved in including more than four cities would be very difficult to manage.

Contributor

Christine Meloni teaches EFL at George Washington University in the United States (e-mail: meloni@gwis2.circ.gwu.edu). She collaborated on the project described above with fellow teacher James Benenson in Paris.

Getting Started on *EVENT-SL*

Levels
Low intermediate +

Aims
Learn to express
opinions in writing
Exchange opinions
about current events

Class Time
Two sessions of 20–30
minutes

Preparation Time
1–2 hours over 2 weeks

Resources
E-mail access for each
student

Having students subscribe to *EVENT-SL*, one of the International Student Discussion Lists, can effectively expand ESL reading class discussions about current events. *EVENT-SL* is an electronic forum in which ESL students around the world discuss current events. Because there are no time limits, as there are for in-class discussions, students can discuss a topic for as long as they are interested. In addition, *EVENT-SL* allows equal time to those students who are reticent or speak slowly. By participating in *EVENT-SL*, students develop their ability to express their opinions in writing and their written fluency as a result of the immediacy of the reaction from and the interaction with multiple readers.

Procedure

Before Session 1 (Week 1)

1. Familiarize yourself with the International Student Discussion Lists by looking at the World Wide Web page at http://www.latrobe.edu.au. www/education/sl/sl.html.
2. Register your class for the lists by sending a message to Thom Robb, one of the list owners, at trobb@cc.kyoto-su.ac.jp. In the message, include your name, your institution, the number of students in your class, the length of the class term, and the domain name (the part of the e-mail address after the @ sign) that your students will use (e.g., @mail.texas.edu at the University of Texas at Austin). You will automatically be subscribed to *TCHR-SL*, the list for teachers. You will receive detailed information about the 10 branches of the student lists, including suggestions for using them with your students, and a useful handout for your students that explains how to send and reply to messages on the list. The handout includes examples of both appropriate messages, which are relevant to the

topic being discussed and ask questions that prompt additional comments, and some that are inappropriate. If you wish, use these sample messages as teaching tools in Session 1.

3. Subscribe to *EVENT-SL* by sending the message *subscribe EVENT-SL Firstname Lastname* to listserv@latrobe.edu.au.

4. Read the messages posted to *EVENT-SL* for 1 or 2 weeks to learn the conventions of the list.

Session 1 (Week 2)

1. Present *EVENT-SL* to your class as an electronic forum for discussing current events. Use the sample messages from the handout or messages you have received since subscribing to show the topics that have been discussed. Explain that being a member of an e-mail discussion list with ESL students from all over the world will be interesting and beneficial to the development of writing and reading skills.

2. Describe how to subscribe to *EVENT-SL* (see Step 3), and give the students copies of the handout you received from *TCHR-SL*.

3. Give the students a deadline, such as the next class session, for subscribing to *EVENT-SL*. Expect subscription problems (e.g., as a result of poor typing, not using capital letters, misspelling *subscribe*).

4. Ask the students to read messages for 1 week and take notes on the topics and styles in them.

Before Session 2 (Week 3)

1. Discuss some of the messages on *EVENT-SL*, focusing on the topics, the style, information that was and was not included, attributes that made messages appropriate, attributes that furthered or hampered discussion, and so on.

Session 2 (Week 3)

1. Designate approximately one third of your students to post messages to *EVENT-SL* for the first round. (Change the fraction to one

quarter if you have a large class, but do not designate more than four presenters per week or the result may be weak discussions of many topics instead of strong discussions of a few.) For the first round, choose confident students to present topics that will start discussions.

2. Have the presenters post one message each to *EVENT-SL* by Wednesday of the following week or earlier. Tell them to include their opinion on a topic of current interest and at least two questions for other students on the list. If they want, allow the presenters to show their messages to you for editing before posting them to the list (see the Appendix for a sample message and response).

3. Tell the other students to read the messages from their classmates as well as from others on the list and to post at least one message by Friday, commenting on and responding to questions in messages from classmates or from anyone on the list. Allow them to show their messages to you for editing.

4. Keep track of which student has sent which message to ensure that each has posted at least one by the end of the week.

5. Repeat Session 2 regularly (e.g., weekly), designating new presenters for each round. In the 3rd week, have the first set of presenters post messages again.

Caveats and Options

1. Either choose students to be presenters, or let them volunteer. Work toward having the students eventually post voluntarily on a regular basis.

2. Arrange the students in pairs to write one message about related topics.

3. Have the students summarize articles as part of their presentations or work in pairs to write messages about articles related to the same topic.

4. Coordinate the exchanges with those of other teachers on the list.

5. Ask the students to find out a certain number of list members' opinions on a current issue.

6. Have the students compete to see whose message triggers the most responses.

7. Stagger the presentations over a week so that the discussions of each topic can run their course without being interrupted by discussions of other topics.
8. Remind the students to check their e-mail at least two times a week, or the number of messages that accumulate may be overwhelming.
9. If necessary, set a limit on how much the students must write to receive credit for a message (e.g., 10 lines). One-line messages that say *I agree with Juan* do not count.
10. If some students are reluctant to post messages because of their writing ability, pair them with other students, or encourage them to show their messages to you first, either in person or via e-mail.

References and Further Reading

EVENT-SL [On-line]. Available E-mail: majordomo@latrobe.edu.au Message: subscribe EVENT-SL

Appendix: Messages on *EVENT-SL*

A high-intermediate presenter posted this message on *EVENT-SL*.

Subject: interracial relationships.

Last weekend I was reading an article about interracial relationships in the United States (Monitor, September 1995). The article states that a relationship between a man and a woman from different cultures such as Asian and American, and Black and White may have to face problems like: societal discrimination, cultural differences and language barriers. However, the number of interracial couples and families continues to rise in this country. Do you think that white families have more chance to succeed than mixed-marriages? Do you think that this issue will continue being a problem in the future?.

(E. Ledezma, October 17, 1995).

A student's response to the message follows.

Subject: Re: interracial relationships.

On Tue, 17 Oct. 1995 ELEDEZMA wrote:

>Do you think that white families have more chance to succeed than

>mixed-marriages? Do you think that this issue will continue being

>a problem in the future?

Hi, everybody: I have some opinions about this article.

1. I think living in a family that has some problems such as racial conflict may be not so lucky as living in a white families. However, everyone can succeed if he/she is ambitious and makes effort to be successful.

2. Racial issue has long been a big problem and it will continue in the future. But we ourselves must not discriminate against any kind of races.

(S. Chang, October 18, 1995)

Contributor

Ellen Butki teaches for ESL Services at the University of Texas at Austin, in the United States. She is co-monitor of EVENT-SL *(e-mail: ebutki@mail. utexas.edu).*

◆ MOOs
Getting Started With MOOs: MOO and YOO—What to DOO

Levels
Any; teachers

Aims
Learn how to connect
to and use a MOO
Introduce students to
MOOs

Class Time
Variable

Preparation Time
Variable

Resources
Computer
Internet access
Visual client software
(recommended)

Imagine a medium in which you can communicate in real time 24 hours a day with people anywhere in the world, become the person you've always wanted to be, and live in the home of your dreams. All of this and more is being done in networked, text-based, near-virtual realities throughout cyberspace called MUDs or MOOs. Depending on which source you consult, MUD stands for *multiuser dialogue, multiuser domain, multiuser dimension,* or even *multiuser dungeon,* which alludes to early networked programs attempting to simulate Dungeons-and-Dragons-type games. MOOs are *MUDs, object-oriented.* They are similar in use, differing primarily in the type of programming language used internally, but "programming is by no means required of MOO players or essential to the enjoyment of the MOO" (Horan, 1995, p. 100). Any user connected to the Internet can reach a MUD or MOO via telnet, a program that uses the Internet standard protocol to communicate with the remote computer. Once connected, the users employ various simple commands to communicate with each other. All communication is synchronous (instantaneous). This activity focuses on MOOs, the format most frequently used for educational purposes.

Teachers can use MOOs as an integral part of a language course, as an extension of the language classroom, or both. At a MOO, students can meet for class discussion, conduct group or pair work, exchange ideas and opinions with international peers, conduct research for reports, log MOO sessions for future analysis, and participate in conferences with their teachers (see Falsetti, 1995; Turbee, 1995). MOOs have many advantages for the nonnative-speaking language learner:

- They are text-based, and the user is required to use English (or the native language of the MOO in question).

- Unlike e-mail, MOOs provide for immediate feedback because the person to whom you are speaking is logged on at the same time you are. Miscommunications are often less painful than in real life. If one types something incomprehensible, the typical MOO response is "Huh?" or "I don't understand" rather than the blank stare or scowl often encountered in face-to-face communication.
- There are no visual cues (which first might appear to be a disadvantage). On a MOO you "see" only what the other person wants you to see. Because it is impossible to "lose face," MOO participants are more willing to engage in conversation and less afraid of making language errors, leading to relationships that might never be possible in real life.
- A MOO can aid in the creation of a true global village. MOO users are permanent residents of a virtual community. They have identities, residences, and a voice in how the community is run, which can be very important to students, who may experience alienation and loneliness when they study English outside their native countries. In addition, many MOOers go on to exchange e-mail, telephone calls, and visits.

To get a true picture of what the MOO experience is all about, your best bet is to try it. Though frustrating at first, with patience and a willingness to learn, students find MOO a rich and rewarding supplement to the language classroom. The initial time commitment is well worth the effort. Some teachers find that MOO meshes well with their pedagogical goals; for others it best serves different purposes, such as providing contact with other language instructors. Whatever your goals and needs, there is surely some aspect of MOO that can be beneficial to you and your students.

Procedure

Connecting to a MOO

1. Log in to your Internet account.
   - Via telnet: At the system prompt (e.g., % or $) type *telnet [address of the MOO]* (for example, *telnet schmooze.hunter.cuny.edu 8888, schMOOze University*—see below) and press <enter>. (See Appendix A for the addresses of MOOs with an educational focus.)

- With a client program such as TinyFugue (Keys, 1996) or MUDDweller (Macquelin, 1994).

If at all possible, use a visual client program instead of telnet to connect to a MOO. Telnet unfortunately allows incoming text (i.e., the text describing what other players are saying or doing) to be displayed over what you are typing as you type it. This is obviously very distracting and confusing, especially to new players.

2. At the opening screen, which usually contains instructions on connecting, type *connect guest* and press <enter>. (The first time you connect, you'll do so as a guest; afterward, you will sign on with a user name and password.)

Chatting in a MOO

1. Once in the MOO, use the basic commands as follows (see the Appendix for the commands in the context of a MOO conversation):
   - Type *@who* to find out who else is in the MOO.
   - Type *@join* [*name*] to move to the same room as [name] and begin a conversation.
   - Type *look* [*name*] to read the text that [name] has written as a self-description.
   - Type *"[what you want to say]"* to represent speech. When you type "[*what you want to say*]", the person you are chatting with will see the following on the screen:

   [name] said, "[what you want to say]"

   - Type *@describe me as "[description]"* to enter your own self-description.
   - Type the emote command, a colon (:), to describe an action. When you type :[*action*], the person you are chatting with will see the following on the screen:

   [name] [does the action]

Taking Students to a MOO

1. As with any function of the Internet, make sure you are comfortable using a MOO yourself before unleashing your students on one. Be aware that this will not happen overnight. In fact, it could take up to a month or even a semester to feel at ease in the MOO environment (Gardner, 1995). Think of it as learning a new language that you hope to share with others. Give yourself time to learn the basic "grammar" (the commands) and feel comfortable communicating and navigating in the MOO.

2. Provide the students with a conceptual picture of what the MOO will be like (perhaps using transparencies on an overhead projector) to prepare them for a potentially chaotic first experience.

3. Take small groups into the MOO for their first time so that they can provide all the help students need and so the students won't be overwhelmed by all the text in a crowded virtual room. The more familiar they are with MOO before they log on for the first time, the more risks they will probably take once there.

4. Review the netiquette guidelines for the MOO. Each MOO has different rules regarding courteous behavior, established by its inhabitants. For example, at *schMOOze University* it is considered polite to knock on the door of a private room or office before entering (type *knock* [*your name*]). As a pre-MOOing activity, have the students predict the *schMOOze University* guidelines based on what is considered respectful behavior at a traditional university.

5. Provide a handout of the basic MOO commands. At first, your students will feel secure knowing they have a handout to refer to, but they will quickly internalize the basic MOO commands and put the handout aside.

   ● Throughout your students' MOO use, encourage them to contribute to an ever-increasing master MOO command list as they discover commands on their own.

   ● Ask the students to send you the commands via MOOmail (see Visiting *schMOOze University*).

   ● By the end of the course, distribute to your students a self-generated list of basic and perhaps advanced commands to take with them for future reference.

Visiting *schMOOze University*

1. Take your students to *schMOOze University* (see References and Further Reading), which was constructed for ESL students with the following issues in mind:
   - Most MOOs are quite structured, with many available player commands (which can be hard to master) and an intimidating hierarchy.
   - Most Internet resources are plagued by a lack of "real" English. Internet users often find more-than-inventive spelling, such as *c u l8r* (*see you later*).
   - Many people worry about running into lewd or abusive players in MOOs. *schMOOze University* was built expressly as a place for ESOL students and teachers. Its creators designed the public spaces with the perception that students would benefit from a textually rich but conceptually simple, friendly, and easy-to-learn environment.

2. Tell your students the structure of *schMOOze*:
   - Unlike many MOOs, *schMOOze* has a small number of rooms divided into only six areas, allowing players to "walk" wherever they go.
   - In place of the bells and whistles popular on other MOOs, *schMOOze* has an on-line dictionary and language games. In addition, the Wizards (administrators) and their assistants are a helpful, friendly, approachable lot. There generally is one around when you need one, and they not only help show players how things work but also can disconnect any vulgar or abusive player.
   - *schMOOze* has facilities for classes and conferences. Resident programmers are happy to help ESOL instructors with programming for a class project.
   - *schMOOze* functions as an international teacher's room, where teachers can discuss techniques, share ideas, and, when the pressures of the real world bear down, just schmooze.

3. Tell your students to go directly to the <classroom> after entering *schMOOze* for detailed information on the basic MOO commands. If your students are visually oriented, direct them to the campus

<map>, which shows them their location and the location of the buildings at *schMOOze*.

4. Introduce your students to the special features of *schMOOze University*. Students can
   - converse with other language learners all over the world
   - access internal "MOOmail," newsgroups, gopher, and a library of information
   - share their own writing with others in the Stacks section of the library or in internal discussion lists
   - play text-dependent games such as Scrabble and Hangman
   - navigate a maze in which students must identify correct grammar usage to propel themselves from one end of a tunnel to the other.

Caveats and Options

1. Remember typing speed. Students who have low-level keyboarding skills will be at a disadvantage in a MOO, as they will find it difficult to keep up with conversation. However, conversing in a MOO could be just the motivation some students need to get their fingers flying.

2. Introduce the "lag monster": Prepare your students to expect some amount of lag (temporary freezing of the screen) during MOO sessions. Assure them that others in the same room and all over the MOO are experiencing the same thing to prevent the students from feeling hurt if they misinterpret the silence on the screen for being ignored. Tell the students that it is considered polite to send out a note letting others know you're lagging.

3. Set your cyber-English standard. Let students know in advance about the variations of English they might see in the MOO, and make sure they know your philosophies on what they can and can't use as part of your class (e.g., would you mark down a student for using *hafta* instead of *have to*?).

4. Check your institution's lab policy on MOOs and MUDs. Make sure the computer lab or classroom can technically support MOO. If not, you might have to put in a pitch for its educational value to be able to use it with your students.

References and Further Reading

Falsetti, J. (1995, March). *What the heck is a MOO and what's the story with all those cows?* Paper presented at the 29th Annual TESOL Convention, Long Beach, CA.

Galin, J. R. (1996). *MOOcentral* [On-line]. Available: http://www.pitt.edu/~jrgst7/MOOcentral.html

Gardner, T. (1995). *MOO teacher's tip sheet* [On-line]. Available: http://www.daedalus.com/net/MOOTIPS.html

Horan, M. (1995). Network update. *IALL Journal of Language Learning Technology, 28,* 95–103.

Keys, K. (1996). TinyFugue (Version 3.5) [Computer software]. Available FTP: tcp.com/pub/mud/Clients/tinyfugue

MacMahon, K. (1996). *MU* resource links* [On-line]. Available: http://homepages/together.net/~shae//guard.html (Addresses of MOOs with an educational focus and other useful information on MOOing)

Macquelin, O. (1994). MUDDweller [Computer software]. Available FTP: mac. archive.umich.edu:/mac/util/comm

Peters, R. (1996). *Unofficial TinyFugue information page* [On-line]. Available: http://fly.ccs.yorku.ca/mush/tf.html

Turbee, L. (1995). *MundoHispano* [On-line]. Available: http://web.syr.edu/~lmturbee/mundo.html

Appendix A: MOOs With an Educational Focus

Little-Italy [MOO]. Available Telnet: ipo.tesi.dsi.unimi.it 4444

MOO francais [MOO]. Available Telnet: logos.daedalus.com 8888

MundoHispano [MOO]. Available Telnet: io.syr.edu 8888

schMOOze university [MOO]. Available Telnet: schmooze.hunter.cuny.edu 8888

Vilmi, R. (1997). *HUT Internet writing project.* Available: http://www.hut.fi/~rvilmi/Project/

Appendix B: A MOO Conversation

Let us join two hypothetical users, Alice and Bob, to see how a MOO functions. Bob logs on to the MOO using his user name and password. Once connected, he types

@who

and sees that Alice also is connected. To talk to Alice, he must be in the same room, so he types

@join Alice

He "moves" to Alice's room, and the following appears on his screen:

Alice's Room

A cluttered but comfortable larger than average light-filled room decorated in a lagomorph motif. You see Alice. Obvious exits: Oak Door.

If Bob is the curious sort, he can type

look Alice

and the text that Alice has written to describe herself will appear:

look Alice

A petite blond given to peering into rabbit holes.

Alice set this description previously by typing

@describe me as "A petite blond given to peering into rabbit holes."

To describe a room or any other object the user has created is just as simple.

Alice begins a conversation with Bob. She types

"It's snowing outside now."

and the following appears on her screen:

You say, "It's snowing outside now."

Bob (and anyone else in the room besides Alice) will see

Alice says, "It's snowing outside now."

Bob can respond by using the same command (" ", to speak) or the emote command (:). Thus typing

:reaches for a snow shovel.

will produce

Bob reaches for a snow shovel.

on both his and Alice's screens.

Contributor

Julie Falsetti is an instructor at the International English Language Institute of Hunter College, New York City, in the United States. She is the cofounder of schMOOze University *and the coauthor of* Getting Together: An ESL Conversation Book *(Harcourt Brace Jovanovich, 1986) (e-mail: jfalsett@shiva.hunter.cuny.edu). Karla Frizler (MA-TESOL, San Francisco State University) serves as the instructional designer for City College of San Francisco, in the United States. She founded and co-owns* NETEACH-L *and maintains the* Frizzy University Network (FUN) *(http://thecity. sfsu.edu/~funweb) (e-mail: frizzy@earthlink.net, kfrizler@ccsf.cc.ca.us; http://hills.ccsf.cc.ca.us:9878/~kfrizler). Eric Schweitzer teaches computer science at Hunter College in New York City. He is a cofounder of* schMOOze University *(e-mail: eschweit@shiva.hunter.cuny.edu). Greg Younger is the computer-assisted language learning coordinator and an ESL instructor at the Economics Institute in Boulder, Colorado, in the United States. He is an administer/programmer on* schMOOze University *and* MundoHispano, *works with the International Student Discussion Lists project as comonitor of* MUSIC-SL, *and coordinates* NETEACH-L's *biweekly on-line discussions at* schMOOze University *(e-mail: youngerg@ spot.colorado.edu; http://spot.colorado.edu/~youngerg/).*

Getting Students MOOre Involved in Conferences

Levels
Intermediate +;
preuniversity or
university

Aims
Increase input in essay
conferences
Write for an authentic
audience

Class Time
15 minutes per student

Preparation Time
5–10 minutes

Resources
Computer and Internet
access for each student
Communication
software that can print
or capture conference
transcripts
Printer
Visual client software
(optional)

Holding a conference on a first draft of a student essay is an essential part of any ESL process writing course. The more input students have in their conferences, the more likely they are to revise, and thus improve, their essays (Goldstein & Conrad, 1990). However, many students can be shy, nervous, or self-conscious when meeting with their instructors face-to-face. Conferencing at a MOO provides students with a comfortable and relaxed atmosphere in which they can take more responsibility for the discussion and their essay. Because the conversation can be saved as a file, neither the student nor the teacher needs to take notes during the conference and can focus on the discussion itself.

Procedure

1. Introduce the students to the basics of MOOing. Take the class to a MOO in small groups and have them communicate with each other so that they get used to the unique environment. (For basic MOO directions, see Frizler, 1996; see also MOO and YOO, What to DOO? in this volume.)
2. Collect the first drafts of an essay from the students (via hard copy or e-mail). Have a copy of the draft with you for reference during the conference (either printed out or on screen in a separate window).
3. Set up conferences for each student. Ask the students to bring three questions regarding their essay to the conference.
4. Meet each student at the MOO to discuss the draft, focusing on the questions they bring.
5. Through nonverbal gestures, encourage the student to do most of the "talking" (see Appendix A).
6. Lead the students to state clearly by the end of the conference what they will focus on during the revision process.

7. Have the students save a log of the conversation to their hard drive or a floppy disk, or do it yourself and send it to the student in an e-mail message.

Caveats and Options

1. This method of conferencing can be used with either traditional (in-person) or on-line classes. In the case of the latter, it may be the only way to achieve real-time communication between the teacher and the students.
2. Both you and your students will benefit from using a visual client, software that splits the screen so that others' typing does not interrupt or scramble yours (see Appendix B). For information on visual clients (including software to download), see Galin (1996), McDonough (n.d.), and Thorne (1996).
3. For MOOs that focus on language learning, see MOO and YOO—What to DOO?, Appendix A.

References and Further Reading

Frizler, K. (1997). *Frizzy University Network* [On-line]. Available: http://thecity.sfsu.edu/~funweb

Galin, J. R. (1996). *MOOcentral* [On-line]. Available: http://www.pitt.edu/~jrgst7/MOOcentral.html

Goldstein, L., & Conrad, S. (1990). Student input and negotiation of meaning in ESL writing conferences. *TESOL Quarterly, 24,* 443–460.

McDonough, J. P. (n.d.). *MOO/MU* document library* [On-line]. Available: http://lucien.sims.berkeley.edu/moo.html

Thorne, S. (1996). *More about MOOs* [On-line]. Available: http://www.itp.berkeley.edu/~thorne/MOO.html

Warschauer, M., Turbee, L., & Roberts, B. (1994). *Computer learning networks and student empowerment* (Research Note 10). Honolulu: University of Hawaii, Second Language Teaching and Curriculum Center.

Appendix A: MOO Conversation Using Visual Client

This excerpt is from an interview with a student.

Teacher asks, "Can you give me three examples of Internet resources that have helped you improve your *writing* in English?"

Teacher agrees about MOOs being addictive.

Student says, "Of course, the Internet will be the most important thing in the coming future."

Teacher asks, "Why do you think so?"

Student asks, "Did you watch the film called 'Johnny Mnemonic'?"

Teacher glances at the poster of Keanu Reeves on her wall.

Student exclaims, "Internet is convenience!"

Teacher asks, "In what ways?

Student says, "Oh ... convenient."

Student says, "It is the trend."

Appendix B: MOO Conversation With and Without Visual Client

MOO conversation seen through raw telnet:

Frizzy [to Gregor]: "How is your thesis coming along?"

Gregor [to Frizzy]: It's coming. I wrote some more writing pedagogy stuff today.

to Gregor "Oh yeah? Did you say anything I should read befoGregor says, "I am g

oing to go to the library after awhile and pick up some re articles Ifound on UNCOVER> ..."

... tomorrow?

Frizzy [to Gregor]: "Oh yeah? Did you see anything I should read before ... tomorrow?

Gregor says, "Um ... no, nothing earthshattering."

Same MOO conversation seen through visual client:

Frizzy [to Gregor]: "How is your thesis coming along?"

Gregor [to Frizzy]: "It's coming. I wrote some more writing pedagogy stuff today."

Gregor says, "I am going to go to the library after awhile and pick up some articles I found on

UNCOVER."

Frizzy [to Gregor]: "Oh yeah? Did you see anything I should read before tomorrow?"

Gregor says, "Um ... no, nothing earthshattering."

Contributor

Karla Frizler (MA-TESOL, San Francisco State University) serves as the instructional designer for City College of San Francisco, in the United States. She founded and co-owns NETEACH-L *and maintains the* Frizzy University Network (FUN) *(http://thecity.sfsu.edu/~funweb) (e-mail: frizzy@ earthlink.net, kfrizler@ccsf.cc.ca.us; http://hills.ccsf.cc.ca.us:9878/~kfrizler).*

Structured Chatting On-Line With ESL Students

Levels
Intermediate +

Aims
Develop basic literacy, interactive, and critical thinking skills
Retain language structures and vocabulary
Learn independently

Class Time
2½ hours over two sessions

Preparation Time
1 hour

Resources
Computer for every three students
Internet access
Word-processing software
Printer

Chatting is a powerful means of teaching communication strategies to ESL students. It allows for natural interaction and offers students the opportunity to exchange information on a wide variety of topics with both native and nonnative speakers of English. In structured on-line chatting, one class chats live on-line with another in an interactive area by typing on the computer screen. After the chat is finished, a log (document of the chat) can be printed out to use for follow-up activities.

Procedure

Before Class

1. Find another teacher who is willing to take a class on-line to chat with yours.
2. Decide together on a topic that is relevant to both classes.
3. Have the students develop questions on the topic.
4. Send your students' questions to the other class, and receive the other class's questions.

In Class

1. Lead a class discussion of the classes' questions and answers. Note any similarity in the types of questions asked by each class to avoid unnecessary duplication of questions.
2. Divide the students into groups of three for practice. Have each group become experts on one or two questions by practicing writing the answers to the questions. Be sure to include practice with typing.

Live Chat

1. The following week, establish an on-line connection during class. Prepare to log the chat in process or save it automatically into a word-processing program.
2. Give each group of students a turn typing a question and answering a question.

After Chatting

1. Print out the log, make copies, and give one to each student or group (see Appendix A).
2. As follow-up activities, have the students correct the punctuation, capitalization, and spelling in the log or expand on the answers to the questions

Caveats and Options

You can have chats with classes worldwide in an Internet Relay Chat (IRC) area, a MOO (multiuser domain, object oriented) with a telnet application or using a commercial service that has a chat function. Some U.S.-based commercial services that offer chat functions are CompuServe and America Online.

References and Further Reading

Berge, Z. (1995, February 1). Computer-mediated communication and the online classroom: Overview and perspectives. *Computer-Mediated Communication*, 6-17.

Harris, J. (1992–1995). Mining the Internet for educational resources [Column]. *The Computing Teacher/Learning and Leading With Technology, 20–23.*

Harris, J. (Ed.). (1994). *Way of the ferret: Finding educational resources on the Internet.* Eugene, OR: International Society for Technology in Education.

Warschauer, M., Turbee, L., & Roberts, B. (1994). *Computer learning networks and student empowerment* (Research Note 10). Honolulu University of Hawaii, Second Language Teaching and Curriculum Center.

Appendix: ESL Chat

Chat between the Roxie Oberg, Adult Educator Even Start Family Literacy Program, Binghamton City Schools, Binghamton, NY, and the contributor:

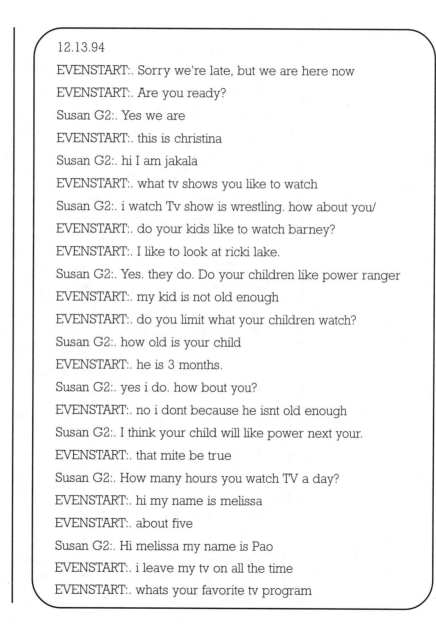

12.13.94

EVENSTART:. Sorry we're late, but we are here now

EVENSTART:. Are you ready?

Susan G2:. Yes we are

EVENSTART:. this is christina

Susan G2:. hi I am jakala

EVENSTART:. what tv shows you like to watch

Susan G2:. i watch Tv show is wrestling. how about you/

EVENSTART:. do your kids like to watch barney?

EVENSTART:. I like to look at ricki lake.

Susan G2:. Yes. they do. Do your children like power ranger

EVENSTART:. my kid is not old enough

EVENSTART:. do you limit what your children watch?

Susan G2:. how old is your child

EVENSTART:. he is 3 months.

Susan G2:. yes i do. how bout you?

EVENSTART:. no i dont because he isnt old enough

Susan G2:. I think your child will like power next your.

EVENSTART:. that mite be true

Susan G2:. How many hours you watch TV a day?

EVENSTART:. hi my name is melissa

EVENSTART:. about five

Susan G2:. Hi melissa my name is Pao

EVENSTART:. i leave my tv on all the time

EVENSTART:. whats your favorite tv program

Susan G2:. I leave my tv on some time.

Susan G2:. My favorite tv program is nature.

EVENSTART:. do you like soap operas

Susan G2:. How about you?

Susan G2:. No, i don't.

EVENSTART:. ilike roseanne

Susan G2:. how many Tv do have?

EVENSTART:. i like comedy shows

EVENSTART:. i have three TVs

Susan G2:. ooh that is a lot of tv.

EVENSTART:. is your tv black and white

EVENSTART:. how many TVs do you have?

Susan G2:. I have two tv . booth are color

EVENSTART:. does watching tv influence your childrens behavior

Susan G2:. Next week we have vacotion

EVENSTART:. we do too

Susan G2:. Ok Roxie we have to leave now...... Thanks, Merry Christmas and see you . in three weeks

EVENSTART:. ok susan, see ya soon. have a nice vacation

Susan G2:. Bye

EVENSTART:. Bye

Contributor

Susan Gaer is an assistant professor of ESL at Rancho Santiago Community College. She has been using chats with adult ESL students since 1991 (e-mail: SusanG2@aol.com; http://www.otan.dni.us/webfarm/emailproject/email.htm).

Part III: Working With the Web

Front, from left to right: Elsa Raquel Suozo, Sharon A. McKay, and Mulumba Mbombo; back, from left to right: Janna Victorovna and Thuy Tien (Tina) Cash at the Arlington Education and Employment Program (REEP), Arlington, Virginia USA.

Classroom and Teaching Applications of the World Wide Web

Contributor's Note

The introduction of the World Wide Web (WWW, or the Web) has been the catalyst for the recent surge of interest in and use of the Internet. Perhaps one reason for its popularity is that the WWW brings together many aspects of the Internet: audio, video, text, and images. Users can even send e-mail and transfer files within a Web site.

What Is the World Wide Web?

The WWW is a system of locations (also known as *sites* or *pages*) for accessing various resources on the Internet. Each page has an "address" called a *Uniform Resource Locator* (URL). The Web is organized (or disorganized, as the case may be) the way many of us think, that is, in nonlinear fashion. Exploring the WWW is like reading a book and coming across a word that reminds you of something from your past. That memory triggers a connection to another, and soon you are no longer reading the page on which you started. Like this chain of memories, the Web is a chain of topics associated or connected in some way.

What Can I Do on the Web?

There is probably a Web page somewhere in the world on just about any topic imaginable. The Web is a mostly unmoderated and uncensored source of information on everything from commercial advertisements to song lyrics, to on-line professional journals, to ESOL lesson plans (see Appendix A). On the WWW, you will find classroom materials such as maps, magazines, movie listings, weather reports, and recipes. In addition, stu-

131

dents can visit ESOL-specific sites to practice and get help with their English (see Appendix B; for information on how to get on-line and what to do there, see also Owen, Owston, & Dickie, 1995; Tillyer, 1996).

Retrieving information isn't all you can do on the Web. You can create your own Web page. (Frizler, 1997, is a collection of ESOL-related URLs that serves as a springboard for other ESOL teachers and students to use when getting started.) Some teachers also place course materials and assignments on their Web page and require students to download them on their own.

Besides being a resource for teachers and students, the Web can be an educational tool in the ESOL classroom. Teachers who are interested in incorporating the WWW into their teaching of ESOL have many avenues to explore depending on their pedagogical goals. As the activities in this section show, students can do WWW-related projects ranging from researching book reports (Cyber-Reports for Web Newbies) and conducting treasure hunts (WWW Quest for Knowledge) to creating Web pages (Getting Started in Multimedia ESL Materials Distribution on the Web) and publishing electronic (on-line) magazines (Publishing a Web Magazine). In doing activities on the Web, students develop and build many skills, among them critical thinking, vocabulary, reading skills such as skimming and scanning, and writing skills such as paraphrasing, summarizing, and quoting.

What Do I Need to Use the Web?

What you need is directly related to what you plan to do on the Web. Whether you use an IBM-compatible or a Macintosh computer, you will need several key items:

- an Internet account
- a modem, which allows your computer to dial your Internet account and connect to the Web
- a browser (see below)
- a SLIP or PPP connection if you want to use a graphical or multimedia browser
- a word-processing program that allows the creation of text-only (ASCII) documents, if you plan to create Web pages

For more detailed information on connecting to the Web, see References and Further Reading.

What Is a Browser?

A browser is a software program that works in much the same way as a publisher who ultimately determines how the text and graphics in an author's manuscript will look in the final publication. It reads the Web document, which is coded in a special language called *hypertext markup language* (HTML), and determines how that document will appear on the screen. A text-based browser, such as Lynx, will show only text, whereas a graphical browser, such as NCSA Mosaic or Navigator, offers the user a multimedia package, including text, images, audio, and video. Navigator is available at no charge to educators by anonymous file transfer protocol (FTP) (ftp.mcom.com).

A Web page viewed with Lynx looks like this:

```
                          Lynx-Web Browser                              ▼ ▲
                                        Linguistic Funland TESL Page  (p1 of 5)
 Linguistic Funland TESL: Resources for Teachers and Students of
 English

GO DIRECTLY TO THE MENU, OR GO TO THE LYNX (TEXT-ONLY) VERSION OF THIS PAGE.


 Welcome to the Linguistic Funland's TESL page. This site is intended
 to be a stepping off point for TESL/TEFL people into the wonderful
 chaos available on the Internet. If you have questions on what to do
 here, an introductory file is available.

 I have included links to other search mechanisms (such as the Applied
 Linguistics Virtual Library) which contain an enormous amount of
 useful information, and many of the other sites I have listed will
 connect you to still more. I hope that this page will continue to be a
 good demonstration of the resources available on the Net.

 This page has recently undergone its quarterly revision. The initial
 -- press space for next page --
   Arrow keys: Up and Down to move. Right to follow a link; Left to go back.
   H)elp O)ptions P)rint G)o M)ain screen Q)uit /=search [delete]=history list
LAT: 1  AXP     |Sts:Act|Kb:Rdy|Ptr:Aux|Scr: On|Emu:VT240|Md:Txt|Hlp: Alt-H|N↓C↓
```

The same page viewed with Navigator looks like this:

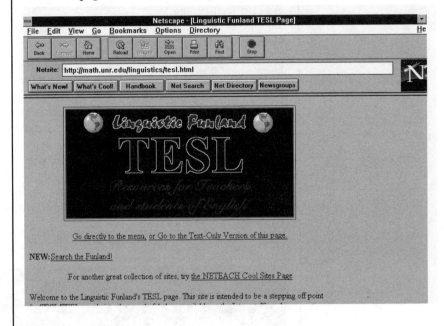

Although Lynx is commonly found on many servers, graphical browsers are the most popular. They stimulate the senses more than text browsers do, and using them is as easy as pointing and clicking with a mouse.

To use a graphical browser, you need

- a SLIP or PPP connection
- a 9600-baud or faster modem
- at least 8 megabytes of RAM

A text-based browser requires only a direct Internet connection and can be used with most modem speeds and memory amounts.

The browser is the vehicle in which you move around the Web. When you click on a link (usually a highlighted and underlined word or a graphic) in a Web page, hypertext transports you to another page of information related to that word or graphic. This new page can reside within the same directory as the first page or on a computer on the other side of the planet.

Hypertext also allows you to move between different types of data. For example, you can click on text and be transported to a related picture (and vice versa).

Where Do I Start?

In Appendix A are the URLs of ESOL-specific and education-related Web sites for teachers to explore; Appendix B contains the URLs of sites with a pedagogical focus and other sites students may enjoy.

References and Further Reading

Ellsworth, J. (1994). *Education on the Internet*. Indianapolis, IN: Sams.

Frizler, K. (1997). *Frizzy University Network* [On-line]. Available: http://thecity.sfsu.edu/~funweb/

Lynx (Version 2.x) [Computer software]. (1996). Available: ftp2.ukans.edu/pub/lynx

Navigator (Version 3.0) [Computer software]. (1996). Mountain View, CA: Netscape Communications. Available: ftp.mcom.com

NCSA Mosaic (Version 3.0) [Computer software]. (1996). Urbana-Champaign: University of Illinois, National Center for Supercomputing Applications. Available: ftp.ncsa.uiuc.edu/Mosaic

Owen, T., Owston, R., & Dickie, C. (1995). *The learning highway: A student's guide to using the Internet in high school and college.* Toronto, Canada: Key Porter.

Sperling, D. (1997). *Dave's ESL Café* [On-line]. Available: http://www.eslcafe.com

Tillyer, A. (1996). Teachers' net gains: TESL-L and other Internet resources. In S. Fotos (Ed.), *Multimedia language teaching* (pp. 35–53). San Francisco: Logos.

Warschauer, M. (1995). *E-mail for English teaching: Bringing the Internet and computer learning networks into the language classroom.* Alexandria, VA: TESOL.

Williams, B. (1995). *The Internet for teachers.* Foster City, CA: IDG Books Worldwide.

Appendix A: Sites for Teachers

Collections of Many ESOL-Related Sites

Frizler, K. (1997). *Frizzy University Network* [On-line]. Available: http://thecity.sfsu.edu/~funweb/

Harris, K. (1995). *Linguistic Funland TESL: Resources for teachers and students of English* [On-line]. Available: http://www.linguistic-funland.com/tesltext.html

Electronic/On-Line Journals and Magazines

Computer-Mediated Communication [On-line serial]. Available: http://www.december.com/cmc/mag/

EX*CHANGE [On-line serial]. Available: http://deil.lang.uiuc.edu/exchange/

TESL-EJ [On-line serial]. Available: http://violet.berkeley.edu/~cwp/TESL-EJ/index.html

ESOL-WWW Curriculum Development

Rosen, L. (1996). *Teaching with the Web* [On-line]. Available: http://polyglot.lss.wisc.edu/lss/lang/teach.html

Web resources for composition [On-line]. (1996). Available: http://deil.lang.uiuc.edu/resources/TESOL/Heidi/student.html

On-Line ESOL Projects

Li, R.-C. (1996). *Learning English on the Web: English as a second language home page* [On-line]. Available: http://www.lang.uiuc.edu/r-li5/esl/

OHIO University CALL lab [On-line]. (1997). Available: http://www.tcom.ohiou.edu/OU_Language/OU_Language.html

University of Illinois at Urbana-Champaign, Department of English as an International Language. (n.d.). *LinguaCenter* [On-line]. Available: http://deil.lang.uiuc.edu/lchomepage.html

Vilmi, R. (1997). *HUT Internet writing project* [On-line]. Available: http://www.hut.fi/~rvilmi/Project/

Visalia Adult School [On-line]. (1995). Available: http://www.otan.dni.us/cdlp/visalia/home. htm

Welcome to schMOOze! [On-line]. (1997). Available: http://schmooze.hunter.cuny.edu:8888/

Appendix B: Sites for Students

Focus on ESL Grammar

Mills, D., & Salzmann, A. (n.d.). *LinguaCenter grammarsafari* [On-line]. Available: http://deil.lang.uiuc.edu/web.pages/grammarsafari.html
Purdue on-line writing lab (*OWL*) [On-line]. (1996). Available: http://owl.english.purdue.edu/

Focus on ESL Listening/Speaking

Li, R.-C. (1996). *Learning English on the Web: English as a second language home page* [On-line]. Available: http://www.lang.uiuc.edu/r-li5/esl/

Focus on ESL Reading/Writing

*EX*CHANGE* [On-line serial]. Available: http://deil.lang.uiuc.edu/exchange/ (student publishing)

Additional Web Sites to Explore

Kinesava Geographics. (1996). *The virtual tourist* [On-line]. Available: http://vtourist.com (Get maps and pictures of places all over the world.)
MIT Media Lab. (1996). *The electric postcard* [On-line]. Available: http://postcards.www.media.mit.edu/postcards/ (Send postcards to anyone with e-mail or WWW access.)
Pioch, N. (1996). *The WebMuseum network* [On-line]. Available: http://sunsite.unc.edu/louvre/ (View famous collections of art on-line.)
Welcome to the White House [On-line]. (1997). Available: http://www.whitehouse.gov/

Contributor

Karla Frizler (MA-TESOL, San Francisco State University) serves as the instructional designer for City College of San Francisco, in the United States. She founded and co-owns NETEACH-L *and maintains the* Frizzy University Network (FUN) *(http://thecity.sfsu.edu/~funweb) (e-mail: frizzy @earthlink.net, kfrizler@ccsf.cc.ca.us; http://hills.ccsf.cc.ca.us:9878/ ~kfrizler). She thanks D. J. Beech for his technical advice and support.*

Getting Students Started on the World Wide Web

Levels
Any; teachers

Aims
Prepare students to do WWW activities

Class Time
Variable

Preparation Time
Variable

Resources
Computer and browser
Internet access

No matter which WWW activities teachers incorporate into their ESOL classroom, they need to consider several topics during the planning stage: teaching the students how to use a browser, deciding which terminology to teach the students, and, if they will be creating Web pages, teaching the students how to use hypertext markup language (HTML). The activities below help teachers prepare their students to integrate the WWW into their ESOL learning.

Procedure

The Browser

1. Familiarize yourself with the browser you want to use with your class, as each browser has its own features. As a warm-up activity, search the Web for an article that will give your students a conceptual picture of the WWW. The hands-on, focused task will help you familiarize yourself with the technology.

2. Before the first class session on the Web, give the students the article or a handout based on it. Explain what the WWW is, using analogies or metaphors with which the students are already familiar, if possible.

3. Plan your strategy for introducing the browser to your students:
   - Create a handout with step-by-step instructions on moving around in the browser, such as using Navigator's navigation buttons.
   - Take the students on a hands-on tour of the browser.
   - Design an activity for focused practice in using the browser, such as a scavenger hunt or information-gap activity (see WWW Quest for Knowledge).

Terminology

1. Decide which terminology to teach your students (e.g., *link, browser, URL, home page*; see References and Further Reading).
2. Find definitions that you feel comfortable using (i.e., if you call a URL *U-R-L*, teach it that way). Remember to keep the definitions simple, and try to use analogies or metaphors whenever possible (e.g., some have described the WWW as a library). Make sure the students understand how the terms fit together to in the big picture—the Web.

HTML

1. To provide a conceptual picture of various HTML commands, compare creating a Web page to baking a cake. Frosting and sprinkles are not necessary for a cake to taste good, but they can add flavor and make the cake more visually appealing. In HTML, certain basic commands (e.g., <HTML>, <BODY>) are the basic cake, and other commands (e.g., <bold>, <italic>) and various images or graphics are the frosting and sprinkles. (See References and Further Reading for sources of HTML command lists.)
2. Remember that, like any language, HTML can be taught inductively (see Students Discover HTML). Make sure the students have ample computer time to explore HTML on their own—individually, in pairs, or in groups.
3. If you're using Navigator, show the students how to view the markup of existing Web pages (by clicking on *View* and then *Source*) so that they can build their critical thinking skills by figuring out HTML commands on their own.
4. Teach the basic commands (i.e., the minimum necessary to create a WWW page). Add more complicated ones as the students become more comfortable using HTML or become curious about how to do certain functions (i.e., create a bulleted list).
5. If you wish, give the students an HTML template to expand on. A template is helpful not only when the students are getting started but when they create pages, as using one can save time.

Caveats and Options

1. Depending on your teaching style, you may choose to take your students on a hands-on tour of the browser or the Web first and tell them they will receive a handout at the end of the activity. That way, they can focus on exploring instead of on following a page of notes (or feeling compelled to take notes themselves).

2. Make a conscious effort to see that the students understand the connection between pedagogy and technology. Clearly state the goals of every Web-related activity you have your students do. If they do not understand the focus of a lesson, they may get caught up in the computer-related aspect of the activity and feel as if they're in a computer class instead of an English class. You cannot remind your students (and yourself) too often of what you're doing and why you're doing it.

3. The WWW is a good introduction to the Internet for students with minimal keyboarding skills, as the students can navigate easily by pointing and clicking with a mouse (Navigator) or using the arrow keys (Lynx).

4. Subscribe to at least one discussion list that addresses the use of WWW in the ESOL classroom. Two are recommended here:
   - *NETEACH-L* is a discussion list through which teachers worldwide discuss potential applications of the Internet in the ESOL classroom. To join *NETEACH-L*, send an e-mail message to listserv @thecity.sfsu.edu with *subscribe Firstname Lastname* as the body of the message.
   - *TESLCA-L* is a branch of *TESL-L* (an international discussion list for EFL/ESL teachers) devoted to computer-assisted language learning. Subscribe to the main list (*TESL-L*) first, and then follow the instructions to join *TESLCA-L*. To join *TESL-L*, send an e-mail message to listserv@cunyvm.cuny.edu with *sub TESL-L Firstname Lastname* as the body of the message.

5. Encourage your students to take risks. As in traveling in real life, getting lost in the Web is half the fun of using it. The more willing your students are to explore and take chances, the more likely they are to learn.

6. Have a teaching assistant or technical resource person who is fluent in using the WWW assist you and the students while you are in the computer classroom or lab.

7. Schedule a 2-hour block of time in the computer lab, if possible, when doing Web activities. What you think will take 20 minutes may take 50, especially if some students have never touched a computer before.

8. Anticipate transfer delays when connecting to other places via links or by typing in URLs. As with a telephone line, if too many people dial into the same place at the same time, the line will be busy. In addition, if you or your students type in a URL with even one letter incorrect, you will not be able to access the information.

9. Provide the students with a few WWW links you think will be of interest to them. Be prepared for the students to discover sites you would consider inappropriate for the classroom, and plan how to deal with such situations.

References and Further Reading

See also References and Further Reading in the Contributor's Note to Part III.

Lynx (Version 2.x) [Computer software]. (1996). Available: ftp2.ukans.edu/pub/lynx

Navigator (Version 3.0) [Computer software]. (1996). Mountain View, CA: Netscape Communications. Available: ftp.mcom.com

NETEACH-L [On-line]. Available E-mail: listserv@thecity.sfsu.edu Message: subscribe [Firstname Lastname]

TESL-L [On-line]. Available E-mail: listserv@cunyvm.cuny.edu Message: sub TESL-L [Firstname Lastname]

Resources for Terminology Appropriate for Students

Crispen, P. D. (1994). *Patrick Crispen's Internet roadmap* [On-line]. Available: http://www.brandonu.ca/~ennsnr/Resources/Roadmap/Welcome.html

University of Minnesota, College of Education. (n.d.). *Web 66: A K12 World Wide Web project* [On-line]. Available: http://web66.coled.umn.edu/

Web publishing at SFSU [On-line]. (n.d.). Available: http://www.sfsu.edu/training/session1.htm#guides. (list of HTML guides available on-line)

Contributors

Karla Frizler (MA-TESOL, San Francisco State University) serves as the instructional designer for City College of San Francisco, in the United States. She founded and co-owns NETEACH-L *and maintains the* Frizzy University Network (FUN) *(http://thecity.sfsu.edu/~funweb) (e-mail: frizzy @earthlink.net, kfrizler@ccsf.cc.ca.us; http://hills.ccsf.cc.ca.us:9878/ ~kfrizler). Heidi Shetzer is a specialist in computer-assisted language learning and an ESL instructor in the Intensive English Language Program at the University of New Orleans, in the United States (e-mail: hshetzer@ix.netcom.com). They thank D. J. Beech for technical advice and support.*

◆ Visiting Web Sites World Wide Web Quest for Knowledge

Levels
Intermediate +

Aims
Investigate interesting
Web home pages
Harvest Web page
resources

Class Time
45 minutes +

Preparation Time
30 minutes +

Resources
Computer and browser
for each student
Internet access
Printer (optional)

This is a guided information-gap activity, sometimes called a *treasure hunt* or *scavenger hunt*, in which students search certain addresses and home pages to find answers to specific questions. In doing so, they practice such skills as reading and scanning English text, clicking on links, typing in and going to new addresses or locations, and writing simple or extended answers in English. Secondarily, students can practice copying and pasting text and graphics; downloading files or software; e-mailing registration forms, survey responses, and messages; using bookmarks; and printing.

Procedure

1. Before class, create a list of World Wide Web addresses and a worksheet containing tasks to complete at each one (see Appendixes A and B). Provide a varied "menu" of at least four or five choices for beginning "surfers."
2. In class, give the resource list and worksheet to the students. Have them choose two or three of the tasks to complete. In this way, the students can work at different home pages at different times, thereby decreasing the chances of someone's being refused a connection. Remind surfers to move on to another address any time they have trouble getting into a home page (always a good strategy to use on the Internet).
3. Discuss the problems encountered in searching for information on the Web, and present effective techniques and strategies.
4. Follow up with an independent research activity, such as a Cyber-Report (see Cyber-Reports for Web Newbies).

Caveats and Options

1. Vary the level of difficulty and the number of the tasks according to the students' English proficiency and level of expertise with the computer.
2. Search for sites and develop tasks that strengthen topic knowledge or skills your students are currently developing.
3. URLs (Web addresses) change constantly. Run a search for the topic or name of the home page if you can't get to it via the address in Appendix A. Also, run searches for your local city, county, and state pages.

References and Further Reading

Navigator (Version 3.0) [Computer software]. (1996). Mountain View, CA: Netscape Communications.

Appendix A: WWW Resources

ESL and Education Pages

Classroom connect: Internet made easy in the classroom [On-line]. (n.d.). Available: http://www.classroom.net

Frizler, K. (1997). *Frizzy University Network* [On-line]. Available: http:// thecity .sfsu.edu/~funweb/

Harris, K. (1995). *Linguistic Funland TESL: Resources for teachers and students of English* [On-line]. Available: http://www.linguistic-funland.com /tesltext.html

Intercultural e-mail classroom connections [On-line]. (n.d.). Available: http://www.stolaf.edu/network/iecc/

Purdue on-line writing lab (OWL) [On-line]. (1996). Available: http:// owl.english.purdue.edu/

University of Sussex Language Centre. (1997). *The virtual CALL library* [On-line]. Available: http://www.sussex.ac.uk/langc/CALL.html

Vilmi, R. (1997). *HUT Internet writing project* [On-line]. Available: http:// www.hut.fi/~rvilmi/Project/

WWW Information

Boutell, T. (1996). *World Wide Web FAQ* [On-line]. Available: http:// www.boutell.com/faq

Crispen, P. D. (1994). *Patrick Crispen's Internet roadmap* [On-line]. Available: http://www.brandonu.ca/~ennsnr/Resources/Roadmap/Welcome .html

Current Events

Cable News Network. (1997). *CNN interactive* [On-line]. Available: http://www.cnn.com/

Discovery Communications. (1997). *Discovery Channel online* [On-line]. Available: http://www.discovery.com/

National Public Radio. (1997). *National Public Radio online* [On-line]. Available: http://www.npr.org/

NetPressence. (1997). *CReAteYour Own Newspaper* [On-line]. Available: http://www.crayon.net/index.html

Time Inc. New Media. (1997). *Time Warner's pathfinder* [On-line]. Available: http://www.pathfinder.com/

Travel and Tourism

Cyberville Tech. (1996). *Asiaville: The global village in Asia* [On-line]. Available: http://king.ncb.gov.sg/cyber/ville.html

International Council of Museums. (1997). *Museums around the world* [On-line]. Available: http://www.comlab.ox.ac.uk/archive/other/museums /world.html

International Home Exchange Network. (1995). *The travel exchange network* [On-line]. Available: http://www.magicnet.net/homexchange /ten.html (ecotourism, research tours)

Kinesava Geographics. (1996). *The virtual tourist* [On-line]. Available: http://vtourist.com

Museums and Other Attractions

Kieslinger, M., & Kolnicker, M. (n.d.). *1002situations* [On-line]. Available: http://fgidec1.tuwien.ac.at/1002situations/ (interactive museum)

Rainforest Action Network. (n.d.). *Rainforest action network home page* [On-line]. Available: http://www.ran.org/ran/about_ran/

Smithsonian Institution. (1996). *Radio Smithsonian* [On-line]. Available: http://www.si.edu/resource/topics/onair/start.htm

Smithsonian Institution. (1996). *The Smithsonian Institution: America's treasure house for learning* [On-line]. Available: http://www.si.edu/newstart .htm

Smithsonian Institution. (1996). *Smithsonian tours* [On-line]. Available: http://www.si.edu/youandsi/join/tsa/start.htm

Universal Studios. (1997). *Universal* [On-line]. Available: http://www .mca.com/ (cyberwalk and back-to-the-future tour)

University of California Regents. (1997). *California museum of photography* [On-line]. Available: http://cmp1.ucr.edu/

University of South Wales, College of Fine Arts. (n.d.). *Fantasmagoric museum: A museum of metaphysical machines* [On-line]. Available: http://hepworth.cfa.unsw.edu.au/FM/home.html

U.S. National Aeronautics and Space Administration. (1996). *Aerospace educational services program* [On-line]. Available: http://www.okstate.edu /aesp/AESP.html

U.S. National Aeronautics and Space Administration. (1996). *NASA eureka! NASA online resources* [On-line]. Available: http://nic.nasa.gov/Eureka/

U.S. National Aeronautics and Space Administration. (1996). *SeaWiFs project home page: The living ocean* [On-line]. Available: http://seawifs .gsfc.nasa.gov/SEAWIFS/LIVING_OCEAN/LIVING_OCEAN.html

Welcome to the White House [On-line]. (1997). Available: http://www .whitehouse.gov/

High-Interest/Silly Pages

Berkeley Systems. (1997). *Ask Miss Hane* [On-line]. Available: http:// www.berksys.com/cafeslack/askmisshane.html

Berlin, S. (1997). *The useless pages* [On-line]. Available: http://www .go2net.com/useless/

Giffen, S. (1997). *Spider's hot links* [On-line]. Available: http://newreach .net/~sgiffen2/mylinks.htm

J.B.'s jelly donut page [On-line]. (n.d.). Available: http://vms.www.uwplatt .edu/~kleinr/jelly.html

Joe Boxer [On-line]. (n.d.). Available: http://www.joeboxer.com/

MIT Media Lab. (1996). *The electric postcard* [On-line].Available: http://postcards.www.media.mit.edu/postcards/

Paramount Pictures. (1996). *Coming attractions, current releases* [On-line].Available: http://paramount.com/motionpicture/homemp.html

Walker, C., & Leslie, B. (1997). *Centre for the easily amused* [On-line]. Available: http://www.islandnet.com/~cwalker/

Appendix B: Student Worksheet

Computer and Language Learning Class,
The Internet (World Wide Web)
University of Oregon Home Page:
http://www.uoregon.edu/home.html

Guidelines
- Do not send secured information (e.g., passwords, personal address or phone number, bank or credit card account numbers) over the Internet.
- Print only when necessary. Copy down addresses that you may want to revisit, but understand that sites can come and go very quickly on the Internet.

Navigator
Double-click on the Navigator icon to open the application. It is your "door" to the Internet.

University of Oregon Home Page
You will begin here, where Navigator often starts you on a University of Oregon computer. Answer the questions under *What's New?* Always type in home page addresses carefully. Take notes of addresses you may want to revisit.

What's New?

1. Go to *J.B.'s Jelly Donut Home Page*, a humorous home page at http://vms.www.uwplatt.edu/~kleinr/jelly.html. Scroll down to the "Jelly Donut Jokes" and find the answer to this joke: What do you get when you cross a jelly donut with King Kong?

   Answer: _____ (Ha ha!)

   If you're feeling brave, send a short e-mail response, as requested.

2. Go to *Joe Boxer*, another weird and wacky home page, at http://www.joeboxer.com/entry.html. Find the fly (insect) and click on it. I dare you! What happens?

   Answer: _____

3. Go to *Virtual Tourist II* at http://vtourist.com. Find your country. Send an e-mail message to add some interesting information about your hometown.

4. Go to *CRAYON* (*CReAte Your Own Newspaper*) at http://www.crayon.net/index.html. You can receive a personalized newspaper on worldwide issues related to politics, weather, comics, sports, and more. Fill out the form and choose the items you want to know more about.

5. Go to *1002situations* (interactive museum) at http://fgidec1.tuwien.ac.at/1002situations/. Tour the castle. You will be invited to put things in the rooms. What did you add?

Contributor

Leslie Opp-Beckman is an ESL instructor at the University of Oregon's American English Institute, in the United States (e-mail: leslieob@oregon .uoregon.edu; http://darkwing. uoregon.edu/~leslieob/index.html).

Cyber-Reports for Web Newbies

Levels
Low intermediate +

Aims
Practice using Internet
search engines
Learn about aspects of
home pages
Share information on
topics of personal
interest

Class Time
30–60 minutes +

Preparation Time
15–20 minutes

Resources
Computer and browser
for every one to two
students
Internet access
Word-processing
software
Printer

This hands-on activity makes a great follow-up for introductory lessons on the Internet. It encourages neosurfers to be brave language and computer explorers. Everyone succeeds because there is no right or wrong, only a great deal of information to share. Students experiment with one or more search engines, prepare a Cyber-Report (the traditional book report), and share it with the class. The overall format is flexible.

Procedure

1. Prepare a computer template or hard copy Cyber-Report worksheet for the students to complete (see the Appendix).
2. Make sure the class is familiar with the Internet by doing any introductory activities you like to use (e.g., treasure hunts, information-gap activities, netiquette discussion; see World Wide Web Quest for Knowledge). Introduce the search engine(s) the students will use, demonstrating the required forms for simple queries.
3. Divide the students into pairs and have them jot down a list of possible one- or two-word topics to search for on the Internet. Some examples are
   - a current class topic (e.g., the environment, pollution, rain forests, water, the media, racism)
   - a country
   - a famous person (e.g., president, Golda Meir, King Fahad, Michael Jackson)
   - hobbies and interests (e.g., skydiving, rafting, aliens, stamp collecting, MTV, animation)
   - vacation or travel destinations (e.g., Hollywood, Vancouver Island, San Francisco, New York)

4. Have the students choose one or two of the topics and search for them on the Internet, using a chosen search engine. If more than one search engine is available, have the students run second and third searches with the same query in different engines and compare their findings. Remind the students to copy addresses they may want to revisit, or have them print out the search reports as a record of all the addresses that were found. This is especially useful if the students will be completing the assignment outside class.
5. Give the students the handout or give them instructions for accessing the template. Ask the students to investigate various home pages and choose one. Have them complete the Cyber-Report worksheet and share it with the class.

Caveats and Options

1. Modify, add, and delete information in the Cyber-Report worksheet as needed.
2. Have the students complete the worksheet outside class or work in pairs as needed.

Appendix: Cyber-Report Worksheet

Cybernaut's Name and e-mail address:

Name of home page:

Home page address:

Attach a printed copy of the home page you are reviewing to this report.

1. What was interesting about this home page? Why did you choose it to share?

2. Comment on the following:
   ● other links (connections)

   ● sound

   ● videos

3. Copy and paste a short, interesting section of text here:

4. Copy and paste a "cool" graphics image here:

5. Were there any e-mail addresses at this site? If yes, for what purpose? Subscribe to an electronic magazine (e-zine)? Register? Complete a shopping survey? Fill out an information form of some kind? Join a club?
   Did you send a message?

6. Was there any free software to download?

7. Was there anything to avoid (because it was not interesting or still under construction)?

8. Will you visit this site again? Did you make it one of your bookmarks?

9. Copy and paste or type here 5–10 new vocabulary words you discovered:

Contributor

Leslie Opp-Beckman is an ESL instructor at the University of Oregon's American English Institute, in the United States (e-mail: leslieob@oregon.uoregon.edu; http://darkwing. uoregon.edu/~leslieob/index.html).

What a Site!

Levels
Intermediate +

Aims
Evaluate WWW sites as
resources for research
Search for information
on the WWW

Class Time
60 minutes over three
sessions

Preparation Time
60 minutes

Resources
Computer and graphical
browser for each
student
Internet access
Hypertext authoring
software (optional)
Projection system
(optional)

When asked to do research, students traditionally rely on library resources for their information. This activity helps students cope with one of the most difficult aspects of doing research: deciding which sources support the topic. To apply their library research skills to new resources available on the Internet, students generate topics and judge the usefulness of World Wide Web sites as resources.

Procedure

Session 1

1. Review the research process, and generate broad research topics such as the environment, health, or nuclear energy.
2. Divide the class into groups and have the students generate subtopics. For example, subtopics for the the topic *environment* might include *the economy, natural resources, pollution,* and *politics*.
3. After class and before Session 2, generate a list of Web resources by using search engines like *Yahoo!*, *WebCrawler*, or *Lycos* (see References and Further Reading). Choose sites that you think the students would choose at various levels of research ability. Include
   - a variety of sites on each topic
   - at least one or two sites that are attractive but not necessarily appropriate for the research topic. (The sites students find attractive are often entertaining, visually appealing, small, and simple, but such sites are often inappropriate resources for research.)
   - sites that contain the search term but have little to do with the topic
   - if you come across one, a site that returns an error message (to expose the students to possible problem sites)

4. Make a worksheet listing the sites and their Uniform Resource Locators (URLs). Include space for the students to indicate the appropriateness of each site and the criteria on which they base their judgment.

Session 2

1. Review with the students how to use a graphical browser (e.g., Navigator or NCSA Mosaic). (This step works best with a projection system so the students can look at a site together.)
2. Hand out the worksheet. As a class, go on-line, look at a few of the sites on the worksheet, and discuss their usefulness:
   - Choose one site that has several layers, and show the students how to navigate from a main menu page to its branches.
   - Stress to the students that they should analyze the relevance of the site and its individual branches.
   - To look at the type of information presented, ask the students if they can find information in the form of facts, statistics, graphs, photos, or maps.
   - To analyze the site's information, ask the students who wrote the information, whether the writer is an authority on the topic, and when the site was last revised.
   - Remind the students that a site may be entertaining but not informative. Tell them that their main question about the site should be "Does this site have information that can provide support for research on my topic?"
3. Have the students fill in their worksheets. Assign the rest of the worksheet for homework, and tell the students to be prepared to discuss their findings.

Session 3

1. As a class, discuss the students' answers:
   - As the students mention criteria they used to judge the sites, list them on the blackboard. If the students overlook any criteria, add them to the list.

- Remind the students that different research topics will lead to different resources on the Web. For example, a search on the environment leads to many sites with statistics on pollutants, but a search on an American Indian tribe leads to photographs and historical documents.
- Stress that the students should analyze the sites' appropriateness for a given research project.

Caveats and Options

1. To provide the students with experience searching for information on the World Wide Web, have the students generate the list of URLs:
   - In Session 1, train the students to use some search engines.
   - Ask the students to generate a list of two or three relevant sites and to turn in a list of the names of sites and their URLs.
   - Combine the students' URLs to make the worksheet.
2. If you do this activity before a research assignment, such as a research paper, have the students form a list of guidelines for on-line research in preparation (see Session 2).
3. If you know hypertext markup language (HTML), prepare the worksheet as a Web page. The students will click on a hypertext link to the site and return to the worksheet to record their answers.

References and Further Reading

Lycos [On-line search engine]. (1996). Available: http://www.lycos.com
Navigator (Version 3.0) [Computer software]. (1996). Mountain View, CA: Netscape Communications. Available FTP: ftp.mcom.com
NCSA Mosaic (Version 3.0) [Computer software]. (1996). Urbana-Champaign: University of Illinois, National Center for Supercomputing Applications. Available FTP: ftp.ncsa.uiuc.edu/Mosaic
WebCrawler [On-line]. (1997). Available: http://www.webcrawler.com
Yahoo! [On-line]. (1997). Available: http://www.yahoo.com

Contributors

Suzan Moody and Lori Sandholdt Branham teach at the Applied English Center at the University of Kansas (e-mail: smoody@kuhub.cc .ukans.edu).

English Conversations for U.S. Parties

Levels
Intermediate

Aims
Learn to take part in conversations at parties

Class Time
50 minutes

Preparation Time
15 minutes

Resources
Computer with sound for each student
Internet access

This activity makes use of a World Wide Web ESL learning resource, *Learning Oral English Online* (Li, 1996). This on-line conversation book contains typical conversations on a variety of interesting topics, and students can click each sentence to hear it. The book can be easily accessed from any networked computer. This activity helps students learn what to say and how to behave at a U.S. party and how to make use of the Web's ESL learning resources.

Procedure

1. Inform the students that the next class will consist of group activities on the topic "Going to a Party." Ask the students each to prepare for the class by reading the lesson "Going to a Party" from the on-line conversation book *Learning Oral English Online*. Tell the students which computers available on campus can play audio.

2. In class, tell the students what a typical U.S. party is like and what they should pay attention to at a party.

3. Divide the students into groups of three or four. Ask them to simulate a conversation at a party. Encourage them to use the phrases and expressions learned from the on-line lesson.

4. Ask each group to act out their conversation in class.

5. Ask each group to comment on other groups' performance.

6. Give a summary at the end of the class, and ask the students to complete the exercises for the on-line lesson "Going to a Party" for homework.

Caveats and Options

1. Make sure the students know how to access the Web before doing this activity.
2. If necessary, download the text files and sound files and install them in a local computer to make it easier for the students to use the materials.

References and Further Reading

Li, R.-C. (1996). *Learning oral English online* [On-line]. Available: http://www.lang.uiuc.edu/r-li5/book/index.html

Contributor

Rong-Chang Li is a PhD candidate at University of Illinois at Urbana-Champaign. His major is computer-assisted language learning (e-mail: r-li5@uiuc.edu).

Using *Time* Magazine On-Line to Enhance Reading Skills

Levels
Advanced

Aims
Think critically in
English
Access current news
materials
Judge the relevance of
an article to a topic

Class Time
1 hour

Preparation Time
30 minutes

Resources
Computer and browser
for every two to three
students
Internet access
Printer

This activity allows students to reach out from the ESL classroom and deal with events happening in the real world. It requires reading but serves as a springboard for speaking and writing activities. Students work cooperatively; use their judgment to choose an article; read authentic, up-to-date materials; and make connections between the new and the old as well as between the known and the unknown. It gives the teacher the pleasure of using a variety of methodologies and techniques.

Procedure

Before Class

1. In your browser, go to http://pathfinder.com and click on the *Time Analysis* box, which takes you to the *Time* magazine homepage. Add a bookmark so you won't need to type in the World Wide Web address each time you wish to access it.

2. If you want your students to work on a specific topic, on the day of your lesson check the *Time Daily* (the daily news) in the *Time* home page to see if there is a news item that is suitable. If you don't care what news they work on, omit this step.

In Class

1. Divide the students into pairs or small groups.

2. Tell your students to go to the *Time* bookmark and click on *Time Daily*.

3. Instruct the groups to browse through the news items, which are usually short, until they find a relevant or interesting item.

4. Tell them to read the item carefully so as to answer the basic questions *who?*, *what?*, *where?*, *when?*, and *why?*, discuss the answers in their group, and write them down. You may want to limit the amount of time for this part of the activity to encourage concentration and a good pace.

5. Have the groups report to the rest of the class on the news item they read, using their notes to help them.

6. Ask the groups to discuss the key words from the news item so they can search for related articles.

7. Tell the students to click on the search box to the right of each news item, which allows readers to go to other articles dealing with the same topic.

8. Have the students click on the link to one of the articles listed and skim through it to decide whether it is relevant to their purposes.

9. Tell the students to read the article (and perhaps print it) if it is relevant. If it isn't, have the students go back to the list and look for another title. Make sure the students understand that a highlighted title (i.e., a title in a different color) indicates that somebody has already looked at the article. Tell them to avoid such titles if they want an article that no one else has read.

10. Have the groups compare the news item and the article, noting the following information:
    ● When was the article published?
    ● Does the news confirm any predictions made at that time?
    ● Is the focus the same?
    ● What background information helped them understand the current news?

11. Have the groups prepare an oral or a written report stating their main conclusions and either hand it in or choose a representative to report it orally.

Caveats and Options

1. Be prepared for some last-minute preparation, and be willing to change part of your lesson plan if necessary.
2. Have an alternative plan just in case the Internet connection is out that day. For example, print out some news items and some articles beforehand.
3. Use the activity with news items or articles from other sources.

Contributors

Miriam Schcolnik, director of the Language Learning Center and ESL course coordinator at Tel Aviv University in Israel, has published books, courseware, and multimedia software (e-mail: smiriam@post.tau.ac.il). Yedida Heymans, coordinator of Special Programs in the Division of Foreign Languages at Tel Aviv University, develops courseware and special curricula for university students.

Newspapers International

Levels
Intermediate +

Aims
Read newspaper articles
on the Web
Summarize and
categorize information

Class Time
4–6 hours

Preparation Time
1 hour

Resources
Computer, browser, and
Internet access for each
student
Word-processing
software
Printer
Overhead projector
Hypertext authoring
program (optional)

Before students can begin processing newspaper articles at advanced levels, they need to understand the general contents at an elementary level. Reading guides and question prompts can involve students actively in this process. In this activity students find newspaper articles located on the World Wide Web and use them for a variety of oral and written tasks designed to help the students process the information in the articles. The option of using SmarTText (Thibeault, 1994) to complete the written activities benefits the student readers/annotators, who must become intimately involved with the material to gloss the words correctly, and future students, who can improve their general reading comprehension by reading the high-interest, current articles selected by their peers.

Procedure

Before Class

1. Examine the daily newspaper most available to the students, and determine the types of articles and sections it contains. Choose two sample articles to use in class, and copy them onto an overhead transparency.
2. Search the Web for major newspapers in the students' target language (see Appendix A for a list of newspapers in English). Make a list of the newspapers and their Uniform Resource Locators (URLs: Web addresses).
3. Make a newspaper search sheet (see Appendix B) in the form of either a handout or a word-processing file.

In Class

1. Guide the students to state the purpose of one of the sample articles (to persuade, to inform) and its key ideas by asking them *wh-* questions. Work together to categorize the information in the article from general to specific descriptors (e.g., *football, North High School; injury, Robert Smith*).

2. Ask the students if the newspaper has an international focus. Elicit a list of newspapers commonly read in the homes of the students. Ask if they know the names of any major newspapers from other countries.

3. Hand out the list of newspapers and URLs. Ask the students to access at least two newspapers via the World Wide Web and to list the title of the most recent major headline of the day in each.

4. Hand out the newspaper search sheet, or tell the students how to access the word-processing file. Assist the students as they find information in a newspaper on the Web and answer the guided reading questions. If you are using the word-processing file, have the students copy and paste sections from the newspaper into the file.

5. Ask the students to choose one main article in the newspaper that they find interesting or that fits the theme of the unit the class is working on. Have them copy the article, paste it into a word-processing file, and print it.

6. Demonstrate the students' next task with an article on transparency:
   - Circle key items in the article, and label them with the words *who, what, where, when, why,* and *how.*
   - Place an asterisk (*) near any interesting details.
   - Locate any difficult language, and decide on information that would be helpful in comprehending the text (e.g., a definition, a translation, an example, a picture).

7. Have the students complete the task in Step 6 with the article they found on the Web.

8. Ask the students to trade articles with a classmate and decide if any additional difficult or confusing vocabulary should be listed and explained. Ask partners to judge the *wh-* labeling by putting a

+ (agree) or a – (disagree) next to the *wh-* listed. Have them discuss conflicting answers with their partner and come to an agreement.

9. Model a verbal summary, and introduce the idea of article descriptors that progress from general to specific. For example, an article about collecting tortoise eggs in the Galapagos Islands may have descriptors as follows: *Galapagos Islands, endangered animals, tortoise, breeding program*.

10. Ask students each to verbally summarize their article to their partner in response to question prompts from their partner (see Appendix C).

11. For homework, ask the students to summarize the article in writing, following the question prompts used by their partner, and to list article descriptors that progress from general to specific.

Caveats and Options

1. Ask the students to categorize the newspapers they review in class according to the focus of the newspaper (e.g., politics, business, computer news).

2. Ask the students to compare the daily newspaper most readily available with the newspaper they find on the WWW.

3. If your main goal is simply to familiarize the students with various newspapers, focus the newspaper search on cultural aspects of the country in which the target language is spoken. In a cultural clue search, ask the students to find information in newspaper articles related to the occupations, religions, animals, events, leisure pursuits, foods, or other aspects of the country. Then have the students provide a comparison summary (verbally and in writing) of two countries or locales that are dissimilar.

4. If possible, use SmarTText (Thibeault, 1994) or a similar program to set up the question prompts and do Steps 4–7 via computer. For example,

   - Have the students use SmarTText to compose a reading guide. Tell them to gloss difficult words themselves by entering translations, explanations, grammar notes, or multimedia annotations into the database. The reader can then click on unfamiliar words to access the annotations.

- Check the guides for appropriate definitions, explanations, and graphics.
- Have the students share the articles via computer networking, providing the SmarTText guides for reader support.
- Save and supplement the completed reader guides and related articles. The result is a "library" of high-interest articles with guides that provide realistic learning/teaching opportunities for the students.

References and Further Reading

Thibeault, T. (1994). SmarTText (Version 1.1) [Computer software]. Available: http://www.siu.edu/~nmc/smarttext.html

Appendix A: International Newspapers in English With WWW Sites

List of On-Line Newspapers

Editor & Publisher Interactive. (1997). *Online newspapers* [On-line]. Available: http://www.mediainfo.com/ephome/npapernphtm/online.htm

Africa

Weekly Mail & Guardian (South Africa)	http://www.mg.co.za/mg/mgmenu.htm
Zambia Post	http://www.zamnet.zm/zamnet/post.html

Asia

Asiaweek	http://www.pathfinder.com/Asiaweek/
Cambodia News	http://www.jaring.my/at-asia/camb_at_asia/camb_times/ct_list.html
Hong Kong Standard	http://www.hkstandard.com/
Tokyo Kaleidoscoop	http://www.smn.co.jp/
The Star (Malaysia)	http://www.thestar.com.my

Australia

The Age	http://www.theage.com.au/
Australia Tourist Radio	http://www.world.net/touristradio/

India/Sri Lanka

Sri Lanka Daily News   http://www.lanka.net/lakehouse/anclweb
                         /dailynew/select.html

News India-Times   http://www.newsindia-times.com

Sunday Observer   http://www.lanka.net/lakehouse/anclweb
                         /observr/select.html

North America

Kamloops Daily   http://www.netshop.net/dailynews
  News (Canada)   /local_news.html

United Kingdom

Electronic Telegraph

   Home page   http://www.telegraph.co.uk/login.html
   World news   http://www.telegraph.co.uk/et/access?
                         ac=120876745334&pg=//foreign.html

Appendix B: Newspaper Search Worksheet

Directions: Fill out the chart below as you browse through your newspaper on the World Wide Web. You may wish to copy and paste your answers rather than write them with pencil and paper.

Title	
Focus and description	
City and country of publication	
Date published	
Main sections	
Feature stories (page 1)	
Title of article that interests you the most	

Appendix C: Summary Questions Worksheet

Directions: Ask your partner these questions as he or she summarizes an article for you. Ask yourself the questions as you later prepare a written summary on your own.

1. What is the title of the article? When was it written? Who wrote it? Give a complete citation that includes the author of the article, the date of publication, the title of the newspaper, and the page numbers.
2. Who is the writer? Is the writer an expert on this topic? Should I believe him or her?
3. Does the writer want to persuade me to do something? What? Does the writer want to inform me about something? What?
4. What is the article about? What happened?
5. Who is the article about?
6. When did this happen?
7. What will happen next?
8. Where did it happen?
9. Why is this important?
10. Are there any other details that are useful or interesting?
11. What key words or ideas can be used to describe the article (list from general to specific)?

Contributors

Kim Hughes Wilhelm has taught ESL in Hong Kong and Malaysia and is Intensive English Program curriculum coordinator and assistant professor of linguistics at Southern Illinois University–Carbondale (SIUC), in the United States (e-mail: kimw@siu.edu). Thom Thibeault is the director of the Language Media Center, a developer of courseware for computer-assisted language learning, and an assistant professor of German at SIUC.

Supplementary Reading on the Web

Levels
Intermediate +

Aims
Read, summarize, and
write a personal
reaction to a WWW
article

Class Time
1–2 hours

Preparation Time
1–2 hours

Resources
Computer, Web access,
and browser for each
student
E-mail access
(optional)

This activity presents a way of using World Wide Web resources to supplement readings in an ESL textbook. By creating a World Wide Web page with hypertext links to articles on the Web, the teacher gives the students access to materials that echo or enhance the readings in the textbook. As presented below, the activity was written as a supplement to chapter 7 of Weidauer (1994), which contains articles about coping with difficult and challenging situations, including racism, violence, and depression.

Procedure

1. Select a chapter from your ESL textbook that contains themes of interest to your students.

2. Search the Web for articles to supplement that chapter. Use the same criteria to select articles that you would use for material from other print sources, such as magazines or newspapers. The number of articles you choose is up to you.

3. Create a Web page that has hypertext links to the supplementary articles. Your Web page can be simple or elaborate, depending on how much time you have to create it. If you wish, include the goal of the asssignment and instructions for students to follow (see the Appendix).

4. In the computer lab, have the students start their browsers and go to the Web page for the assignment.

5. Tell them to read the goal of the assignment and the instructions. Explain how you want them to complete and hand in the assignment (on paper, by e-mail, or on a Web form; see Caveats and Options).

6. Have the students complete the assignment and hand it in.

Caveats and Options

1. If e-mail is available, have your students complete the assignment in a message and send it to you when they have finished.
2. Have the students write the assignment in a word-processing program.
3. Create a Web form that students can complete and either print or send to your e-mail account. To process the text on the form, you can download a public domain script at the *WebMonitor* site (Pero, 1995; see References and Further Reading). Warn the students to be careful when completing assignments on forms: If they reload the Web page containing the form, their work will be lost.
4. Have students complete their assignment on paper to turn in to you, a good option to allow if some of your students are new to the keyboard or prefer to write on paper.
5. If students complete their assignment as an e-mail message or a word-processing file, make sure the computer can run both the Web browser and the e-mail or the word-processing program at the same time so the students can refer to the article while writing their assignment.

References and Further Reading

Pero, C. A. (1995). *Webmonitor* [On-line]. Available: http://hoohoo.ncsa
.uiuc.edu/webmonitor/module-mail.html

Weidauer, M. H. (1994). *Modern impressions: Writing in our times.*
Boston: Heinle & Heinle.

Appendix: Sample Assignment

Goal of this assignment: To practice reading and writing about a challenge on the World Wide Web, summarizing what you read, and writing about how it relates to your life.

Instructions: Explore the links below and choose one to read in depth. Choose a link to a topic that you can relate to or identify with. Answer the following questions:

- What is the challenge described on the page? Explain.
- How does that challenge relate to you? What experience(s) have you encountered in your life that are related?

Contributor

Heidi Shetzer is a specialist in computer-assisted language learning and an ESL instructor in the Intensive English Language Program at the University of New Orleans, in the United States (e-mail: hshetzer@ix .netcom.com).

◆ Creating Web Sites
Students Discover HTML: Teaching Web Page Creation the Inductive Way

Levels
High intermediate +

Aims
Guess meaning from
context
Think critically
Work cooperatively
Become familiar with
HTML

Class Time
50 minutes

Preparation Time
15–30 minutes

Resources
Computer and browser
for each student
Internet access
Handouts
Projection capability
(recommended)
Printer (optional)

Before students can benefit from creating their own pages for the World Wide Web, they must learn how to use hypertext markup language (HTML). In this activity, students work together to inductively learn the meanings of HTML codes required for basic Web page creation.

Procedure

1. Have the students view a variety of Web pages and the source code (markup) of at least one or two of them (e.g., to see pages with their coding visible in Navigator, click on *View* and then on *Source*).
2. Give the students Handout 1 (see Appendix A), which contains both source code (HTML) and the browser's translation (i.e., how the text will look when viewed on a graphical browser such as Navigator), and Handout 2 (see Appendix B), a list of the HTML codes (without their definitions or functions) used to create the document on Handout 1.
3. Instruct the students in pairs to compare the HTML and browser versions in Handout 1 to figure out the functions of the basic HTML codes on Handout 2. Model how to approach the assignment by leading the students through the first pair of codes. Once the class has determined that <HTML> and </HTML> are required at the beginning and end of every HTML document, let the pairs work on their own.

169

4. Circulate to answer questions and provide guidance as necessary.
5. Open a copy of Handout 2 on your computer so that all the students can see it on the overhead projector.
6. Discuss as a class the meanings or functions of each or pair of codes. Also elicit from the students that </> is necessary to end most commands.
7. Give the students Handout 3 (Appendix C), which contains basic codes and their definitions or functions.
8. For homework, have the students create a template, their own basic Web page, or both, using the commands they learned in class.

Caveats and Options

1. If you have a printer in the room, for Steps 5 and 6 type in the students' responses to Handout 2 in their own words (clarifying as necessary). Print out the document and distribute it to the students in lieu of Handout 3.
2. Make sure the students are aware of the locations of computer labs on campus and their days and hours of operation so that the students can complete the homework assignment.
3. At first, the students may be stunned by the task you have asked them to do (i.e., figure out HTML coding without ever having used it). Encourage the students to attempt to figure the codes out on their own. Assure them that you will provide any answers they cannot figure out themselves.

References and Further Reading

Navigator (Version 3.0) [Computer software]. (1996). Mountain View, CA: Netscape Communications. Available: ftp.mcom.com

Appendix A

Handout 1: HTML Source Code

```
<HTML>

<TITLE>FRIZZY UNIVERSITY NETWORK: FUN TUTORING
</TITLE>

<H1>Welcome to FUN Tutoring!</H1>

<p>

<BODY>

<center><IMG SRC=3D"at_work.gif"></center>

<p> This page is still <b>under construction</b>. In the future, you
will be able to sign up for an individual tutor to help you on-line with
your writing in English.

<p>

<IMG SRC=3D"dotpurp.gif">Return to
<A HREF=3D"Welcome.html">FUN Home Page</A>.
<IMG SRC=3D"dotpurp.gif"><p>

</BODY>

</HTML>
```

```
─|                    Netscape - [FRIZZY UNIVERSITY NETWORK: FUN TUTORING]          |▾|≑
File  Edit  View  Go  Bookmarks  Options  Directory                                  Help
  ⇦o           🏠           ⊚           ⇨o      🖶      🔍
  Back         Home        Reload        Open    Print    Find
```

Welcome to FUN Tutoring!

This page is still **under construction**. In the future, you will be able to sign up for an individual tutor to help you online with your writing in English.

⬤Return to <u>FUN Home Page</u>.⬤

Appendix B

Handout 2: Basic HTML Codes

<HTML> </HTML>

<TITLE> </TITLE>

<BODY> </BODY>

<H1> </H1>

<p>

<A HREF="...">

<IMG SRC="...">

<center> </center>

<b> </b>

Appendix C

Handout 3: Basic HTML Codes and Definitions		
Name	Code	Function
General (all HTML documents must have these)		
Document type	<HTML> </HTML>	Beginning and end of HTML document
Document title	<TITLE> </TITLE>	Top of page
Body	<BODY> </BODY>	Most of the page—text + pictures
Heading/header	<H1> </H1>	Descriptive information; subtitle
Formatting		
Center	<center> </center>	For both text and pictures
Bold	<b> </b>	Make text look darker and thicker
Italic	<i> </I>	Make text tilt to the right
Alignment		
Line break	 	Single return down to next line
Paragraph	<p>	Double return—leaves one blank line
Links and graphics		
Link something	<A HREF="...">	Connect to another document or URL
Show image	<IMG SRC="...">	See a picture

Contributor

Karla Frizler (MA-TESOL, San Francisco State University) serves as the instructional designer for City College of San Francisco, in the United States. She founded and co-owns NETEACH-L *and maintains the* Frizzy University Network (FUN) *(http://thecity.sfsu.edu/~funweb) (e-mail:frizzy @earthlink.net, kfrizler@ccsf.cc.ca.us; http://hills.ccsf.cc.ca.us:9878/ ~kfrizler).*

Getting to Know You Better From Across the Globe

Levels
Intermediate +

Aims
Publish on the Internet
Practice writing
personal information

Class Time
1–2 hours over two
sessions

Preparation Time
30 minutes before
Session 1
45 minutes between
Sessions 1 and 2

Resources
Computer and browser
for each student
Word-processing
software
Scanner and
photographs
Printer
Recorder (optional)

Many teachers have started to incorporate keypal (e-mail pen pal) projects into their teaching. Some student keypals enjoy writing to each other very much and exchange photos by regular mail as a way of getting to know each other better, but the Internet is making this unnecessary. With only a basic knowledge of hypertext markup language (HTML), the keypals can put together a document with their photo and some text and create a home page so that anyone with access to a graphical World Wide Web browser can see it. This activity is best associated with an e-mail project.

Procedure

Before Class

1. In your word-processing program, compose a 100-word introductory statement and save it on a floppy disk in the ASCII format.
2. Scan a photograph of yourself to the same directory on the floppy disk. Add the basic HTML tags to the statement and include your picture as an image source. Give the file a name, such as *palphoto.htm*.
3. Use a graphical browser, such as Navigator or NCSA Mosaic, to open the file to see how it looks. Fix any problems you find. Prepare and print a handout showing the basic HTML tags the students will need for this activity for the students.

Session 1

1. Introduce the activity to the students. Open the file you have produced for yourself as a sample. Give the students the handout with the basic HTML tags so that they can use them to create their own Web document.

2. Have the students compose their 100-word statement and scan their picture to a floppy disk.
3. Tell the students to check their files by accessing them with a Web browser.
4. Collect the students' disks.
5. Before Session 2, put all the students' files on your Web directory. Open a new file and make each of the student names a link to the files the students have prepared. To save time, put all the links/names on one page so that the students' keypals can all go to the same page, click on their name of their keypal, and retrieve the corresponding file with their keypal's picture and statement. Compress the files and put them on your server.

Session 2

1. Show the students the page you compiled in Step 5. Have the students look at each other's pages to find out how they can improve their own.

Caveats and Options

1. Use this activity only after student keypals have got to know each other well over e-mail.
2. To make the activity more interesting and challenging, ask the students to record a spoken version of their statement, save it as a sound file, and put it on their home page. This option requires more hardware and software support for both keypals.
3. To add more fun and difficulty to the activity, tell the students not to include their names in the statements and photos. Also have them compose the statements in such a way that they do not repeat what they have said in previous e-mail messages. The overseas keypals then look at the photos and statements and guess who their keypal is based on the personal information they have received by e-mail.
4. Treat this activity as the students' first experience in publishing on the Internet. Because they have created a home page, it makes sense to continue the effort and build up the page with further materials. Have them write up short articles and put them on the page to solicit responses. This could give them a strong sense of audience in their future writing efforts.

References and Further Reading

Navigator (Version 3.0) [Computer software]. (1996). Mountain View, CA: Netscape Communications. Available: ftp.mcom.com

NCSA Mosaic (Version 3.0) [Computer software]. (1996). Urbana-Champaign: University of Illinois, National Center for Supercomputing Applications. Available: ftp.ncsa.uiuc.edu/Mosaic

Contributor

John Wong is a lecturer in the English section of the Language Institute of City University of Hong Kong (e-mail: lijohnw@cpccux0.cityu.edu.hk).

A Multimedia Autobiography in 60 Minutes

Levels
Beginning +

Aims
Meet classmates at the
start of a course
Embellish a self-
description with
multimedia

Class Time
2 hours over two
sessions

Preparation Time
None

Resources
Computer with sound
and video for every two
to three students
Browser
Word-processing
software
Scanner and
photographs
Drawing software
(optional)

From the primary to the university level, students are asked to write about themselves a number of times, which may eventually kill their interest in the assignment. This activity takes advantage of the multimedia capabilities of graphical World Wide Web browsers and raises an ordinary self-introduction to a new and motivating level. It is especially suitable for adult and migrant language learners.

Procedure

1. Create a home page for yourself. Include a short self-description, a photograph, and a welcome message (see Appendixes A and B).
2. In Session 1, ask the students to write a 100-word description of themselves.
3. In Session 2, show the students how to produce basic hypertext markup language (HTML) files by teaching them to
   - add tags (HTML codes) such as title, heading, and paragraph breaks to their writing and save it as ASCII text with the extension *.htm(l)*
   - scan a photograph of themselves
   - audiotape a few sentences about themselves on the computer
   - save the text, photo, and recording as disk files
4. Have the students take turns scanning in their photos, or have them submit the photos for you or the computer technician to scan. While they wait, have them add HTML codes to their text files and audiotape their message.
5. Upload the files to a Web server.
6. Tell the students to read one another's home pages either in class or after class.

Caveats and Options

1. You need to have basic skills in HTML, photo scanning, and sound editing to do this activity. See References and Further Reading for helpful resources.

2. To adapt this activity for intermediate-level students, encourage them to write their statement in paragraph (narrative) form and add links to essays, projects, reports, and other documents they have written.

3. To save time, use a template file or an HTML editor instead of teaching HTML codes. In this option the students need only replace the content with their personal information, leaving the codes intact.

4. Save the photos as *.gif* files. Generally speaking, 4R (8 in. x 10 in.) photos are preferred, as they just fit in most browser windows. 8R (4 in. x 6 in.) photos can display more details, and *.jpg* photos are of better quality, but the files may be too large to fit on a floppy disk and take a long time to download.

5. Audio files take up quite a lot of disk space. Make sure the students keep their messages short.

6. If the class has no access to a Web server, run the home pages from the floppy disks or the local area network (LAN).

7. Check your equipment carefully before you do this activity. Some computers (e.g., high-end Macintosh computers) have built-in sound cards and microphone, but others may not.

8. Let higher level students include their favorite pictures or cartoons. Modify the activity so that they write about their hobby, school, work, or any topic that fits the picture or cartoon.

References and Further Reading

Lilley, C. (n.d.). *Hypermedia authoring tools* [On-line]. Available: http://fs2.spl.lncc.br/~tatiana/HypAuth.html

National Center for Supercomputing Applications (NCSA). (1996). *A beginner's guide to HTML* [On-line]. Available: http://www.ncsa.uiuc.edu/General/Internet/WWW/HTMLPrimer.html

Smith, M. (1995). *A guide to HTML and CGI scripts* [On-line]. Available: http://snowwhite.it.brighton.ac.uk/~mac/courses/html/html.html

Web66: A K12 World Wide Web Project. (n.d.). *Putting sounds on your pages (Mac)* [On-line]. Available: http://web66.coled.umn.edu/Cookbook/Sounds/Sounds.html

World Wide Web Consortium (W3C). (1996). *Hypertext markup language* [On-line]. Available: http://www.w3.org/pub//WWW/MarkUp/MarkUp.html

Appendix A: Traditional Self-Introduction

I am Stephen Mak, assistant professor in the Department of Building and Real Estate, The Hong Kong Polytechnic University. I teach construction economics, quantitative techniques, and information technology. I have two children, a 5-year-old boy and a 18-month-old girl. After obtaining my first degree from the Chinese University of Hong Kong, I went to the University of London to read for my Master of Science and Doctor of Philosophy degrees in Construction Economics. My research interests include risk analysis in construction and information technology application in the construction and real estate industries.

Appendix B: Multimedia Autobiography

Location: http://www.bre.polyu.edu.hk/~bssmak/

Department of Building and Real Estate
Stephen Mak

[Myself] [My Video] [My Children]

| Voice | (852) 2766 5820 | with Voice Mail |
| Fax | (852) 2764 5131 | Send Fax to me |

Send mail to me at: **bssmak@polyu.edu.hk**

Send fax to elsewhere via Internet

Qualifications:

- BSSc (CUHK), MSc (Lond), PhD (Lond)

Document: Done.

Contributors

Linda Y. O. Mak teaches undergraduate English proficiency courses at the Hong Kong University of Science and Technology (e-mail: lclindam @usthk.ust.hk). Stephen Mak is an assistant professor in the Department of Building and Real Estate at the Hong Kong Polytechnic University. He set up Hong Kong's second Web server (e-mail: bssmak@bre.polyu.edu.hk).

Teaching Story Writing With Hypertext

Levels
Intermediate +

Aims
Stimulate creative
writing

Class Time
30 minutes (prewriting
discussion)
60–90 minutes
(storytelling and
writing)

Preparation Time
30 minutes–2 hours

Resources
Networked computer
with sound and video
for every three to four
students
Word-processing
software
Browser
Scanner and recorder
(optional)

When teachers ask students to write stories describing their camping experience, the usual classroom restricts teachers to giving students one set of guiding questions to use when writing, resulting in nearly uniform written products. Hypertext as used on the World Wide Web offers teachers a way to tool to give students multiple sets of prompts, leading to different possibilities, perspectives, and dimensions in students' stories. This activity can be used whether there is only one computer for the whole class or there are several computers for students to share in groups.

Procedure

1. Before the lesson, use hypertext markup language (HTML) to type the instructions for the writing assignment (see the Appendix and References and Further Reading):
   - Write an introduction like the following:
     > One evening, you were camping out with a group of friends. Suddenly, you heard some strange noise. When you got out of the tent, you saw footprints on the sand. . . .

     Continue the story by telling what you did next and saw.
   - Write some questions for prewriting discussion (e.g., *What kind of noise did you hear? What kind of footprints did you see?*).
   - Create several sets of guiding questions, each leading to a different type of story (e.g., science fiction, detective, mystery, love).
   - Type in some suggested vocabulary for each type to trigger the students' imagination and help lower level students.
   - If you wish, audiotape some appropriate sounds or scan in some appropriate photos for each type.
   - Using HTML, link the guiding questions to the corresponding vocabulary, photos, and sounds.

Session 1

1. Lead the students through the prewriting discussion. Ask the students which type of story they would like to write.
2. Divide the students into groups of three or four according to the type of story chosen. Tell each group to make up a story within 30 minutes, referring to the guiding questions, vocabulary, sounds, and photos on the computer. Do not ask the students to write the story yet.

Session 2

1. Have each group report its story to the class orally and then write it up (on paper or in a word-processing program) in 200 words or more (depending on the level of the students).
2. Publish the stories on the class WWW page or in a class newsgroup, or post them on the notice board for peer feedback.

Caveats and Options

1. To adapt the activity for advanced students, have them scan in their favorite pictures or cartoons (if resources and class time allow) and role play the story in front of the class.
2. If you have only one computer for the whole class, put it in one corner of the room. Have all the groups write their stories on paper and use the Web page as a source of information and help. If several computers are available, have the groups sit in front of the page and write their stories in a word-processing program.
3. Remember that audio files take up quite a lot of disk space.
4. If the class has no access to a Web server, run the Web pages from a floppy disk or the local area network (LAN).
5. Check your equipment carefully before you do this activity. Some computers (e.g., high-end Macintosh computers) have built-in sound cards and microphone, but others may not.
6. Modify the activity for use with other topics, such as an accident report or crime report.

References and Further Reading

Aronson, L. (1994). *HTML manual of style*. Emeryville, CA: Ziff-Davis Press.

National Center for Supercomputing Applications (NCSA). (1996). *A beginner's guide to HTML* [On-line]. Available: http://www.ncsa.uiuc.edu/General/Internet/WWW/HTMLPrimer.html

Appendix: Web Page Writing Assignment

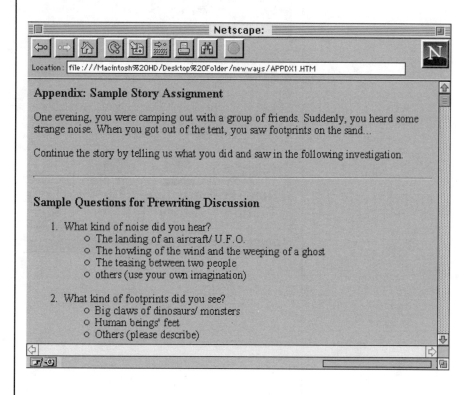

Netscape:

Location: file:///Macintosh%20HD/Desktop%20Folder/newways/APPDX1.HTM

Appendix: Sample Story Assignment

One evening, you were camping out with a group of friends. Suddenly, you heard some strange noise. When you got out of the tent, you saw footprints on the sand...

Continue the story by telling us what you did and saw in the following investigation.

Sample Questions for Prewriting Discussion

1. What kind of noise did you hear?
   - The landing of an aircraft/ U.F.O.
   - The howling of the wind and the weeping of a ghost
   - The teasing between two people
   - others (use your own imagination)

2. What kind of footprints did you see?
   - Big claws of dinosaurs/ monsters
   - Human beings' feet
   - Others (please describe)

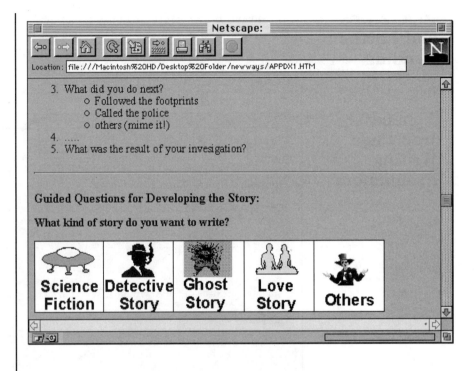

3. What did you do next?
   o Followed the footprints
   o Called the police
   o others (mime it!)
4. .....
5. What was the result of your invesigation?

Guided Questions for Developing the Story:

What kind of story do you want to write?

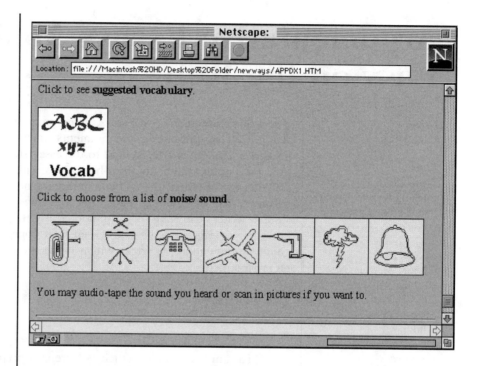

Contributors

Linda Y. O. Mak teaches undergraduate English proficiency courses at the Hong Kong University of Science and Technology (e-mail: lclindam @usthk.ust.hk). Stephen Mak is an assistant professor in the Department of Building and Real Estate at the Hong Kong Polytechnic University. He set up Hong Kong's second WWW server (e-mail: bssmak@bre.polyu .edu.hk).

Argumentative Essays Made Easy on the Web

In writing argumentative essays, many students follow the traditional approach of presenting proarguments, then counterarguments, then refutation. If there is a word limit to the essay, students often have a hard time presenting arguments from both sides while making it clear which side they are on. Their pro- and counterarguments also tend to be too well balanced. The concluding paragraph becomes the only place where student writers can state their opinion clearly. By incorporating hypertext into their writing, students can lighten their cognitive load by presenting counterarguments as hypertext, which allows the writer to focus more fully on proarguments.

Procedure

Before Session 1

1. In a simple text editor (such as Notepad), prepare the following files with the necessary hypertext markup language (HTML) tags:
    a. essay.htm (contents page)
    b. outline.htm (a very brief version of the essay)
    c. intro.htm (the introduction)
    d. proargu1.htm (Proargument 1)
    e. proargu2.htm (Proargument 2)
    f. proargu3.htm (Proargument 3)
    g. conclude.htm (the conclusion)
    h. conargu1.htm (counterargument to Proargument 1)
    i. conargu2.htm (counterargument to Proargument 2)
    j. conargu3.htm (counterargument to Proargument 3)
    k. refute1.htm (refutation to Counterargument 1)
    l. refute2.htm (refutation to Counterargument 2)
    m. refute3.htm (refutation to Counterargument 3)

2. In essay.htm, add hotspots (links) pointing to Items b–g so it can serve as the contents page.
3. Add a "mailto" hotspot in each proargument file to facilitate the e-mailing process.
4. Add hotspots in each proargument that jump to the corresponding counterargument.
5. Add hotspots in each counterargument that jump to the corresponding refutation.
6. Add hotspots in each refutation that jump back to the contents page.
7. Copy all the files to a directory in the hard disk of a few computers.
8. Ask the students to write an outline for an argumentative essay on paper for Session 1.

Session 1

1. Have the students copy Files a–m to their floppy disk.
2. Open essay.htm with a graphical web browser (such as Navigator) and show the students the purpose of the HTML files by clicking the various items and jumping back and forth.
3. Leave the browser open. Open the text-editing software and retrieve essay.htm. Type in the topic of the essay. Save the file and switch back to the browser. Reload the file essay.htm to let the students see that the topic has been added.
4. Open outline.htm, intro.htm, or both in the text-editing software to show the students what to type into the files. Caution them not to delete any of the HTML tags. Tell them to keep switching back to the browser to check the effect of whatever they have typed in with the text-editing software.
5. Have the students use the text-editing software to type their topic in their copy of essay.htm and their outline in their copy of outline.htm and then check the files using the browser. Tell them to write only a brief version of the introduction, the three proarguments, and the conclusion in outline.htm and to give the complete versions in the corresponding HTML files.

6. Ask the students to finish typing in essay.htm, outline.htm, intro.htm, proargu1.htm, proargu2.htm, proargu3.htm, and conclude.htm and to hand in their disks before the next session.
7. After collecting the files, check them to correct tag problems. Some students may have accidentally deleted some tags in the process of typing.
8. Put the files on the students' home page.

Session 2

1. Have the students read each other's proarguments on the Web and send each other responses by using the "mailto" hotspot in the proargument files. If the mailing function of your browser allows the sender to quote the current document, encourage the students to quote the proarguments they are responding to.
2. When the students have all sent and received responses, have them check their e-mail and save all the messages to the corresponding conargu.htm files.
3. Have the students summarize and edit the responses in the conargu .htm files.
4. Have the students type up the corresponding refutation htm files.
5. Have the students check all the files, using the browser to fix all problems.
6. Collect the students' disks.
7. Put the files on the students' home page.

Caveats and Options

1. This activity is best done in association with Getting to Know You Better From Across the Globe and E-Mail Keypalling for Writing Fluency. If you wish, invite keypals to read the proarguments and send in their responses.
2. Build a hotspot, such as "My First Essay on the Web," into every student's home page that jumps to essay.htm. Encourage the students to keep building up their home page by adding other hotspots of their own, such as interesting pictures and Web sites they have visited.

3. Encourage the students to reread their own proarguments from time to time and submit improved versions.

4. As a follow-up activity, ask the students to match their counter-arguments to the corresponding proarguments in the essay proper. When the students are ready, put them to the test of writing the essay in a more traditional way.

5. If incorporating HTML tags into 13 files and putting them onto the Web sounds too complicated, an easier way to encourage the use of hypertext in argumentative essays is to use WordPerfect hypertext features. To teach the students to create hypertext, specify the hypertext action as *Go to other document*. The teaching and learning can easily be done in 15 minutes.

6. Although the students don't get to respond to each other's proarguments, allowing them to present counterarguments to their own proarguments as hypertext still enables them to focus their attention on proarguments. In addition, presenting hypertext in other documents gives a clean and complete look to the current document.

References and Further Reading

Navigator (Version 3.0) [Computer software]. (1996). Mountain View, CA: Netscape Communications. Available: ftp.mcom.com

Windows Notepad (Version 3.11) [Computer software]. (1994). Redmond, WA: Microsoft.

WordPerfect (Version 6.1) [Computer software]. (1996). Ottawa, Canada: Corel.

Contributor

John Wong is a lecturer in the English Section of the Language Institute at the City University of Hong Kong (e-mail: lijohnw@cpccux0.cityu.edu.hk).

Publishing a Class Web Magazine

Levels
Advanced

Aims
Communicate technical
information to the
public
Integrate technical
writing and research
report skills with
Internet knowledge

Class Time
Variable over one
semester

Preparation Time
Variable

Resources
Networked computer
with sound and video
for every two to three
students
Browser
GIF graphic converter
Authoring and drawing
software
Scanner
Sound editor (optional)

Publishing students' work in a World Wide Web magazine or newsletter is both a highly motivating and an interactive venture. Over a semester, the class works collaboratively to produce a computer-related Web magazine on hardware, software, the Internet, and other subjects of interest to staff and students (both computer professionals and non–computer professionals). The activity has been piloted in several technical communications classes with college students at the upper intermediate to advanced level in English and in general education courses. It can be adapted for any course or language at any level.

Procedure

Week 1

1. Give the students an orientation to the Internet.

Week 2

1. Hold a WWW workshop in the computer lab. The aim is to introduce the students to the WWW, show them how to navigate it, and allow them to explore the WWW both inside and outside class.
2. In groups of three or four, have the students find, summarize, and evaluate one WWW page that is useful for English language learning.

Week 3

1. In groups of three or four, have the students take turns reporting orally on different WWW pages, on difficulties they have found in working with the Web, or on tips on accessing WWW resources. Have one representative from each group summarize the discussion for the class.

2. Have the students write up one report that they gave. Tell them that the best written reports will be included in the class magazine.

Week 4

1. Set up an editorial board consisting of an adviser (the teacher); several writing teams, each consisting of two or three reporters or writers (at least one with computer knowledge); and an editorial team:
   - an editor-in-chief and an assistant editor (to plan the overall layout of the publication, take turns chairing editorial meetings and producing minutes, coordinate the writing of the magazine by class members, and ensure that the magazine is consistent in style and presentation)
   - a computer officer (to handle computer graphics, desktop publishing, and other computer-related matters)
   - a treasurer
   - a publication manager (to handle photocopying and binding the magazine)
2. Tell the editorial board to hold its first meeting. The aims are to brainstorm and decide on a table of contents for the magazine and determine the magazine's standards and layout. Topics for articles might include
   - instructions or guides for using e-mail
   - descriptions, evaluations, or promotions of new software
   - tips on navigating the Internet
   - FAQs (frequently asked questions)
   - tips on designing a WWW page for technical communication classes
   - a proposal to set up an Electronic Resource Center and a survey of what staff and students want
   - advice on surviving on the Information Superhighway or in the Information Explosion Age
   - advantages of, difficulties with, and tips on learning with the WWW, including whether doing so is worth the trouble or is cost effective

- a discussion of whether and how the Web changes the way people learn, work, and play
- the joys of, the problems with, and advice on publishing on the WWW
- a discussion of whether interactivity on the WWW is a myth or only a teachers' idea, not a students' idea
- a discussion of whether the WWW helps or hinders different aspects of research

Make sure a member of the board takes minutes (focusing on the decisions made and the working schedule decided on) and writes them up after the meeting.

3. Have each writing team produce a one- to two-page proposal stating the names of the writers on the team and outlining the articles the team will produce and the methodology it will use to gather information. To collect information, the teams may conduct surveys, interviews, case studies, or site visits, or use other methods. Each team is responsible for word processing, proofreading, and graphics within its section.

4. Have the members of the editorial board start writing the editorial, foreword, table of contents, and acknowledgments for the magazine.

Week 5

1. Work on technical writing skills in class as the students collect information for the magazine outside class.

Week 6

1. Work on bibliography skills (e.g., paraphrasing, citing sources and references) in class. Have the students give informal progress reports (orally or via e-mail) on their research (writing team members) or on the magazine (editorial board members).

Week 7

1. Hold a workshop on hypertext markup language (HTML) in the computer lab. Show the students how to produce HTML files, scan

pictures, digitize audio and video components, and perform any other tasks they will need to produce the magazine.

2. Have the students create their own home pages and convert a previously written paper into HTML format.

Week 8

1. Have the writing teams submit the first draft of their articles for peer comments and editing. Have the editorial board hold its second meeting to review the articles.

Week 9

1. Have the writing teams give group oral presentations, spending 15–25 minutes presenting the results of their study or research and allowing 5–10 minutes for questions and discussion. Although the editorial board need not give group oral presentations, grade them on the skills of chairing meetings and coordinating and compiling the whole magazine.

Week 10

1. Have the writing teams revise their magazine articles; have the editorial board compile the first draft of the whole magazine.

Week 11

1. Tell the editorial board to hold its last meeting to finalize the magazine and review it.

Week 12

1. Upload the magazine to the WWW server.
2. Survey the students on the usefulness of the project and on whether their interests match what teachers think they need. Remind the students of this important aspect of WWW page production.

Caveats and Options

1. Make sure you have prior knowledge of some Internet applications (e-mail, newsgroups, gopher, file transfer protocol [FTP], browsers) before using this activity.

2. For a less formal publication, have the students produce a class newsletter, which is similar to a class magazine in that it contains the students' course assignments. The former may be more casual and include as many individual articles as possible, whereas the latter tends to be shorter and more condensed and contain a greater variety of articles.

3. Train the students not only to write HTML codes but also to think in hypertext and hypermedia.

4. Encourage the students to think of the readers' interests and needs and preferred paths of reading (i.e., ways of navigating through the pages in the magazine), balance text and graphics, and include variety and consistency in both content (types of articles) and style. Students tend to include a lot of graphics but overlook that they do so at the expense of file size and thus download time. Emphasize that what attracts people to visit a page again is not beautiful graphics or video but content.

5. Although some students like to use desktop publishing software to produce the hard copy of the magazine, the formatting will complicate the HTML conversion for the WWW. Thus it is more efficient to develop the HTML version right from the start or in parallel to the hard copy.

6. Tell the students to consider how the WWW magazine looks both on the screen and in print form, as some readers will prefer to read it on-line whereas others may print it and read it off-line.

7. Students normally care a lot about graphics and overlook interactivity. To increase interactivity, have the students add the e-mail addresses of the authors and cross-links to related Web pages, especially those dealing with similar subjects.

8. Be aware of copyright law and the potential for plagiarism. It is far too easy for students to copy text or graphics from the WWW into their paper or WWW page. Warn them of the consequences, and expose them to the WWW pages on intellectual property and related government policies. If they reprint someone's work, remind them to obtain copyright from the author or the publisher beforehand.

References and Further Reading

Chinese University of Hong Kong, ELT 3113B,H. (1995). *Technical express* [On-line]. Available: http://www.cuhk.hk/eltu/SW/TC.html

Kehoe, B. (1993). *Zen and the art of the Internet: A beginner's guide.* Englewood Cliffs, NJ: Prentice Hall.

Krol, E. (1994). *The whole Internet guide: User's guide and catalog* (3rd ed.). Sebastopol, CA: O'Reilly.

Appendix A: Web Technical Magazine Table of Contents

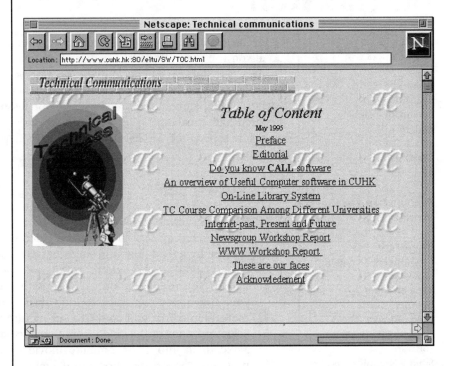

Contributors

Linda Y. O. Mak teaches undergraduate English proficiency courses at the Hong Kong University of Science and Technology (e-mail: lclindam@usthk.ust.hk). Stephen Mak, an assistant professor in the Department of Building and Real Estate at the Hong Kong Polytechnic University, set up Hong Kong's second Web server (e-mail: bssmak@bre .polyu.edu.hk).

Getting Started in Distributing Multimedia ESL Materials on the Web

Levels
Any; teachers

Aims
Collaborate in producing teaching materials

Class Time
Variable

Preparation Time
Variable

Resources
Computer with sound and video
Tape recorder
Scanner
Video camera
Hypertext authoring software
Sound-, graphics-, and video-editing software
Web server access

The procedure below for distributing teacher-made multimedia materials on the World Wide Web is based on my experience setting up an ESL Web site for an on-line conversation book, *Learning Oral English Online* (Li, 1996), which is a collaborative network project. Each ESL teacher participating in the project wrote one lesson with the guidelines I prepared and e-mailed the lesson to me. Now available on the Web, the project is a resource for ESL learners to use in practicing listening and speaking.

Procedure

1. Write a conversation or a story, prepare some content-related pictures, and make a short, related video with a video camera.
2. With a hypertext markup language (HTML) program, make your conversation or story into an HTML document.
3. Record your conversation or story with a tape recorder. Convert your audiotaped material into individual sound files.
4. Scan the pictures, and convert your picture files into *.gif* format.
5. Select portions of the video from the videotape you have prepared. Make them into 1- or 2-minute movie clips with a video-editing program. Convert the clips into digital files.
6. Organize your sound files, picture files, and video files into different folders or directories. Link them to the appropriate points in the HTML documents.
7. Put the whole package on a Web server to which you have write-access privilege.
8. Back up all your files.

9. Test the new Web site by asking your students to use it. Show it to your colleagues and ask them for comments. Make any necessary changes. Back up the whole package again.
10. Announce the site to the intended audience. Make use of it in your class. Share the resource with other ESL teachers.

Caveats and Options

1. Remember that graphics and video clips are large files. Too many of them will slow down the display and even freeze users' computers. Make sure they are not too big, and do not include too many.
2. If you are going to use other people's materials, including texts, pictures, video clips, pay attention to copyright considerations. Ask for permission before putting others' materials on the Web.
3. Pay attention to your file formats. Some formats are cross-platform, which means the files in these formats can be displayed both on Macintosh and IBM-compatible computers, but some formats are not cross-platform and cannot be used on the Web. For sound files, *.au* is the cross-platform format, which can be created and played with a sound program called SoundMachine (Kennedy, 1996). For picture files, the *.gif* format is cross-platform. While you are scanning a picture, you may not be able to save it directly to a *.gif* format. Save it to a common format such as *pict*, and then use a program called GIFConverter (Mitchell, 1996) to convert it into *.gif* format.

References and Further Reading

Kennedy, R. (1996). SoundMachine (Version 2.6.2) [Computer software]. Available: ftp.ncsa.uiuc.edu/Mosaic/Mac/Helpers/sound-machine-21.h

Li, R.-C. (Ed.). (1996). *Learning oral English online* [On-line]. Available: http://www.lang.uiuc.edu/r-li5/book/

Mitchell, K.A. (1996). GIFConverter (Version 2.3.7) [Computer software]. Available: ftp.ncsa.uiuc.edu/Mosaic/Mac/Helpers/gif-converter-237.h

Contributor

Rong-Chang Li is a PhD candidate at University of Illinois at Urbana-Champaign. His major is computer-assisted language learning (e-mail: r-li5@uiuc.edu).

Part IV: The Multimedia Machine

Editor's Note

Most personal computer systems sold today incorporate a CD-ROM player and are frequently bundled with reference materials (e.g., an electronic encyclopedia) and a series of games. CD-ROM materials are excellent as references and stimuli for writing and speaking, and educational/entertainment ("edutainment") software, such as SimCity Classic (and the other Sim- packages) and the Carmen Sandiego series, can stimulate vocabulary and fluency development through contextualized practice. The activities in Part IV illustrate how to integrate such materials in a pedagogically sound way while allowing students to enjoy learning. A caveat: These programs provide only the context for practice; they often present new language in an inaccessible form, so students may only practice at their own level of competence, fixing their own mistakes.

The second group of activities uses audio signal processing, a new area with great potential for developing pronunciation and other speech skills (see Pennington & Esling, 1996, for a state-of-the-art survey of this developing field).

References and Further Reading

Pennington, M. C., & Esling, J. (1996). Computer-assisted development of spoken language skills. In M. C. Pennington (Ed.), *The power of CALL* (pp. 153–189). La Jolla, CA: Athelstan Press.

SimCity Classic [Computer software]. (1995). Santa Clara, CA: Maxis.

Where in the World Is Carmen Sandiego? [Computer software]. (1996). Novato, CA: Brøderbund Software.

◆ CD-ROM "Edutainment" and Reference Software Serious Fun in the ESL Classroom

Levels
High intermediate +

Aims
Collaborate to solve a problem
Practice critical thinking, listening, reading, and speaking skills
Develop content-specific vocabulary

Class Time
2–3 hours

Preparation Time
About 60 minutes per program

Resources
Computer with CD-ROM drive and sound for every two to four students
Edutainment software

The underlying goal of most ESL classes is to get students to use English. This activity requires students to work together and think critically and creatively in English to solve a problem in an edutainment program. The programs, which are inherently entertaining but educational as well, focus on a variety of themes (e.g., science fiction, the environment, history, science), and new ones come on the market all the time. Adapting any of these highly popular software programs to the language classroom makes language learning enjoyable, purposeful, and meaningful. ESL students particularly enjoy these programs because they are designed for native speakers of English, and the programs allow teachers to evaluate a student's ability to use English to solve challenging problems. In addition, most of the programs can be played repeatedly without duplicating any games. Consequently, once students learn how to play a program, they can play it many times, reinforcing the vocabulary they have learned and refining their critical thinking, collaboration, listening, and speaking skills as well as problem-solving strategies.

Procedure

1. Familiarize yourself with the edutainment program.
2. Take note of special vocabulary that the students will need to know in order to play the game. For example, in the Carmen Sandiego games, the students will need to know the terms *arrest warrant, query,* and *case.*

3. Take note of the background knowledge needed to play the game. For example, in the Oregon Trail games, the students will need to know about the Oregon Trail and its place in U.S. history.

4. Introduce the theme of the program to the class. For example, if you are using Where in the USA Is Carmen Sandiego?, discuss what crime detectives do, and ask the students for vocabulary that detectives, police, and criminals might use.

5. Explain the general rules and goals of the program. For example, for Sherlock Holmes: Consulting Detective, explain that the goal of the game is to determine who committed a murder by searching for clues through the process of interviewing people, reading newspaper articles, and doing research.

6. Demonstrate how the program works:
   - Show the students how to start the program and the game.
   - Show the students any special features of the game. Many programs have special "hot" buttons to click on for different functions; be sure the students are familiar with these. For example, in the Carmen Sandiego games the user clicks on different buttons to make travel arrangements, look at the evidence collected, and pick up an arrest warrant.

7. Arrange the students in groups of two to four, with each group having access to a program. Either assign specific group members to specific tasks, or have the members rotate during the game. The tasks may include looking up information (a feature that many edutainment programs require), keeping notes on progress, typing information into the computer, and checking vocabulary.

8. Have the students play the game in their groups, working together to complete the task. Tell the students to keep track of the steps they took when playing the game so that they can explain what they did to accomplish the task or, if they were not successful, why they failed.

9. End the activity when the students successfully complete the game.

Caveats and Options

1. Almost all edutainment programs include listening and reading components; generally, the students must combine information from both sources to successfully complete the task. Most programs allow students to replay audio portions as many times as needed, and the reading portions usually remain on the screen for as long as the students wish.

2. Ask the students to keep track of the slang and idioms that are used as well as new vocabulary that they learn. Because the target audience for most of these programs is native speakers of English in middle and high school, some programs use a fair amount of slang, idioms, and plays on words. Many students are highly motivated to learn words that are introduced in these games.

3. If you wish, do the activity several times during the course of the program.

4. Make the activity competitive to add a little excitement. For example, in any of the detective-oriented programs, present challenges such as who can solve the most crime cases, who can solve them the most quickly, and who can solve them with the fewest mistakes. Many edutainment programs keep track of the time for the user.

5. Depending on the level of the students and the composition of your class, you may want to form the groups so that members have different L1s and must collaborate in English. However, if the students find these games very difficult, putting them in groups with speakers of the same L1 will allow them to use it as a tool if they get stuck.

6. Assign the programs as a regular computer lab activity done outside class. They are ideal for this purpose. Almost all the programs give information on the user's level and task time and congratulate the player in a final window, which can be printed out and given to the teacher as verification of completing the task. Doing the activity in the lab also allows the students to progress at their own pace without the constraints of the class schedule. The students usually can save a game and resume where they left off at another time.

References and Further Reading

Oregon Trail II [Computer software]. (1994). Minneapolis, MN: MECC.

Sherlock Holmes: Consulting Detective [Computer software]. (1994). Greeley, CO: Viacom International.

Where in the USA Is Carmen Sandiego? [Computer software]. (1996). Novato, CA: Brøderbund Software.

Contributor

Thom Upton is an assistant professor and the director of ESL at the University of Wisconsin-Eau Claire, in the United States (e-mail: uptonta@uwec.edu).

News From the Trail

Levels
High beginning +;
middle school–adult

Aims
Practice question words
Write news-style prose
Review information
from Trail software

Class Time
Variable

Preparation Time
0–10 minutes before
Session 1
Variable for other
sessions

Resources
Computer with CD-ROM
drive
Amazon, Oregon, or
Yukon Trail software

In this activity, learners work together to create a newsletter chronicling their journeys on the Amazon, Yukon, or Oregon trails for the "folks back home." In an ongoing activity, the students must take notes, turn speech and other types of communication into prose, and organize information so that readers can understand the sequence of events.

Procedure

1. Introduce the class to the software.
2. Have the students work through the software, either in a one-computer classroom or in a computer lab, either in class or as a free-time activity, and either individually or in small groups:
   - Tell the students to note regularly the date (provided by the software), the circumstances (e.g., place, time, people), and the action (e.g., people they're meeting, historical events, catastrophes) as they work with the software.
   - Provide a form for students who need more structure for such an assignment. (Yukon Trail, CD-ROM version, includes a notepad on which the students can take notes at any time.)
3. Review or teach the five Ws of newspaper writing and newspaper form.
4. After a preset time period on the trail (e.g., a week or a month), have the students choose the most interesting events that have occurred and write them up in newspaper style. Tell them to use the specific information that they have collected along the way. Edit the articles as necessary.
5. Have the students put the newspaper articles together and vote on a title for the ongoing newspaper. Distribute the newspaper to other students and teachers who might be interested.

Caveats and Options

1. In a one-computer classroom, use one copy of the software and put groups of students in charge of collecting information on different aspects of their adventure.
2. Have the students do further research on the time period, characters, and events and include them in the newspaper.
3. Have the students write up tips for other students on how to survive the Trail, crossword puzzles for Trail vocabulary, information on identifying animals and edible plants, and interviews with "pioneer" classmates.
4. Post the newspapers to the World Wide Web for other students to use on their journeys.
5. Instead of having the students write a newspaper, tell them to keep a journal of their travels and write informal letters to friends and family "back home." The friends and family (another class or another group of students) can reply, asking pertinent questions about the Trail.

References and Further Reading

The Trail software from MECC comes on disk and on CD-ROM, in networked and stand-alone versions.

Amazon Trail [Computer software]. (1996). Minneapolis, MN: MECC.

Oregon Trail II [Computer software]. (1994). Minneapolis, MN: MECC.

The Oregon Trail teacher's guide. (n.d.). Walla Walla, WA: Whitman Mission National Historic Park. (Available from Whitman Mission, Route 2, Box 247, Walla Walla, WA 99362 USA)

Yukon Trail [Computer software]. (1995). Minneapolis, MN: MECC.

Trail teacher's guide. (n.d.). Minneapolis, MN: MECC. (Educational version with handouts, lessons, and a list of related activities and resources; available from MECC, 6160 Summit Drive North, Minneapolis, MN 55430-4003 USA)

Contributor

Joy Egbert teaches in the Center for English Language Training at Indiana University, in the United States (e-mail: jegbert@indiana.edu; http://ezinfo.ucs.indiana.edu/~jegbert/).

Virtual Travelers

Levels
Intermediate +

Aims
Find information
Write letters and short
essays

Preparation Time
2–3 hours

Class Time
10 1¼-hour sessions

Resources
Computer with CD-ROM
drive for every one to
two students
EveryWhere USA Travel
Guide on CD-ROM
U.S. map
Colored pins

During this minicourse the students acquire basic computer skills, learn to use CD-ROMs, and get acquainted with Niagara Falls and Disneyland through texts and information on CD-ROM. They learn to write travel guide entries and do an oral presentation about a place of interest of their choice.

Procedure

Before the Course

1. Assemble two sets of sample texts relating to Niagara Falls and Disneyland, as follows:
   - one set of travel guide entries about the two places
   - one set of creative writing/personal impressions about them
   Sources of texts include the EveryWhere USA Travel Guide, travel agents, and library sources.

Day 1: Getting Started

1. Hold a general discussion on traveling and famous places in the United States that the students have heard of and would like to visit. On the map, mark places the students have visited with pins of one color and places they would like to visit with pins of another color.
2. Ask the students to write a journal entry about their visit to a famous place in the United States (or, for those students who have not had a chance to travel, the day of their arrival in the United States). Follow up with peer sharing and a class discussion.

Day 2: Introducing Travel Guides

1. Introduce the two places the students will focus on in this minicourse—Niagara Falls and Disneyland. Elicit from the students and write on the blackboard some basic information about these places, such as their location (East Coast vs. West Coast), general features (historical natural place vs. pop-culture, fabricated place), and significance in U.S. history and culture.
2. Discuss with the students the concept and purposes of travel guides and the type of information they include.
3. Ask the students to compose their own travel guide entries about the two places (using the information on the blackboard). Have the students hold small-group discussions before the writing activity, afterward, or both.

Day 3: Rewriting Travel Guides

1. Hand out the sample travel guide entries to the students and ask them to read the texts. Briefly discuss new terms, and answer any questions the students have.
2. Go over some of the specific requirements of different audiences (e.g., filmmakers, environmentalists, high school teachers who might be planning to take their students there, foreign tourists). Ask the students to rewrite the travel guide entries for a different audience.

Day 4: Emotional Experiences

1. Compare travel guide entries to creative writing about the same tourist attractions. Include such questions as *If travel guides are written for people who plan to go places, what would be different about a text written by somebody who visited a place and wants to share impressions with the audience? What would be similar?* The students might say that the second type of writing is more emotional, is more personal, and contains more details or personal associations.
2. Introduce new vocabulary from the other sample set of creative writing/personal impressions, and ask the students to read the texts at home.

Day 5: Introducing Virtual Travel

1. Tell the students that in today's world of technology it is possible to travel without leaving home and that the next stage of the course will be devoted to "virtual travel."
2. Introduce computer-related terminology (e.g., *click, double-click, icon, browse, search, menu*), and take the students to the computer room to work on the EveryWhere USA Travel Guide CD-ROM.
3. Show the students the general commands and ways to look for information. Give them a list of questions to answer as a way of becoming more comfortable with the computer. Questions could include the following:
   - Who is the musical director of the San Francisco symphony?
   - What is Biosphere II? How many biospherians participated in the experiment?
   - Which two points does the Alaskan Railroad connect?
   - When was the Gamble House in Pasadena (California) designed and built?
   - What is the address of the Heritage Square Museum (California)?
   - What is the Aloha Week Festival (Hawaii) dedicated to?
   - When (months, days, hours) is the Alexis Bailly Vineyard (Minnesota) open?
   - How many times a year does the Oklahoma City ballet perform *The Nutcracker*?

Days 6–9: Using the EveryWhere USA Travel Guide

1. Ask the students to find theme parks, natural parks and forests, or both in the software and compile a travel guide devoted exclusively to these places (using information and graphics from the CD-ROM).
2. Ask the students to prepare presentations of the travel guides they compiled for the class.

Day 10: Giving the Presentations

1. Have the students give their presentations.

Caveats and Options

1. Have the students find information about places of interest in a certain state or city and compile a corresponding travel guide.
2. Additional classroom activities might include
   - writing letters requesting information about certain historical places, museum schedules and programs, or travel information
   - working out an itinerary given certain data (e.g., a certain traveler, the purpose, time limitations, specific interests)
   - doing outside research about a place or historic event and writing a paper about it.

References and Further Reading

EveryWhere USA Travel Guide [CD-ROM]. (1994). Portland, OR: Deep River Publishing.

Contributor

Julia Gousseva is a graduate student in the ESL program at the University of Arizona, in the United States. Her main interest is computer-assisted language learning (e-mail: julia@gas.uug.arizona.edu).

Digging for Data

Levels
Beginning–intermediate

Aims
Practice using a mouse
and navigating
hypertext
Learn information-
searching techniques

Class Time
1–2 class periods

Preparation Time
1 hour

Resources
Networked CD-ROM or
CD-ROM-equipped
computer for
every three to five
students
Encyclopedia on
CD-ROM
Text-editing or word-
processing software
(optional)

Many writing and speaking activities require students to first gather relevant information. Computers using CD-ROM-based encyclopedias can now supplement the traditional trip to the library and go far beyond the limited information in the class textbook. On its own, this activity introduces students to the powerful abilities of visually based point-and-click encyclopedias and associated searching techniques. Combined with a writing assignment, this activity can also show the multitasking abilities of the Macintosh and Windows environments (i.e., the ability to search for data and copy them into a simple text-editing or word-processing program).

Procedure

Before Class

1. Become familiar with the CD-ROM encyclopedia your students will use.

Session 1

1. Give an example of how to find information using the CD-ROM-based encyclopedia. This can be done through a central display or networked through terminals so that the whole class can watch.
2. Choose a topic that has some relevance to your class, such as the country you are in. On the blackboard write the main topic and subtopics you want to find information on (e.g., population, languages, economics).
3. Demonstrate more than one way to search for the data. Most of the encyclopedias can search using subject groupings, alphabetic listings, and search strings as well as use hypertext to jump to related topics. Touch on each of these methods.

4. If you are including a writing or speaking project, show the students how to start the text-editing software and how to copy text from the CD-ROM and paste it into the software.

Session 2

1. Supply a new subject that is related to the assignment you want to give. Allow the students to search their CD-ROMs in small groups. Circulate to help those who encounter problems.
2. Have the students use the data gathered as input to complete a traditional writing or speaking project.

Caveats and Options

1. Because of the freedom given to students during the data search, working in groups may actually be more productive than individual access. Three or four students generate more ideas about directions to take when searching the CD-ROM for data.
2. Give beginners a topic that is as specific as possible. Information overload can occur if the topic is broad simply because of the ease of jumping between topics in a CD-ROM-based encyclopedia. For beginners, picking up the use of CD-ROM-based encyclopedias should not prove difficult because of the highly graphic nature of most encyclopedias.
3. If your lab does not have the same copy of an encyclopedia available on all the computers, use different CD-ROM-based software for different computers. In this variation, write a relevant topic on a piece of paper and attach it to the computer.

Contributor

Judy Chen is a business English instructor at the Overseas Chinese College of Commerce, Taichung, Taiwan.

Getting to Know *Grolier*

Levels
High intermediate +

Aims
Use a multimedia
encyclopedia
Learn subject-specific
terms and concepts

Preparation Time
About 1 hour

Class Time
About 45 minutes

Resources
Computer with sound
and CD-ROM drive for
every two students
CD-ROM encyclopedia
Handout

This activity is meant to be done on the first visit of an English for special purposes class to the Learning Center. Although the teacher's aims are as listed, the student perceives the goal of solving a puzzle: finding the word that runs down the left-hand side of the handout. The puzzle aspect focuses the activity and lends motivation, encouraging the student to continue looking for what may seem unconnected pieces of information.

Procedure

1. Set up the computers with the CD-ROMs in the drives and the opening screen of the encyclopedia on-screen.
2. After the students are seated in pairs at the computers, distribute the handout (see the Appendix) and explain how to complete it.
3. Explain how the search facility of the encyclopedia works, and do the first question on the handout with the students.
4. Have the students continue on their own. Circulate and help those students who have questions.

Caveats and Options

1. Tell the students that they do not have to answer the questions in any specific order.

Grolier new electronic encyclopedia [CD-ROM]. (1995). Danbury, CT: Grolier Interactive.

**References
and Further
Reading**

**Appendix:
Handout**

Getting to Know *Grolier*
Advanced Humanities

Resource: *Grolier New Electronic Encyclopedia*, 1995

Answer each question and write the designated letter on the line. The word formed down the right side of the page is a unit in this course.

1. What is the name of the book in which Jean Jacques Rousseau explained his political philosophy? (three words) Word 2, Letter 5 _____

2. One of the first principles in Rousseau's political philosophy is that politics should never be separated from what? Letter 3 _____

3. Whose heroic adventures are described in *The Iliad*? Letter 2 _____

4. Socrates' ideas helped to define what concept? Letter 1 _____

5. *Anschluss*, in connection to the events preceding World War II, refers to Hitler's intention to incorporate what country into the Third Reich? Letter 1 _____

6. Who wrote *Thus Spake Zarathustra*? Last letter _____

7. Who wrote *The Odyssey*? Letter 2 _____

8. What is the name of George Eliot's greatest work? Letter 5 _____

9. In what period did George Eliot live? Letter 5 _____

10. John Dewey, in addition to being a philosopher and an educator, was also a _____. (Fill in a word.) Letter 9 _____

11. What is a *polis*? Letter 4 _____

If you have time left:

12. See what each of the icons on the icon bar at the top does.

13. Look at an animation or video or listen to a tape.

14. Explore the Tree of Knowledge or the Pathfinders.

Contributor

Sara Kol teaches advanced English for specific purposes reading courses in the Division of Foreign Languages at Tel Aviv University in Israel and works on materials development in the Division's Learning Center (e-mail: sarakol@ccsg.tau.ac.il).

Meet the Multimedia Encyclopedia

Levels
High beginning–
intermediate

Aims
Get information on key
concepts of a topic
Learn to use a
multimedia
encyclopedia

Class Time
30–90 minutes

Preparation Time
15–30 minutes

Resources
Computer with sound,
video, and CD-ROM
drive for every one to
two students
Multimedia CD-ROM
encyclopedia

Each year more and more students learn English through content-based courses. One of the challenges this brings to teachers of low-level students is how to creatively present new information to students who have no prior knowledge of the topic. The multimedia features of CD-ROM encyclopedias make it possible for low-level students to learn a significant amount of information without having to wade through text that is beyond their language capabilities. Students can view pictures, listen to sounds, watch videos, and read captions to learn basic facts. These encyclopedias are a rich resource for low-level students and provide an enjoyable, technically appealing way for this group of students to increase their knowledge of a topic.

Procedure

1. Choose a topic on which to focus. Look up your topic in a multimedia encyclopedia. Look specifically for graphics, sounds, and captions. If they are present, decide whether they provide the students with important information about the topic.
2. Using the information available in these multimedia features, write a short list of questions for the students.
3. Prepare a worksheet that includes both instructions for accessing the information and the questions you prepared (see the Appendix).
4. If a lab is available during class time, have the students complete the worksheet in class. If not, assign it for homework, making sure the instructions are clear.
5. After the students have completed the worksheet, have them discuss their answers in small groups.

6. If this computer activity is used as a prereading or prelistening task, have the students prepare a list of other questions they hope to find answers to as they learn more about the topic.
7. To synthesize the information gained from the computer activity, have the students do one or more of the following:
   - prepare a 1-minute news broadcast
   - write a newspaper article
   - write a short summary
   - create a diagram, graph, chart, or illustration based on the information.

Caveats and Options

1. For this activity to be successful and enjoyable, the instructions for accessing the information need to be extremely clear.
2. If the students are novice computer users, encourage them to work in pairs.
3. As the students become more comfortable with the technology and more proficient in English, give them the responsibility for writing the handout questions. One way to set up this activity is the following:
   - Divide the class in half and assign each half a different, but related, topic.
   - Have the students work with partners to generate questions about their topic based on the information available in the encyclopedia's multimedia features and captions. Encourage the students to utilize all the multimedia features (e.g., pictures, sounds, videos) and captions when writing their questions.
   - Have the two groups exchange questions and answer the questions the other group wrote.

References and Further Reading

The new Grolier multimedia encyclopedia [CD-ROM]. (1993). Danbury, CT: Grolier Interactive.

Appendix: Worksheet

Apollo 11

Based on *The New Grolier Multimedia Encyclopedia* (1993)

1. Put the CD in the computer and double-click on the disk icon to open it.
2. Double-click on the *Grolier* icon.
3. When you see the *Welcome* window, click once in the *Close* box.
4. Click once on *Videos*.
5. Click once on *Space Exploration*.
6. Double-click on *Apollo 11 Launch*.
7. Click on the → to watch the video.
8. Click on *Caption* to read about the video.
9. Answer any of the questions below that you can.
10. Click on the *close* box of the caption and the video.
11. Double-click on *Apollo 11 Moon Landing*.
12. Click on the → to watch the video.
13. Click on *Caption* to read about the video.
14. Answer any of the questions below that you can.
15. Click on the *close* box of the caption and the video.
16. Double-click on *Apollo 11 Moon Walk*.
17. Click on the → to watch the video.
18. Click on *Caption* to read about the video.
19. Answer any of the questions below that you can.
20. Click on the *close* box of the caption and the video.
21. Go to the *File* menu and drag down to *Quit*. Close all the windows and drag the *Grolier* icon into the Trash.

Questions About Apollo 11

1. What day did Apollo 11 leave earth?
2. When did it reach the moon?
3. How many days did it take to reach the moon?
4. Who were the astronauts?
5. What country was Apollo 11 from?
6. Was this the first time anyone ever walked on the moon?
7. What does *launch* mean?

Contributor

Carolyn Heacock is the director of the ESL computer lab and a curriculum coordinator for ESL reading courses at the University of Kansas, in the United States (e-mail: cheacock@falcon.cc.ukans.edu).

How Can This Word Be Classified?

Levels
High beginning-
intermediate

Aims
Expand content-based
vocabulary
Improve categorization
skills
Learn to use pictures,
videos, sounds, and
captions in a multimedia
encyclopedia

Class Time
15–60 minutes

Preparation Time
15–30 minutes

Resources
Computer with sound,
video, and CD-ROM
drive for every one to
two students
Multimedia
encyclopedia on
CD-ROM

One effective way to help students learn new vocabulary is to have them categorize it. Ideally, students would have all the items they are going to categorize at their fingertips so they could experience the objects with many senses. Unfortunately, because this direct contact isn't always possible, teachers have to look for alternate ways for students to experience new objects and learn new vocabulary. A multimedia encyclopedia is a rich resource when objects aren't available. This activity is designed to present new vocabulary in order to prepare students for a reading, writing, or listening activity. By using a multimedia encyclopedia, students can access graphic and auditory information about related items and use this information to categorize the items.

Procedure

1. Select a set of words that can be categorized into distinct groups. When choosing a vocabulary set, be sure the encyclopedia has clear pictures of at least 10 objects in the set. If sound or the ability to see movement is critical for classifying the objects, be sure these features are available.
2. Create a worksheet that includes instructions for accessing the information, a list of objects to be categorized, and category headings (see the Appendix).
3. Introduce the topic in class. If you have access to one item or picture from each category, bring them to class and discuss the differences and similarities among the items.
4. Have the students discuss ways the objects can be categorized and explain the category headings on the worksheet.

5. Have the students work individually or in pairs to complete the computer worksheet. If you don't have access to a computer lab during class time, the students can do the assignment for homework as long as the instructions are clear.

6. After the students finish categorizing the information, have them compare their answers and discuss any discrepancies.

Caveats and Options

1. The success of this activity depends heavily on the quality of the worksheet instructions. These instructions need to be very clear so that novice computer users and low-level students can follow the steps easily.

2. This activity works well as an introduction to a reading, writing, or listening activity. The students can become familiar with the vocabulary and the categories through the computer activity and then review them during the main lesson.

3. After the students are comfortable with the multimedia encyclopedia, give them a broad topic (e.g., plants) and tell them to look up the multimedia information on that topic. Later, have them create their own categories, define the characteristics of each category, and list items that belong in each.

References and Further Reading

The new Grolier multimedia encyclopedia [CD-ROM]. (1993). Danbury, CT: Grolier Interactive.

Appendix: Categorization Activity for Low-Level Students

Categorizing Musical Instruments

Based on *The New Grolier Multimedia Encyclopedia* (1993)

1. Put the CD in the computer and double-click on the disk icon to open it.
2. Double-click on the *Grolier* icon.
3. When you see the Welcome window, click once in the *close* box.
4. Click once on *Pictures*.
5. Click once on *Fine Arts*.
6. Double-click on *Music*.
7. Double-click on *Musical Instruments*.
8. Double-click on *banjo*. Look at the picture. Then click once on the ⌂ to hear the sound the banjo makes. Write the word *banjo* in the appropriate column in the chart below.
9. Click in the *close* box for the Banjo window.
10. Do Steps 8 and 9 for the instruments listed below.

cello	harp	trombone
cymbal	marimba	trumpet
flute	organ	violin
French	horn	piano
gong	saxophone	xylophone
guitar	tambourine	zither

drums (Double-click on *Drums*. Then double-click on the different types of drums to hear and see each one.)

Stringed instruments	Wind instruments	Percussion instruments
banjo		

11. When you are finished, go to the *File* menu and drag down to *Quit*. Close all the windows and drag the *Grolier* icon into the Trash.

Contributor

Carolyn Heacock is the director of the ESL computer lab and a curriculum coordinator for ESL reading courses at the University of Kansas, in the United States (e-mail: cheacock@falcon.cc.ukans.edu).

Using a Multimedia Encyclopedia as Fuel for Descriptive Writing

Levels
High beginning +

Aims
Expand descriptive
vocabulary
Write descriptions
Learn to use a
multimedia
encyclopedia

Class Time
45–90 minutes

Preparation Time
15–30 minutes

Resources
Computer with sound
(optional), video, and
CD-ROM drive for every
one to two students
Multimedia
encyclopedia on
CD-ROM

Incorporating descriptive words into writing can be a challenge for many nonnative speakers. By taking advantage of the multimedia features of CD-ROM encyclopedias, this activity allows students to see and hear things they might not be able to in the classroom. Students use the computer to gather information about objects through graphics, sounds, and captions and then write preliminary descriptive statements about the objects. Through a classroom game and a vocabulary activity, students review the objects they have described and expand their knowledge of descriptive words. Students can later revise their descriptions or write a paragraph or story using the descriptive words.

Procedure

1. Select a category of concrete nouns. When choosing a category, be sure the encyclopedia has clear pictures of at least five objects in the category. Sound is helpful but not essential.
2. Prepare a worksheet that includes both instructions for accessing the pictures and a list of the objects the students will describe (see the Appendix).
3. On pieces of paper, prepare pictures representing the nouns on the worksheet. Fold up the pieces of paper so that the pictures are not visible.
4. Introduce the topic to the students, and have them create a list of descriptive words they might use when writing their statements. If this list is extremely short, introduce a few key words. The students will learn much of the related vocabulary as they do the assignment or in the follow-up activity, so it's not critical to teach a large number of descriptive words.

5. Have the students do the worksheet during class if a lab is available. If the instructions are clear, however, the students should be able to do the assignment outside class.

6. After the students complete the worksheet, put them into groups of three to five students.

7. Give each group some of the small folded-up strips of paper and the following instructions:
   - Have one student draw a strip of paper from the group's pile and describe the object on the strip of paper to the group.
   - After each description, the members of the group guess the object. If someone guesses correctly, the clue giver keeps the strip of paper. Another student becomes the clue giver and draws a strip of paper from the pile.
   - If the members of the group can't guess the object, they ask the clue giver for more information about the object.
   - If no one can guess the object, the clue giver puts the slip of paper back in the pile without revealing the object so it can be drawn by someone else.
   - The students continue taking turns being the clue giver until they have successfully described all the objects.

8. Because the students will probably need help with unfamiliar vocabulary as they play the guessing game, tell them to write down a question to ask the other groups or you later if no one in the group knows the word. For example, if they are describing animals and don't know the word *trunk*, they could write *What is an elephant's nose called?*

9. After all the groups have successfully described all the objects, have each group take a turn asking the other groups their vocabulary questions. If no student knows the word, tell the groups to refer to the dictionary, or provide the word for them. As words are defined, write them on the blackboard with a short definition.

10. Have the students expand the list of words on the blackboard by including other related descriptive words. If the students haven't mentioned key vocabulary items, add them to the list. For example, in a class of intermediate students, a list for jungle animals might

contain *fur, stripes, spots, mane, claws, fangs, tame, gentle, wild, fierce, ferocious, gnash, stalk,* and *pounce.*

11. Have the students revise their descriptions on their computer worksheet by incorporating more descriptive words and statements.

Caveats and Options

1. The success of this activity depends heavily on the quality of the worksheet instructions. These instructions need to be very clear so novice computer users and low-level students can follow the steps easily.

2. If the students aren't yet confident in their computer skills, encourage them to work in pairs. Be sure computer partners don't end up in the same groups during the game.

3. For beginning-level students, focus this activity on the acquisition of basic nouns and adjectives. For more advanced students, focus on word choice in descriptive writing.

4. To make this activity more challenging, include items on the list that are similar. The students will then have to look for discrete features and ways to describe them clearly.

5. This activity can work for most proficiency levels. As the students become more proficient in English, encourage them to take advantage of the captions and more of the multimedia features in the encyclopedia. For example, have them include descriptions of sounds in their statements.

6. Encourage the students to draw similarities between the characteristics of the items they're describing and other objects (e.g., *It sounds like a born* or *It looks like a tree trunk*.)

7. Have the students select an object from the list and write a paragraph describing that object or a short story about that object, incorporating descriptive words into their writing.

References and Further Reading

The new Grolier multimedia encyclopedia [CD-ROM]. (1993). Danbury, CT: Grolier Interactive.

Appendix: Descriptive Activity for Low-Level Students

Describing African Animals

Based on *The New Grolier Multimedia Encyclopedia* (1993)

1. Put the CD in the computer and double-click on the disk icon to open it.
2. Double-click on the *Grolier* icon.
3. When you see the Welcome window, click once in the *close* box.
4. Click once on *Pictures*.
5. Click once on *Animals*.
6. Double-click on *Mammals*.
7. Double-click on *Mammals Species*.
8. Double-click on *elephant*. Then click once on the ⌒ to hear the sound the elephant makes. Write six short sentences to describe elephants. (*How big is the animal? What color is it? What does it eat? What makes it different from other animals? Where does it live? Is it dangerous? What does it look or sound like?*)

   Sample sentences:
   - It's very big.
   - It's gray.
   - It has very big ears.
   - It has a long trunk (nose).
   - It has two tusks (long sharp things) near its mouth.
   - Its legs are like tree trunks (the bottoms of trees).
   - It has a loud voice that sounds like a horn.
9. Click in the *close* box for the Elephant window.
10. Do Steps 8 and 9 for the animals listed below.

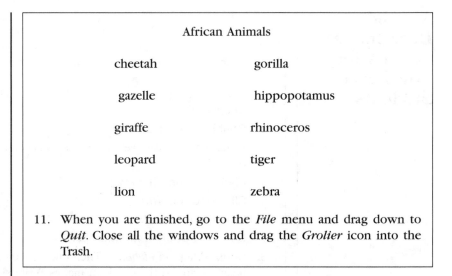

African Animals

cheetah	gorilla
gazelle	hippopotamus
giraffe	rhinoceros
leopard	tiger
lion	zebra

11. When you are finished, go to the *File* menu and drag down to *Quit*. Close all the windows and drag the *Grolier* icon into the Trash.

Contributor

Carolyn Heacock is the director of the ESL computer lab and a curriculum coordinator for ESL reading courses at the University of Kansas, in the United States (e-mail: cheacock@falcon.cc.ukans.edu).

Honeymoon in New Orleans

Levels
Intermediate +

Aims
Develop research and
computer literacy skills
Practice describing and
summarizing
Read for key
information
Rate and categorize
information
Match information to
varied audiences

Class Time
2-6 hours

Preparation Time
1 hour

Resources
Computer with CD-ROM
drive for each pair of
students
Reference software
Word-processing
software (optional)
Internet access and
browser (optional)

Procedure

Before Class

1. Write a fictional letter from Michael, a student who lives in another country or city and wants to visit your city (see Appendix A).
2. Prepare a "top 10" handout like the one in Appendix B for the students to use in class for Step 2.
3. Check your reference software (e.g., *Encarta 97 Encyclopedia*, *Grolier Multimedia Encyclopedia*) to see if it contains information on the city in which you live. If not, find another city for which information is available. Research and prepare a city guide for that city. Prepare a handout (to use in class for Step 6) that contains the headings in the guide but omits the information (see Appendix C).
4. Write descriptions of different types of travelers for the students to use in class for Step 8 (see Appendix D).

In Class

1. Distribute or read (or distribute and read) Michael's letter to the students.
2. Distribute the "top 10" handout. Ask the students to consider the type of information in which Michael would be most interested, working with a partner to rate (from 1 to 10) the top 10 categories of information they would include in a response.
3. Debrief and discuss the students' choices, creating a top 10 list with the class. Elicit more detailed information class members think should be included under each of the class's top 10 categories.
4. Have the class work with you on paper or computers to list the top 10 categories, organizing the titles so as to construct the layout for a

city guide. Decide which categories from the list should come first, which should be grouped together, and what type of information (e.g., list, chart, map, picture) would be the most useful in developing each category.

5. Encourage the students to recall the ideas presented in Step 2 and work singly or in groups to fill in information on the city guide for Michael from their own knowledge of their city. For lower level groups, do this step as a teacher-directed activity; for higher level groups, assign it for homework.

6. In the next class, have the students share their guides with their classmates. Guide the students to look up information on their city in the reference software. Ask the students to explore the program in order to add to their city guides for Michael by importing useful maps, explanations, charts, and other elements. If information about your city is not available, ask the students to look up another city that is available and complete the city guide you researched and prepared before class.

7. Assign or ask pairs of students to choose a city in which their target language is spoken. Encourage and assist each pair of students in using the software to locate information about that city. Ask them to learn as much as possible so that they become "travel experts" on that city.

8. Once the students are able to find additional information about their target cities in the multimedia encyclopedia, give the pairs of students the traveler descriptions (see Appendix D) and ask them to work with their partners to decide the most important categories of information their particular traveler(s) would require. For example, a mother traveling with a baby would want to know about climate, transportation around the city, safety, and "family-oriented" activities (e.g., museums, parks).

9. Ask the students to organize the most important categories of information into a city guide for their traveler(s), using information and materials gleaned from software reference programs. Remind them to always cite their sources.

10. Have each pair can present its travel guide to the class, explaining who the traveler is, what categories of information they believe are most important, and what details they provide to the traveler. Encourage the students to accompany the presentation with visual aids.
11. If you wish, follow up in the computer learning center by mixing pairs and having the students "teach" their new partner the information available about his or her target city.

Caveats and Options

1. If your learning center is networked, do the class sharing via computer.
2. Encourage the pairs to write their own traveler descriptions rather than supply them.
3. Invite another class to visit. Turn the classroom into a "travel agency," with the visitors asking questions about a city of their choice and your students finding the answers on computer. Be sure to limit the cities the visitors can ask about.
4. Do this activity with a World Wide Web browser instead of or along with the reference software.
5. Free city guides on most major cities that are available at large hotels or by writing the city's chamber of commerce. These are useful if you want to introduce the concept of a travel guide with print-based materials before moving to computer-based materials.

References and Further Reading

The Guide in Brief sections of the Insight Travel Guide series (Prentice Hall, 1989–1992; Houghton Mifflin, 1993–1997) provide excellent examples from which to brainstorm categories of information for the class-created travel guides.

Encarta 97 encyclopedia [CD-ROM]. (1996). Redmond, WA: Microsoft.

Grolier multimedia encyclopedia [CD-ROM]. (1997). Danbury, CT: Grolier Interactive.

Appendix A: Letter From Michael

Dear Students,

   I am 20 years old and am visiting the U.S. for the first time this coming summer. I have saved for several years so that I can take a trip to the U.S. during my summer break from university. I am writing to learn more about your city, as I know absolutely nothing about it. You should know that I enjoy the outdoors, am quite athletic, enjoy night life and dancing, am interested in history and political science, enjoy animals, and will be traveling with my sister, who is 18 years old. Could you help me to learn more about your city so that we can spend our time well? We will only have 1 week in your city. Thank you so much for your help.

Sincerely,
Michael

Appendix B: "Top 10" Information for Michael

Directions: With your partner, consider the categories of information listed below and decide the 10 most important for Michael. Rate them 1, which equals the most important, through 10. You'll be asked to share and explain your ratings with the class.

____ shopping

____ climate

____ entertainment and night life

____ famous people

____ city government

____ city history

____ historical places of interest

____ transportation within the city

____ transportation to and
      from the city

____ restaurants

____ places to stay/accommodation

____ universities

____ location/arriving and departing

____ seasonal activities and festivals

____ arts and culture

____ outdoor recreation

____ sports

____ population

____ economy/doing business

____ occupations and lifestyles

Appendix C: Travel Guide Headings

Location (map)
Getting there
    by plane
    by train
    by auto
    by ship
Climate and seasons
Banks
Tourist assistance and information
Tours and special activities
Sports
Shopping
Doing business

Famous people
Getting away
History
Medical concerns and assistance
Transportation in the city
Accommodation
Cultural events
Festivals, holidays
Courtesy, complaints
Night spots
Famous buildings
Religious services

Appendix D: Traveler Descriptions

- a mother who is interested in arts and crafts and local culture and who is traveling with a 1-year-old child
- a businessman who is interested in all kinds of sports, runs at least 5 miles a day, and enjoys fine dining
- a foreign couple on their honeymoon. They both work as lawyers and are looking forward to exploring nature, relaxing, and resting while learning about local people and culture and practicing their language skills.
- a family with three teenagers. They enjoy educational trips and being out and about all day. They must watch their budget, however.

Contributors

Kim Hughes Wilhelm taught ESL in Hong Kong and Malaysia and is currently the curriculum coordinator for the Intensive English Program and an assistant professor of linguistics at Southern Illinois University, Carbondale (SIUC), in the United States (e-mail: kimw@siu.edu). Kelly Maine received her MA degree in TESOL from SIUC. She has taught ESL in the United States, Spain, and Germany.

Tell Me About Your Country

Levels
Intermediate +

Aims
Learn the names of
countries and cities
Write physical
descriptions

Class Time
50 minutes

Preparation Time
None

Resources
Computer with sound,
video, and CD-ROM
drive for every four to
five students
Encyclopedia on
CD-ROM
Word-processing
software
Printer

In ESL situations, students need to learn how to describe physical entities both orally and in writing. With *Encarta 97 Encyclopedia* or any similar encyclopedia on CD-ROM, students in a heterogeneous class can find their country, or their favorite country, in the program and write a description using the maps, flags, national anthems, and charts available. Students can also read the text about their chosen country in order to learn the way physical descriptions are written. This activity incorporates reading, writing, speaking, and listening skills.

Procedure

1. Seat groups of four or five students at a computer system.
2. Ask each group to choose a country to look up in the encyclopedia.
3. Have the students run the encyclopedia and spend 15–20 minutes learning about their chosen country. Ask them to take notes and discuss among themselves the features of that country.
4. Have the students switch to the word-processing software and write three paragraphs about three main features of that country (e.g., location, weather, political system, agriculture, economy, industry). When they have finished, have them print out their paragraphs.
5. Have each group choose one member to present the country to other students.
6. When all the groups have finished their presentation, have the groups exchange papers and give each other feedback.
7. Have the students rewrite their description and print it out.
8. Collect all the writings and make copies for all the students.

Caveats and Options

1. With more advanced students, use the same procedure and information but ask the students to write tourist brochures. They can use the pictures available in the software to make the brochures more appealing and, if they wish, use desktop publishing software (e.g., PageMaker, Publisher) for the layout.

References and Further Reading

Encarta 97 encyclopedia [CD-ROM]. (1997). Redmond, WA: Microsoft.
PageMaker 6.0 [Computer software]. (1996). Seattle, WA: Adobe Systems.
Publisher (Version 2.0) [Computer software]. (1996). Redmond, WA: Microsoft.

Contributor

Yousef H. Almozaini is a PhD student in the Rhetoric and Linguistics Program of the English Department, Indiana University of Pennsylvania, in the United States (e-mail: CVRF@grove.iup.edu).

Look at Your Refrigerator

Levels
Intermediate

Aims
Understand process
description
Understand the
operation of a
refrigerator
Practice technical
writing

Preparation Time
30 minutes

Class Time
40–60 minutes

Resources
Computer with sound,
video, and CD-ROM
drive for every four to
five students
Encyclopedia on
CD-ROM
Word-processing
software
Printer
Overhead projector
(optional)

This activity is based on the multimedia encyclopedia, *Encarta 97 Encyclopedia*. In teaching English for specific purposes, teachers need to link the students' area of study with the English instruction to motivate the students to learn. Using Encarta will do this in two ways. First, because Encarta contains a number of animated technical topics ranging from refrigeration, to the internal combustion engine, the microphone, the television, gears and gear systems, and rockets, students will be motivated to listen to the description of a topic they are familiar with. Second, the animation and captions help them understand the language they are listening to. The activity links the students further to their content area by adding writing to the sound and animation.

Procedure

1. Seat four or five students at each computer.
2. On either the overhead projector or the blackboard, brainstorm with the class about the operation of a refrigerator by using semantic mapping, gathering information from the students, and posing relevant questions. Elicit answers from the students as a whole class.
3. Ask the students to start their computers, run the encyclopedia, and listen to and watch the animation on the operation of a refrigerator.
4. If the students wish, let them run the animation a second time and take notes.
5. Ask the students to summarize orally in their groups the description they have just seen.
6. Ask the students to switch to the word-processing program and write a description of the refrigerator operation process. Let them use their notes to help them in the writing.

7. Have the students print their descriptions.
8. Provide peer or teacher feedback on the students' writing.
9. Have the students write and hand in a final draft for assessment.
10. Choose the best description, and either read it to the class or ask a volunteer from that group to do so.
11. Have the students start the animation again to enhance their understanding of it.

References and Further Reading

Encarta 97 encyclopedia [CD-ROM]. (1997). Redmond, WA: Microsoft.

Contributor

Yousef H. Almozaini is a PhD student in the Rhetoric and Linguistics Program of the English Department, Indiana University of Pennsylvania, in the United States (e-mail: CVRF@grove.iup.edu).

Listen to Your Computer

Levels
Intermediate

Aims
Listen for specific
information
Write a technical
process description
Link written and spoken
discourse

Class Time
30–40 minutes

Preparation Time
1 hour

Resources
Computer with sound,
video, and CD-ROM
drive for every four to
five students
Encyclopedia on
CD-ROM
Word-processing
software
Printer

At the intermediate level, reading activities can prepare students to listen to authentic texts that students may find difficult. This activity motivates students to listen to a description of a process familiar to them, and the animation that accompanies the listening will help them to understand the language they are listening to. The activity enhances students' listening strategies because they have to listen carefully to put the scrambled sentences in order.

Procedure

1. Before class, transcribe one of one of the encyclopedia's animated sequences (e.g., Bernoulli's Principle, Internal Combustion Engine, Honey Bee, Microphone, Greenhouse Effect, Rockets, Solar System, Calendar, Color).
2. Prepare a scrambled version as a student handout, listing the transcribed sentences in random order.
3. Copy the scrambled word-processed file onto the hard drives of the computers that the students will be using. Make hard copies for the students, too.
4. In class, seat four or five students at each computer system.
5. Distribute a hard copy of the scrambled transcription to the students. Have the students read the transcription and familiarize themselves with the topic. Explain any unknown words.
6. Ask the students to start their computers, run the encyclopedia, and listen to and watch the animated sequence you transcribed.
7. Ask the students to put the sentences on the handout in the right order.

8. Have the students run the animation a second time to check their answers.
9. Tell the students to switch to the word-processing software and edit the file on the hard drive so that it becomes a full-length description of the sequence. When they finish, have them print their edited copy.
10. Tell the students to go back to the encyclopedia and check their writing by listening to the description again.

Contributor

Yousef H. Almozaini is a PhD student in the Rhetoric and Linguistics Program of the English Department, Indiana University of Pennsylvania, in the United States (e-mail: CVRF@grove.iup.edu).

Say It Yourself

Levels
Intermediate +

Aims
Practice speaking
Develop listening
strategies
Understand descriptions

Class Time
30-40 minutes

Preparation Time
10 minutes

Resources
Computer with sound,
video, and CD-ROM
drive for each student
Encyclopedia on
CD-ROM
Audio cassette recorder
(optional)

This activity aims to increase the students' listening and speaking strategies by having them listen to an animation in a multimedia encyclopedia, turn off the sound, and make their own version of the sound track. They can record their voice on the computer or on an audio cassette and compare it with the original recording.

Procedure

1. Before class, choose an animation for the students to work with.
2. Seat each student at a computer system.
3. Brainstorm with the students about the topic to be practiced to make sure everyone is familiar with it.
4. Have the students start their computers, run the encyclopedia, and listen to and watch the chosen animation.
5. Have the students run the animation a second time and take notes.
6. As a whole class, discuss the contents of the sound part of the animation so that all the students understand of the topic and feel able to repeat the information themselves.
7. Tell the students to start the animation again with the sound turned off. Ask them to describe the animation themselves and record it either on the computer or on an audio cassette. Circulate to help the students and give them feedback. Make it clear that the students don't have to repeat the computer's description verbatim; tell them to describe the topic in their own words.
8. Have the students play back their recordings and compare their content with that of the original sound track.

9. Divide the students into groups. Have them discuss their recordings, comment on them to their group, and select the best one to present to the whole class.
10. Play the selected recordings to the whole class. Have the class discuss the recordings and give more feedback.

Caveats and Options

If you do not have enough computers to have each student work individually, form groups of four or five students and have them record their descriptions one at a time.

Contributor

Yousef H. Almozaini is a PhD student in the Rhetoric and Linguistics Program of the English Department, Indiana University of Pennsylvania, in the United States (e-mail: CVRF@grove.iup.edu).

◆ Pronunciation and Speech Skills
Getting Started With Sound

Levels
Any; teachers

Aims
Use the computer's
sound capabilities to
teach pronunciation
Learn about speech
recognition and speech
synthesis software

Class Time
Variable

Preparation Time
Variable

Resources
Computers with sound
card, microphone, and
recording/playback
facilities

Computers that make use of text and voice have great potential for language teaching and learning. Fulfilling that potential depends on having software that allows teachers and students to perform language learning tasks that they find useful. Because the manufacturers of software that takes advantage of the computer's sound capabilities are not always educators, however, teachers who want either to use existing software or to design some themselves need to be sufficiently computer literate to make intelligent decisions.

How Does Software Use Sound to Teach Language Skills?

A few commercial programs make use of sound, mainly for teaching very basic language skills, but not all of the programs use sound "intelligently"; some simply make or access and play back digital recordings of sound. There are two intelligent ways in which the computer and software can deal with sound. One is *speech recognition*, in which the software interprets a sound made by the user and responds to it in some way. The other is *speech synthesis,* in which the computer and software produce speech instead of simply playing back recorded sound. A simple type of speech synthesis is *text-to-speech*, which reads the printed word (in the form of a text file) and converts it into sound. This type of speech synthesis is not truly intelligent because the computer does not understand what it is saying.

Speech Recognition Software

The best commercially available software for teaching and learning basic English language skills is Triple Play Plus! English, which uses a combination of colorful graphics, sound, and text to teach basic vocabulary and patterns of conversational exchange. Students can opt to listen only or to record their voice in response to prompts from the computer. The computer then makes use of its speech recognition capabilities to evaluate the student's audio input. Although it is limited to basic English, Triple Play Plus! is quite useful at this level.

The latest versions of a number of programs by Davidson and Associates, notably Spell It!, also make use of the computer's sound capabilities. Davidson's programs are designed primarily for English-speaking children but can be used quite profitably with ESL/EFL learners.

Focusing more specifically on pronunciation, the Summer Institute of Linguistics has produced a multimedia Windows version of its speech analysis system called CECIL (Summer Institute of Linguistics, 1994, 1995) (for IBM-compatible computers running Windows 3.1 or higher only). This program is very useful for displaying intonation contours and stress graphs of short utterances. The teacher records sample sentences, and the students practice imitating them. The program displays graphs for both the sample utterance and the student's rendition, after which the student can replay the two utterances alternately and compare them both auditorily and visually. (See Teaching Suprasegmental Features of Pronunciation Using Graphical Displays for suggestions on using this program.)

Speech Synthesis Software

Text-to-speech software can be used in a number of ways in the language classroom. One suggestion is given in Analyzing Pronunciation Errors: Computerized Applied Phonetics for Trainee English Teachers. As for other speech synthesis programs, Macintosh computers come with this capability built into a program called Simple Text. This program is intended as a sort of oral spelling checker but can have other uses as well.

Authoring Software

In the ideal world, you would create your their own lessons incorporating sound technology. In fact, this dream is not so very far from reality. Creating lessons that make use of speech recognition still requires programming skills, but even barely computer-literate nonprogrammers can quite easily have the computer produce speech to which students respond by typing text or making a choice. The software needed to accomplish is called a *multimedia development kit*. Among those on the market are Director (Macintosh or IBM-compatible computer), HyperStudio (Macintosh or Windows), and Multimedia ToolBook (IBM-compatible computer; Windows only).

What Hardware Do I Need?

To run the software described here, you need
- a computer with a sound card
- a microphone
- either speakers or a headset

Sound cards allow you to enter sound into the computer as data through microphones and other audio sources (e.g., tape recorders, compact disc players, radios). The card converts the incoming sound to a digital form that can be stored in files and processed by computer software. In addition, the sound card allows you to hear sounds produced by the computer and software through speakers or headsets. Adapters allow two headset-microphone combinations to be plugged into a single computer.

Most computers sold now, both IBM-compatible and Macintosh, have all of these features. Unfortunately, however, not all of the software described here will run on both platforms. The future promises to bring greater compatibility between IBM-compatible and Macintosh computers, but it is not yet possible to take any file produced by one machine and have it read effortlessly by the other or to run any piece of software on a machine of either type.

Caveats and Options

1. Remember that time and technology move quickly in the world of computers, and even as I write these lines, the information they contain may be becoming obsolete.
2. Don't assume that the commercial software available will do what you want it to do. Sometimes you can obtain the best results by using software that was created for a different purpose. (CECIL was intended to be used as a phonetician's portable speech lab.)
3. Don't be afraid to get your feet wet. If you don't like the software that's available, you can probably make your own software.
4. Remember that computers and the accompanying software are expensive. When making a purchase, be very careful about compat-

ibility between hardware (your computer) and software (the program you want to purchase), between software (the program you want to purchase) and software (your computer's operating system), and between hardware (your computer) and hardware (the headsets you want to plug into your computer's sound card).

5. When making a decision, don't ask just one person for advice once. Ask at least three people for advice three times, think about what they have said, and make an intelligent decision on your own.

References and Further Reading

Director (Version 5.0) [Computer software]. (1996). San Francisco: Macromedia.

HyperStudio (Version 3.0) [Computer software]. (1996). El Cajon, CA: Wagner.

Multimedia ToolBook (Version 4.0) [Computer software]. (1996). Bellevue, WA: Asymetrix.

Simple Text (Version 1.1.1) [Computer software]. Cupertino, CA: Apple Computer.

Spell It! (Version 3) [Computer software]. (1986). Torrance, CA: Davidson & Associates.

Summer Institute of Linguistics. (1994). Computerized Extraction of Components of Intonation in Language (CECIL) (Version 2.1) [Computer software]. (Available from International Computing Services, JAARS Center, Box 248, Waxhaw, NC 28173 USA; fax 704-843-6300)

Summer Institute of Linguistics. (1995). WinCECIL (Version 2.1b) [Computer software]. (Available from International Computing Services, JAARS Center, Box 248, Waxhaw, NC 28173 USA; fax 704-843-6300)

Triple Play Plus! English [Computer software]. (1994). Syracuse, NY: Syracuse Language Systems.

Contributor

Gloria Poedjosoedarmo is a senior lecturer in the Division of English Language and Applied Linguistics at the National Institute of Education, Nanyang Technological University, in Singapore (e-mail: poedgr@am.nie .ac.sg).

Analyzing Pronunciation Errors: Computerized Applied Phonetics for Trainee English Teachers

Levels
Advanced; teachers in training

Aims
Analyze nonstandard English sound systems
Diagnose pronunciation problems

Class Time
Two 1-hour sessions

Preparation Time
20–30 minutes

Resources
Computer with sound card for every two to three students
Text-to-speech software
Recording/playback facilities
Recorded texts

Many teacher training courses include phonetics and phonology in their curriculum, but such courses are typically quite technical and theoretical. They rarely analyze students' pronunciation problems. The activities suggested here allow students to apply the knowledge they have gained about phonetics and phonology to first analyze a simple and consistent set of text-to-speech rules followed by a computer and then approach the more complex task of analyzing the features of recorded human pronunciation.

Procedure

1. In Session 1, allow the students in groups of two or three to listen to the computer software's reading of the selected text or texts. Tell them to note any unusual features and, from these, to attempt to reconstruct rules the text-to-speech software is following that differ from the rules a native speaker of a standard variety of English would apply in reading the same text. These rules might include, for example, *Pause after every comma, Always use falling intonation at a full stop, Always use rising intonation at a question mark, Main sentence stress always falls at the end of a clause or sentence,* or *The letter* g *is pronounced* /dʒ/.
2. Toward the end of Session 1, allow each group to present the rules they have formulated and to state how each rule differs from that of a native speaker of a standard variety of English. Record the computer software's rules on the blackboard.
3. If anyone in the class disagrees with some of the recorded rules, discuss them. Point out additional rules the class has missed.

4. In Session 2, have the students listen to actual recordings of the speech of less advanced students, such as the ones that they will be teaching. Depending on your recording and playback facilities (computer, language laboratory, or tape recorder with good speakers), they may listen as a group, in small groups, or individually. Have them analyze the features they hear in small groups or individually.

5. Toward the end of the session, have the students report on the features they have noted. Follow up with discussion and your input.

Caveats and Options

1. Before doing the activity, familiarize the students with the computer hardware and software (although some very user-friendly systems with the required features are now on the market) and with the recording/playback equipment (if it is not computerized).

2. If the students are less advanced, spend three or more sessions on the activity. In Session 1, have the students listen to single, isolated utterances produced by the computer, hypothesize the computer's rule, and type in new sentences to test out their hypothesis.

3. For less advanced students, spend two sessions listening to recordings of actual speech. The first might consist of short, carefully selected utterances containing a fairly consistent set of features. The second session would contain more variation.

Contributor

Gloria Poedjosoedarmo is a senior lecturer in the Division of English Language and Applied Linguistics at the National Institute of Education, Nanyang Technological University, in Singapore (e-mail: poedgr@am.nie .ac.sg).

Teaching Suprasegmental Features of Pronunciation Using Graphical Displays

Levels
Intermediate +

Aims
Pronounce
suprasegmental features
of English

Class Time
30–60 minutes per
pronunciation point

Preparation Time
10–15 minutes

Resources
Computer with sound
card, graphics card, and
microphone for every
one to two students
Acoustic phonetic
analysis software
Recorded words or
utterances

The suprasegmental features of English, in particular stress-timed rhythm and appropriate placement of sentence stress, are often the most difficult features for speakers of many Asian languages to master. Students who have difficulty hearing these features of the language often relate more easily to graphic displays. Computerized speech analysis systems that display stress graphs and intonation contours are thus very useful for the comparison of two recordings, one prerecorded by the teacher and one made by the student during the lesson.

Procedure

1. Have the students run the software, listen to each recorded word or utterance, and observe the graphical display.
2. Tell the students to attempt to produce the word or utterance themselves, recording their voices and producing a graphical display in a second window.
3. Have the students replay the sample and their own recording alternately and observe differences in the graphical display.
4. Tell the students to attempt to correct their pronunciation, record the utterance again, and see if their own graphical display more closely resembles the model.

Caveats and Options

1. Make sure the learners have some knowledge of phonetics, the physics of sound, or both.

2. If the age and level of the students warrant, make the exercise into a game with the students in each group competing to see whose displays most nearly match the original.

3. Apply this activity to the teaching of word stress, sentence stress, and intonation contours, depending on the recording time and variety of displays allowed by the software.

4. Though graphical displays are probably most useful for teaching suprasegmentals, observing waveform displays while listening to models and attempting to imitate them may help students who have difficulty with aspiration or the distinction between pairs of English voiced and voiceless plosives.

Contributor

Gloria Poedjosoedarmo is a senior lecturer in the Division of English Language and Applied Linguistics at the National Institute of Education, Nanyang Technological University, in Singapore (e-mail: poedgr@am.nie .ac.sg).

Part V: Concordancing

Tran Lam at the Arlington Education and Employment Program (REEP), Arlington, Virginia USA.

Getting Started With Concordancing

L arge collections of computer-readable texts, or *corpora*, have become central to the work of a growing number of linguists (John Sinclair and Geoffrey Leech in Britain, Douglas Biber in the United States) and to the publication of learners' dictionaries. British publishers Longman, Collins-COBUILD, Oxford University Press, and Cambridge University Press all use corpora as a central part of their work. Although corpora are little used by publishers of dictionaries for the native English-speaking market, and although few teachers and students use the results of their own corpus research in language teaching and learning, both groups are coming to recognize that language corpora are a resource that cannot be ignored. (For more information on corpus linguistics, see Barlow, n.d.; on concordancing in language learning, see Flowerdew, 1996.) Corpora are a rich source of information about language that was completely inaccessible to most people until the mid-1990s.

Definitions

Here are a few terms that you need to know if you are going to work with corpora.

- *ASCII text:* American Standard for Computer Information Interchange text. ASCII text is the most commonly used format for storing texts in a corpus and makes it possible for all concordancing programs to use the corpus. It is sometimes known as *DOS text* or *plain text*.
- *concordance*: A list of occurrences of a word (or words) printed with a context. This context can be a single line of characters with the target word printed at the center, a sentence, or another context. One of the most common ways to print out information is the key-word-in-context (KWIC) concordance:

customs, but a handbook of the Anal language _ spoken by several thousand tribes
cratic Republic, Biermann used body language to dramatise his dilemma in front o
utumn programme kicks off with Body Language for Managers on 30 October in Corby
y to use it as a vital and coherent language of expression. For Terry, nothing m
mes had changed. For all the earthy language and talk of struggles to come, it s
Federation a fluency in the English language he had not erstwhile possessed. <p>
ample, offered computerised foreign language dictionaries and others which provi
Making all children learn a foreign language will do nothing to help Britain com

- *concordancer*: A computer program that allows you to create concordances of words held in a corpus.
- *corpus* (pl. *corpora*): A collection of texts (from written or spoken sources); in this case, in a form that can be read by a computer.
- *word list*: A list of all the individual words in your corpus, sorted either by frequency or alphabetically. The words *am, are,* and *is* are treated as separate words, as are *girl* and *girl*s.

What Is a Corpus, and How Can I Get One?

There are two main kinds of corpora: general and specific. A *general corpus* is ideally a large collection of texts that has been "balanced" to ensure a good mixture of styles and genres and examples of spoken and written language. One general corpus, the British National Corpus (1995), is very large (100 million words) and is currently available only to researchers with powerful workstation computers; an ordinary personal computer cannot handle it. A big general corpus is most useful to people who need information about how very specific words are used (e.g, dictionary makers). COBUILD on CD-ROM (1995), a smaller general corpus, comes with its own search software.

A *specific corpus* may often be more useful to a language teacher and is easier to put together than a general corpus. One way of building a specific corpus is through the many CD-ROMs containing newspaper and literary texts that are now available at a very low cost. Using this resource, you can create a sports English corpus, a business journalism corpus, a U.S. 19th-century novel corpus, or a corpus relevant to whatever you or your students are interested in. Another excellent starting point is the pair of million-word collections of texts (MicroConcord: Corpus Collection A, 1993; MicroConcord: Corpus Collection B, 1993) published by Oxford University Press to complement its MicroConcord concordancer (Scott, 1993; see below). Specific corpora like these are easy to work with and can be stored on a few floppy disks.

A third kind of corpus, which is growing in importance, is often called a *learners' corpus*. It is a collection of samples from the language use of learners from a single language background or from many. Learners' corpora are usually collections of written language, which is much easier to collect than spoken language, especially if the learners use word-processing software in their study programs. Such corpora are an invaluable resource for interlanguage study and give teachers a way to identify their learners' current problems and predict what the problems of future students will be.

The most common way to store a corpus is as a set of individual text files. In a DOS environment, use the eight-letter + period + three-letter naming system to provide some form of logical suffix so that you can identify files and their content easily (e.g., *mca_ind1.art, mca_ind1.bus, ca_ind1.for, mca_ind1.hom, mca_ind1.spo*). Remember that Longman's Mini Concordancer (LMC) (1989) can read only 30 files at a time and that Oxford Electronic Publishing's Micro-OCP (1989) can read only a single file at a time. If you meet this sort of problem, use the DOS copy command to concatenate a batch of files into a single file (e.g , *copy c:\corpus\mca*.* c:\temp\mca.all*).

Concordancers

After you have a corpus, the next step is to get a concordancer. A basic concordancer should be easy to use and should be able to
- produce numerically and alphabetically sorted word lists
- produce concordances in which you can sort the contexts to the right or the left of the key word
- handle significant quantities of text—50,000–1 million words or more

- work quickly
- ideally, produce results directly to the screen, where you can review or edit them

Four concordancers are available to users of IBM-compatible computers. None is perfect, but one of them nearly is. Their main strengths and weaknesses are as follows.

Concordancer	Strengths	Weaknesses
MicroConcord	<ul><li>produces concordances</li><li>sorts concordances</li><li>handles large data files and many files easily</li><li>is fast</li><li>contains good collocation information</li><li>has good output-editing facilities</li></ul>	<ul><li>has no word list feature (a big disadvantage)</li><li>uses a clumsy interface</li></ul>
Micro-OCP	<ul><li>produces concordances</li><li>sorts concordances</li><li>produces statistical information</li><li>handles large data files easily</li><li>gives the user excellent control over the appearance of output</li><li>supports internal tagging (e.g., COCOA)</li></ul>	<ul><li>uses a clumsy command-line interface</li><li>is slow</li><li>reads only single data files</li></ul>

WordSmith Tools	• produces concordances • sorts concordances • produces word lists (alphabetic and frequency) • handles large data files and many files easily • handles the Windows ANSI character sets (e.g., the diacritics used in major European languages) • is fast • contains excellent collocation information • has good output-editing facilities • has powerful vocabulary analysis tools • has extremely useful corpus-handling and -editing tools • can produce *aligned* corpora (i.e., an original text and a translation)	• is not as effective as Micro-OCP in handling tags
LMC	• produces word lists • produces concordances • sorts concordances • produces basic statistical information • is fast • uses a simple, menu-driven interface • gives the user some control over the appearance of output	• handles only up to 50,000 words • handles a restricted number of files in any session

Which program should you buy? Following are recommendations based on the type of computer you use:

- Because it is essential to be able to produce word lists from what is in your corpus, you have only one choice if you have a modern personal computer that runs Windows: WordSmith Tools (Scott, 1996), which does nearly everything you ever need to do with a corpus, and quickly.
- If you are not a Windows user and need to work with large texts, the best combination of tools is Micro-OCP and MicroConcord. The two programs will allow you to work with corpora in nearly every way on an older computer.
- If you can manage with small text collections (up to 50,000 words), LMC is still an excellent teaching tool and will run on older personal computers. It is easy to use, fast, and very flexible. (I have to declare an interest here, as I was involved in the development of LMC and wrote the user's manual.)
- As for the Apple Macintosh computer, three concordancers now exist: Concorder (Rand & Patera, 1994), a KWIC concordancer; Free Text Browser (International Computer Archive of Modern and Medieval English, n.d.), a freeware program; and Conc (Summer Institute of Linguistics, 1996), a text analysis program that produces KWIC concordances and indexes.

You can write your own HyperCard routines (see back issues of *CAELL Journal*). Or you can run SoftPC (software that allows IBM-compatible software to run on a Macintosh) and use one of the concordancers listed above. If your computer is fast, this can be the best solution.

If you want to run multiple copies of any commercial software programs, you will need to get a license. This is not prohibitively expensive and allows you to run an agreed number of copies of the software on the computers in your institution.

Similarly, you will need a license to run concordancers in your writing lab or on a network. At Lancaster University in the United Kingdom, where LMC is available to students over the network, the executable LMC program and the corpus files are stored on a central file server. When a user runs LMC, the program runs on the local machine over the network and the user retrieves the corpus files from the network drive.

What Sort of Computer Do I Need?

If you use an IBM-compatible personal computer, you can manage with the simplest sort of computer. LMC, for example, will run well on an old XT with two floppy disk drives and even better on an AT with 1 megabyte of RAM and a 20-megabyte hard disk. For more serious work, a 386 processor is the minimum, and you should get as big a hard disk as you can afford. For serious corpus study, you need a 486 processor or better, 8 or (ideally) 16 megabytes of RAM, and a hard disk of at least 500 megabytes.

What Can I Do With My Software and Corpus?

The list of what you can do with corpora is long. I have used corpora and concordancers

- to help develop vocabulary and raise students' awareness of grammar in general language teaching
- to help specify a syllabus and assist students with specialized reading tasks in teaching English for specific purposes
- to teach aspects of written discourse in English for academic purposes classes

Two published sources of information on how to use a concordancer in language teaching are the introduction and manual for MicroConcord (Murison-Bowie, 1993). Another is *Concordancing in the Classroom* (Tribble & Jones, 1990). Below is a practical example of how a small general corpus and a concordancer can help a language teacher.

Problem: Your students overuse the word *big* in the contexts of words like *city (-ies), difference(s),* and *problem(s).* You want to help them expand their active vocabulary.

Solution: Create a concordance of *problem* and ask learners to identify words that they could use instead of *big.* The following edited concordance from MicroConcord: Corpus Collection A (1993) presents learners with a cross-section of language in use that they can get only by using a computer. It lets them discover for themselves some of the words that they could use instead of their normally restricted range of vocabulary. In this instance, the contexts of the target words have been alphabetically sorted to the left of the target word. This groups and sorts all words or phrases that have been used to qualify *problem*:

r cent of national income) is not a problem; and to convince the markets
y to answer questions. <p> An added problem in this case was that she was
We can't afford to have an attitude problem in a place like this," Gary W
ted the long revaluation. The basic problem, after Haydn lapsed from the
100 _ all at the same time. Its big problem is how to insert Lewis's rip-
rength of the conservatives." A big problem for the liberals is that rece
parently not a significantly bigger problem. <sect> Business and City Pag
t take the strain. The play's chief problem lies in the fact that its Rus
'There is a fisheries conservation problem in the islands," said an outg
on Board, said: 'It is a continuing problem which all the boards are havi
f the total population. The crucial problem, it is generally understood,
surmountable and perhaps crucifying problem for Bobby Robson, the tempora
own for trial. <p> A more difficult problem was ensuring the extra judges
r, are going to present an enormous problem to the courts very shortly, a
ken seriously. <p> Tukur's fleeting problem was with William Shakespeare.
planted the seed of the full-blown problem that besets the profession to
inly pedestrian but the fundamental problem lay elsewhere. Apart from Kev
Ministry of Defence. <p> A further problem is that a BAe takeover would
rent decade raises both the general problem of how one appraises an opera
ening system. <p> Karpov's greatest problem throughout this match has bee
days are numbered. But an immediate problem is that the SCF is still find
sale since the spring, but the key problem in talks with MCD management
very limited range. <p> The latest problem for the Government is increas
at the best of times. <p> The main problem is keyboard player Brent Mydl
esterday, but otherwise their major problem is whether to play both their
them early on," he said. 'The only problem is it's about a year too soon
food shortages may be a persistent problem in Ethiopia. Until now the go
the book, in fact, has a potential problem: its targets of derision _ il
kable responsiblity for the present problem of confidence in Hong Kong,"
eneral Hakim admitted that the real problem will be fuel, which is alread
eir qualities" either. <p> Her root problem is that modern and classical
igh Court judge warned of a serious problem because of a log-jam of refug

> rcrowding is becoming a significant problem with the explosion in mobile
> pproach every problem as a specific problem. It is what makes us differen
> icant. <p> She has faced an unusual problem, however, in trying to get a
> on to ignore the single most urgent problem that our people are facing _
> ague are currently facing a weighty problem of similar proportions. <p> S

Giving learners access to this sort of information makes possible an investigative, problem-solving way of learning that teachers and students find exciting and rewarding. I hope that this contribution stimulates you to experiment with this new professional resource.

References and Further Reading

Barlow, M. (n.d.). *Corpus linguistics* [On-line]. Available: http://www.ruf.rice.edu/~barlow/corpus.html

British National Corpus (Release 1.0) [Computer software]. (1995). Oxford: Oxford University Computing Services.

COBUILD English Collocations on CD-ROM [CD-ROM]. (1995). Worthing, England: HarperCollins Electronic Reference.

Computers and English Language Learning (CAELL) Journal. (Available from International Society for Technology in Education, 1787 Agate St., Eugene OR 97403-1923 USA; http://isteonline.uoregon.edu)

Flowerdew, J. (1996). Concordancing in language learning. In M. C. Pennington (Ed.), *The power of CALL* (pp. 97–113). La Jolla, CA: Athelstan Press.

HyperCard (Version 2.3) [Computer software]. (1995). Cupertino, CA: Apple Computer.

International Computer Archive of Modern and Medieval English (ICAME). (n.d.). Free Text Browser [Computer software]. Available FTP: nora.hd.uib.no Directory: /pub/mac or from the Norwegian Computing Centre for the Humanities, Harald Haarfagresgt. 31, N-5007 Bergen, Norway; e-mail: icame@hd.uib.no

MicroConcord: Corpus Collection A [CD-ROM]. (1993). Oxford: Oxford University Press. (newspaper texts)

MicroConcord: Corpus Collection B [CD-ROM]. (1993). Oxford: Oxford University Press. (academic texts)

Micro-OCP [Computer software]. (1989). Oxford: Oxford Electronic Publishing.

Mini Concordancer [Computer software]. (1989). Burnt Mill, England: Longman Group.

Murison-Bowie, S. (1993). *Oxford MicroConcord user's manual*. Oxford: Oxford University Press.

Rand, D. W., & Patera, T. (1994). Concorder (Version 2.0) [Computer software]. (Available from Les Publications CRM, Université de Montréal, CP 6128-A, Montréal, Québec H3C 3J7 Canada; e-mail: rand@ere.umontreal.ca)

Scott, M. (1996). WordSmith tools (Version 1.1) [Computer software]. Available: http://www1.oup.co.uk/oup/elt/software/wsmith/

Scott, M., with Johns, T. (1993). MicroConcord. [Computer software]. Oxford: Oxford Electronic Publishing.

Sinclair, J. (1991). *Corpus, concordance, collocation*. Oxford: Oxford University Press.

SoftPC (Version 3.1) [Computer software]. (1994). Santa Clara, CA: Insignia Solutions.

Summer Institute of Linguistics. (1996). Conc (Version 1.76) [Computer software]. (Available from Summer Institute of Linguistics, International Academic Bookstore, 7500 West Camp Wisdom Road, Dallas, TX 75236 USA; e-mail: academic.books@sil.org; http://www.sil.org/computing/conc/; or Athelstan Press c/o Michael Barlow, e-mail: barlow@ruf.rice.edu)

Tribble, C., & Jones, G. (1990). *Concordancing in the classroom*. London: Longman Group.

Contributor

Chris Tribble is a lecturer and consultant who has worked in France, Britain, China, Lithuania, Latvia, and Estonia. He lives in Warsaw, Poland, and is currently completing a PhD on the writing of "important" texts in large corporations (e-mail: 100641.2430@compuserve.com).

Collecting Collocations

Levels
Intermediate +

Aims
Appreciate collocation
as a discourse feature
Develop vocabulary and
word grammar
Analyze and correct
writing

Class Time
1 hour +

Preparation Time
Variable

Resources
Computer for every one
to two students
Concordancing software
Word-processing
software
Printer(s)

The nonnative feel of much student writing, particularly in English for specific purposes (ESP), is largely due to the untypical ways students combine words in phrases. This problem falls into the province of collocation, which has become increasingly important in recent years and is now becoming well known among language teachers. Collocation is especially important in teaching ESP, in which each subject area makes particular demands upon the language resources of the learner, and a familiarity with how ideas are typically expressed is a prerequisite for membership of the new discourse community. Learner discovery and self-correction have proved more successful than simply correcting learners' errors in collocation. Concordancing software makes it easy for students to see collocation patterns, and the teacher's main task is to guide the students' research by suggesting fruitful areas for study (e.g., suggesting possible node words) based on the teacher's knowledge of the subject matter and of the collocation errors students often make. The focus in ESP is usually on lexical collocation, but the exercise is just as useful for raising awareness of grammatical collocation.

Procedure

Before Class

1. Tell the students to prepare a disk with a selection of their own assignments (the more, the better) on it.
2. Brainstorm about the kinds of collocation problems the students have or will have, based on what you know of the students you are teaching, the nature of the subject matter in an ESP class, or both. List these collocations (which will often be noun-verb combinations).

3. Choose one of the words from the collocating pairs as the *node word* (the one the students will have to look up) and make a list of these, one copy for each student. The list could be different for each student, reflecting particular problems, or it could be a composite list reflecting problems many learners are likely to have.

In Class

1. Distribute the lists to the students, indicating which node words they should enter into the concordancing software at the query prompt.
2. Tell the students to work down the list, looking up words and generating concordance lists from the documents on the disk containing their own work.
3. Tell the students to identify incorrect collocations (or ask them to identify correct ones). Give them as much help as they need at this stage with identifying good and bad collocations. Show the students how to use the text-sorting commands to highlight different word combinations to the left and right of the node word.
4. Tell the students to print out their concordance lists and make corrections on the printout.

Caveats and Options

1. Be sure you are familiar with the concordancing software before using this activity.
2. Explain the meaning of *collocation*, its importance, and the way to identify one very carefully to the students before they have access to the software. Otherwise they may waste time on inappropriate searches.
3. If it is not practical for the students to work with their own writing, prepare a text or texts for analysis. Prepare an authentic text from a specific subject area by introducing collocation errors. Then proceed as above.
4. Ask the students to rank the collocation problems they find in order of seriousness or to compare their findings with those of other students. This could lead to an oral follow-up exercise.

5. Encourage the students to have with them a good learner's dictionary that gives help with collocations (such as *COBUILD English Learner's Dictionary*, 1989). Or use the activity as an introduction to the resources offered by such dictionaries.
6. If printing results is not an option, make the corrections on a separate sheet.
7. Use the activity as a means of assessing the students as well as teaching them.
8. With a more experienced class, do not indicate which node words to look up; have the students explore the texts themselves.
9. Use the activity as the basis of an action research project on the collocation problems of particular groups of students studying different subjects. The results would directly inform your classroom teaching and your input for future concordancing sessions.

References and Further Reading

COBUILD English learner's dictionary. (1989). London: Collins.

Contributor

Neil Drave is a lecturer in the Division of Language Studies at the City University of Hong Kong (e-mail: lsdrave@cityu.edu.hk).

Put a Corpus in Your Classroom: Using a Computer in Vocabulary Development

Levels
Low intermediate +

Aims
Develop active
vocabulary

Class Time
15–20 minutes

Preparation Time
10–30 minutes

Resources
Computer(s)
Corpus of appropriate
texts
Concordancing software
Examples of learners'
vocabulary limitations

The first vocabulary items that students learn are often superordinate terms that have a high generalizability value—words like *big*, *thing*, and *get*. This activity shows how students can expand their active vocabulary beyond these very frequently used words and use more specific vocabulary appropriately. The activity uses a newspaper corpus published by Oxford University Press (MicroConcord: Corpus Collection A) as an accompanying resource for the MicroConcord program for MS-DOS-compatible computers (Scott, 1993), but the techniques can be used with any concordancing software and any appropriate collection of texts. This particular corpus and software was chosen because it is widely available. The activity demonstrates a basic principle in corpus study: to find out about one thing, you often have to look for something else.

Procedure

1. Instruct the students in the use of the concordancer if necessary.
2. Decide on the overused word you want to study (e.g., *big*). This is the *target word*.
3. Identify some *context words* with which *big* is overused (e.g., *problem*).
4. Select a corpus of texts by expert writers (e.g., MicroConcord: Corpus Collection A, the million-word corpus of newspaper texts that comes with MicroConcord).
5. Have the students, working in groups, select a context word.

6. Have the students go to the computer to investigate their word. Schedule time for the groups according to the number of computers in your classroom or resource center. Tell the students to use *left context sorting* to identify frequently used qualifiers.

7. Tell the students to write a short report on their findings. This report should discuss the range of possible qualifiers, their meanings, and the appropriate contexts in which they might be used. The *see full context* facility in MicroConcord is useful here, as learners can read a fuller context than the concordance line. Provide support to each group and access to other reference sources.

8. Have the students report back to the class and discuss their conclusions.

9. Post the final results on a class vocabulary development notice board or poster where other learners can share them.

Caveats and Options

1. Keep a collection of words or phrases that learners consistently overuse (e.g., *bad, big, like, good*). For example, many students I have taught overuse *big* in the contexts of *city* (*-ies*), *difference*(*s*), and *problem*(*s*), and misuse *big* with words like *punishment*. The word *big* (*big, bigger*) occurs only 3 times in 279 instances of *problem* in the MicroConcord corpus. In contrast, the ratio in a collection of learner writing is 35 instances of *big* to 494 instances of *problem*.

2. Follow this procedure in place of Steps 5–7 if the students do not have access to a computer.

   - Use the concordancer to produce left-context-sorted concordances of the context words under investigation.

   - Divide the students into groups. Give each group one concordance to study (see, e.g., the extract from the concordance on *problem* in Getting Started With Concordancing). Have the students identify useful or interesting words they can use as an alternative for *big*.

References and Further Reading

MicroConcord: Corpus Collection A [CD-ROM]. (1993). Oxford: Oxford University Press.

Murison-Bowie, S. (1993). *Oxford MicroConcord user's manual*. Oxford: Oxford University Press.

Scott, M., with Johns, T. (1993). MicroConcord [Computer software]. Oxford: Oxford Electronic Publishing.

Tribble, C., & Jones, G. (1990). *Concordancing in the classroom*. London: Longman Group.

Contributor

Chris Tribble is a lecturer and consultant who has worked in France, Britain, China, Lithuania, Latvia, and Estonia. He lives in Warsaw, Poland, and is currently completing a PhD on the writing of "important" texts in large corporations (e-mail: 100641.2430@compuserve.com).

Concordance and Correct

Levels
Advanced

Aims
Correct grammatical and
collocational mistakes
Increase grammatical
awareness

Class Time
About 1 hour

Preparation Time
5 hours

Resources
Computer for every one
to two students
Concordancing software

An authentic corpus can offer a multitude of examples of how a certain word is used. Students in advanced-level English for specific purposes courses struggle hard to use specialized vocabulary in the right way, both grammatically and collocationally. In this controlled, interactive concordancing activity, students discover for themselves from a corpus how a particular word should be used. The point of departure is students' own errors in writing. Rather than the teacher's correcting the errors for them or asking them to correct their own errors without giving them any help, a relevant authentic corpus serves as a bank of language data from which help can be sought. When students discover the collocational pattern for themselves, they will be better able to acquire and use it.

Procedure

1. Before class, assemble a specialized corpus of well-formed texts of the type the students will be writing. If it is highly specialized writing, 50,000 words should be enough.
2. In class, ask the students to do a writing task corresponding to the type used in forming the corpus.
3. When marking the students' writing, use the letter *C*, or a symbol of your own choice, to mark an error that you think the students will be able to correct by studying the corpus. Usually this will be a specialized or semispecialized vocabulary item.
4. When you return the students' work, conduct a concordancing session with them:
   - Direct the students to run concordances of each of the words that you have marked with the symbol.
   - Instruct the students to study carefully the examples generated by the concordancer and draw their own conclusions about how the word should be used.

269

5. Ask the students to rewrite the sentences marked with the symbol.
6. Consult with each student in turn, and look at their revisions.
7. Help students who fail to draw the right conclusions from their study of corpus data.

Caveats and Options

1. Have the students do the concordancing activity in pairs so that they can help each other draw sensible conclusions from corpus data.

Contributor

Bruce Ka-Cheung Ma is a lecturer in English in the Division of Language Studies at the City University of Hong Kong (e-mail: lsbrusma @cityu.edu.hk).

Build Your Own Text Corpora

Levels
Any; teachers

Aims
Create corpora for
teaching and research

Resources
Computer
Concordancing software
CD-ROM drive
(optional)
Texts on CD-ROM
(optional)
Word-processing or
text-editing software,
browser, scanner
(optional)
TV with closed-caption
capabilities and
download device
(optional)

Digital texts are ubiquitously available, and you can harvest them to form your own corpora. Text corpora can form a text base that teachers can use to illustrate concepts in a target language or that students themselves can use to feed themselves examples of patterns in a language, find and make sense of exceptions, and so on. Students can also compare concordances of their own writing with those of native speakers' writings in the hope of exposing differences between the two. Teachers and students can use either native or nonnative text bases in a discourse analysis approach to study a particular language, a body of materials presented to students for the purpose of developing a syllabus or critiquing an existing one, or a body of student work for instances of interlanguage and the like. Finally, text bases can be a source of materials for use in the syllabus and used with text manipulation programs such as cloze generators, concordancers, and other authorable computer-assisted language learning materials.

Procedure

1. Decide whether you want to build a corpus to reflect the language actually encountered by the students (i.e., made up of texts the students are known to use) or a more general one. In the latter case, select texts that reflect whatever domain of English you wish to model.
2. Balance the following sources to reflect your decision. In all cases, be aware of copyright and privacy considerations.
   - word-processed files: Collect word-processed materials, such as teaching materials, memos and correspondence (if not private), reports and papers, publicity materials, and products of research on discourse (e.g., lecture transcripts).
   - Internet sources: Locate relevant Internet sites and download files. Join forums on topics of interest to your students, save postings to files, and concatenate them.

- CD-ROM sources: Explore CD-ROM materials (e.g., encyclopedias). Open CD-ROM applications, copy selected texts to your clipboard, and paste them to your word-processing or text-editing software.
- closed-caption TV transcripts: Connect a device to your TV that sends the closed-caption text to your computer and collects the texts.
- scanned materials: Use any relevant documents. Certain publications disseminated by the U.S. Government Printing Office are copyright free.
- students' own writing: Accumulate word-processing files of student writing.

Caveats and Options

1. Ensure a suitable level of difficulty (i.e., in relation to the level of your students).
2. Have the students locate suitable samples, compile their own corpora, exchange or pool them, and set up protocols for examination.
3. Be sure to retain the ASCII text character of your text base, especially when working through word-processing files.

References and Further Reading

Stevens, V. (1990). Text manipulation: What's wrong with it anyway? *CAELL Journal, 1*(2), 5–8.

Stevens, V. (1991a). Classroom concordancing: Vocabulary materials derived from relevant, authentic text. *ESP Journal, 10,* 35–46.

Stevens, V. (1991b). Concordance-based vocabulary exercises: A viable alternative to gap-fillers. In T. Johns & P. King (Eds.), *English Language Research Journal* (Vol. 4, pp. 47–61). Birmingham, England: University of Birmingham.

Stevens, V. (1992/1993, December/January). Concordances as enhancements to language competence. *TESOL Matters*, p. 11.

Stevens, V. (1995). Concordancing with language learners: Why? When? What? *CAELL Journal, 6*(2), 2–10.

Contributor

Before becoming the director of ESL Software Design at Courseware Publishing International, California, in the United States, Vance Stevens coordinated computer-assisted language learning and self-access learning at Sultan Qaboos University, Oman (e-mail: 102005.65@compuserve.com).

A Simple Do-It-Yourself Concordancer

Levels
Any; teachers

Aims
Create a concordancer

Preparation Time
15 minutes

Resources
Computer
MS-DOS (any level)

The building blocks for a concordancer exist in the DOS command language and can be implemented in a single DOS command statement. For those not comfortable with editing a DOS command line, the concordancing command can be issued from a batch file.

Procedure

From DOS Command Line

1. Install DOSKEY, which is convenient when you anticipate issuing numerous DOS commands that are similar to one another to beforehand. To do this, simply type *DOSKEY* at the DOS prompt. The up and down arrow keys can then be used to recall previous commands—which you can then edit for other strings and filenames—to redirect output, and so on.

2. Get a DOS prompt. Type a variation of the following statement at the command line:

   ```
   for %a in (*.asc) do find "your string" %a
   ```

   For example, to have DOS print all lines in all text files in the default directory ending in *.txt* that contain the string *there is,* at the DOS prompt type

   ```
   for %a in (*.txt) do find "there is" %a
   ```

3. To have that output directed to a file, add >> [filename] to the end of the command:

   ```
   for %a in (*.txt) do find "there is" %a >> there_is.dat
   ```

From a Batch File

1. Use word-processing or text-editing software to create a *.bat* (batch) file called *findtext.bat*. The file will consist of only one line:

   ```
   for %%a in (*.asc) do find "%1" %%a >> %2
   ```

   Alternatively, at the DOS prompt,
   - Type *copy con findtext.bat* and press <enter>.
   - On the next line, type the line of text given above and press <enter>.
   - Type <ctrl-Z> (that is, hold down the <ctrl> key, press and release Z, then release the <ctrl> key). ^Z will appear.
   - Press <enter>. The file will be written to disk.
2. Type *findtext*. Specify the word to search for and a place to put the output. For example, to find all occurrences of *however* and save them to a file called *however.dat*, type

   ```
   FINDTEXT however however.dat
   ```

   Or type *findtext however con* to direct the output to the screen, or *findtext however prn* to direct the output to a printer. Because the command in the *findtext.bat* file ends in *>> %2,* the output device must be specified as the second parameter, or the batch command won't work. If you leave off *>> %2* from the batch command, typing *findtext however* will automatically direct output to the CONsole (i.e., screen).

Caveats and Options

1. Upper- and lowercase letters in the commands are interchangeable.
2. For strings of more than one word, use the command line version of this command.
3. This procedure will extract the line of text in which any specified string resides. It will not do a key-word-in-context concordance, in which the target items are conveniently lined up in the middle of the page.

4. If there are more lines of text than will fit on a screen, they will scroll by faster than you can read them. Stop the scroll by pressing <ctrl-S>, or direct the output to a file as noted above and read it with text-editing or word-processing software.
5. Be sure to work with ASCII text files; otherwise, you'll see some strange characters in your output.

Contributor

Before becoming the director of ESL Software Design at Courseware Publishing International, California, in the United States, Vance Stevens coordinated computer-assisted language learning and self-access learning at Sultan Qaboos University, Oman (e-mail: 102005.65@compuserve .com).

Part VI: Other Applications

Mangaba Mengue Albert at the Arlington Education and Employment Program (REEP), Arlington, Virginia USA.

Editor's Note

This section gives a few additional examples of how the creative teacher can apply just about any computer application to the benefit of language learning.

Spreadsheet and database programs are built into the integrated suites common on most office systems (e.g., Microsoft's Office). Students can use these programs to store and organize data generated by research and writing projects and quickly produce graphics for interpretation and illustration. Teachers too can present prepared data sets on disk to stimulate writing or speaking tasks. Databases can also be used by students to store information about language. In Personalized Grammar Book, David Gardner shows how students can create their own database of grammar explanations and examples that is easily accessible for them as a writing support. In another ingenious activity (How Did I Do?), Luisa Culiat-Sadorra shows how a mail-merge system, operating on a word-processed file of comments and practical advice, can aid students' self-evaluation of their presentation skills.

Increasingly, teachers are designing their own computer-based training programs using the many software packages now available. Hypertext systems, of which HyperCard on the Macintosh is perhaps the easiest to use, allow self-directed movement through a collection of pages or cards. Teachers can develop HyperCard stacks to support specific activities (e.g., Hyped Communication About Modern Art), or students can develop stacks in classroom activities (Student-Generated Motivation).

Two other activities included here show how a shareware text reconstruction program can be used with songs and how students can write their own quizzes in multiple-choice format.

Finally, Paul Lewis presents his own package, Let's Talk, which applies information-gap techniques to the computer lab.

References and Further Reading

HyperCard 2.3 [Computer software]. (1995). Cupertino, CA: Apple Computer.

Office 97 [Computer software]. (1997). Redmond, WA: Microsoft.

The Crime Computer

Levels
High beginning +;
elementary–adult

Aims
Categorize and sort data
Write descriptions
Write and think
creatively
Review information
from texts

Class Time
Several class periods;
ongoing

Preparation Time
10 minutes before
Session 1
Variable for other
sessions

Resources
Computer
Database software
Printer
Scanner (optional)

In this activity, students work together to construct a database with "wanted" or "missing" people and objects. The activity, which can serve as a review of literature, a grammar review, or an enjoyable lead-in to other activities, includes practice in discussion, reading, writing, and a host of critical thinking skills.

Procedure

1. Using "wanted" posters from the post office, descriptions of missing persons from milk cartons or flyers, or a model description of a wanted or missing person from your text or other media, introduce the concept of *missing*, *wanted*, or both.

2. Brainstorm with the class to decide what features of a person or object you would need to know in order to find out whether the person or object is "wanted" or "missing." For example, in the elementary grades talk about the features of the food that the caterpillar in *The Very Hungry Caterpillar* (Carle, 1983) is looking for. At upper grade levels, discuss an honest politician who is wanted.

3. Decide with the class how to arrange the information that they determined is necessary. Decide what the most important and least important information is.

4. With the class, design a form in your database program that will allow you to enter the type of information decided on in Steps 2 and 3. Add graphics if desired. Print out a form for each class member (or photocopy one hard copy).

5. Depending on class content, have the students choose a person or object and fill in their forms. Encourage them to include as much information as possible to aid in locating the person or object. Allow the students to use their dictionaries if necessary.

6. Edit the forms for structures that the students control.

7. Have individual students or an assigned student enter the data from the completed, edited forms into the database. Encourage the students to scan in pictures of their subjects to complement their files.
8. Use the information in the database for a variety of activities throughout the term (see Caveats and Options).

Caveats and Options

1. If you have more than one computer system, have the students devise their own database forms and enter information throughout the semester.
2. Have the students use one database for "missing" subjects and the other for "wanted."
3. If the students have trouble coming up with something "missing" or "wanted," have them look through magazines and choose a picture of a person or thing to describe.
4. Depending on the level of the student, responses on the forms can range from one word to several sentences (or as much data as your database allows for one field).
5. In follow-up activities, have the students use the forms to
   - write the crime page of a newspaper
   - develop and videotape a funny spin-off of the television show *America's Most Wanted*
   - record "late-breaking announcements" for a radio show
   - compare and contrast some of the subjects in the database
   - guess a person or object based on a description you read from the database (or change it slightly)
   - predict in writing or discuss where they think the people or objects will be found and where they were when they were lost or hiding

References and Further Reading

Carle, E. (1983). *The very hungry caterpillar.* New York: Philomel Books.

Contributor

Joy Egbert teaches in the Center for English Language Training at Indiana University, in the United States (e-mail: jegbert@indiana.edu; http://ezinfo.ucs.indiana.edu/~jegbert/).

Personalized Grammar Book

Levels
Any

Aims
Engage with
grammatical meaning

Class Time
Variable

Preparation Time
Variable

Resources
Computer
Database software

In a language course students need to take in a lot of grammar. They learn it from teachers and books, but to engage fully with its meaning they need to make their own explanations and practice with it. They can do this in their individual exercise books, but by doing it in a database they can share the results with classmates and even students in other classes or courses.

Procedure

1. Set up a simple database that will contain the kind of information shown in Appendix A.
2. Create a list of the grammar items you will cover in your course. Either enter them in the database or leave that for the students to do.
3. Show the students how the database program works (e.g., how to enter and search for information).
4. As you deal with grammatical items throughout the course, ask the students to provide their own explanation of the item (for monolingual classes, in their L1) and three short sample texts showing how the item is used. (See Appendix B for a handout used to collect the information.)
5. Collect and correct the students' work.
6. Select the best explanations and the best examples (not necessarily from the same students) and ask the writers to enter them in the database.
7. In subsequent work, when the students use erroneously one of the grammatical items you have covered, refer the students to the database.

Caveats and Options

1. Construct a new database for each new course, or keep one database running from one course to another.
2. If you teach classes that move on to further courses, keep the database running with the same students in subsequent years.
3. The database can develop into a substantial reference tool that the students can take with them when they finish their studies.
4. Make a printed version of the information for the students to use as a reference.

Appendix A: Database Format

```
Microsoft Access - [Form: Grammar Database]
File   Edit   View   Records   Window   Help

ITEM     on

CONTEXT      preposition of place

EXPLANATION
touching something, usually the top side or upper surface


EXAMPLES
1. The cup is on the table.
2. They sat on the chair.
3. The people are on the beach.


UNUSUAL EXAMPLES
1. He had a scar on his face.


Record: 1
```

Appendix B: Handout for Collecting Data

Defining Grammar

Please complete this form for the item of grammar that we have been working on today.

Item	*on* as a preposition of place
Your explanation	
Example 1	
Example 2	
Example 3	
Unusual examples	
Your name	

Contributor

David Gardner is a senior language instructor in the English Centre of The University of Hong Kong (e-mail: dgardner@hkucc.hku.hk).

How Did I Do?: Overcoming Speech Anxiety

Levels
High intermediate +

Aims
Evaluate own oral
presentations
Reduce anxiety about
oral presentations

Class Time
5-7 minutes per student

Preparation Time
60-120 minutes (1st
week of classes)
15-60 minutes (after
every class session of
oral presentations)

Resources
Video camera, player,
and tapes
Computer for each
student
Word-processing
software with mail
merge
Printer
Speech laboratory and
overhead projector
(optional)

Teachers of large oral communication classes face the challenge of evaluating every student speaker and creating a supportive learning climate that reduces speech anxiety. The activities here allow each student speaker to participate in the evaluation task, an essential element in a constructive critique of the self as speaker. Immediately after viewing their videotaped presentation, the student speakers evaluate themselves and their presentation using a teacher-prepared database or library of comments. Students generate an immediate self-evaluation of their own presentations and monitor their progress throughout the term.

Procedure

Before Class

1. Recall comments frequently made to student speakers after their presentations. Categorize these comments into criteria to be used for evaluating oral presentations (e.g., organization, content, voice, use of audiovisual aids, introduction, eye contact, substance).
2. Expand each criterion into a description that offers goals for improvement and means for reaching them. Build an initial database of 40–50 descriptions like the following:
   - *subs6*. I need to give more attention to the coherence of my message. It would be a good idea to review the transition markers I learned in my grammar class and to select those that can be used for spoken language.
   - *intro5*. I was somewhat hesitant and uncertain in my introduction. I have to know my opening lines. It might be a good idea to memorize the first and second statements and to practice delivering them to the point that they become spontaneously delivered. A reminder: First impressions are usually lasting.

- *eye 7.* I was addressing the ceiling. I need to maintain eye contact with my audience.
3. Enter each description as a separate word-processing file or document. Name the files in such a way that they will be easy to recall (see the file names above).
4. Prepare and print a summary of the criteria to use in Session 1.
5. Prepare an oral presentation to give in Session 1. In your presentation, demonstrate step-by-step the use of the mail-merge feature of your word-processing software to generate your self-evaluation, which will include a set of descriptions that apply to your demonstration and to you as a speaker. This is the procedure students will follow to evaluate themselves after their own presentations. Print the evaluation, and make enough copies for your class.

Session 1

1. In the first class meeting, introduce the evaluation procedure as part of an overview of the oral communication course.

Session 2 (later in the term)

1. When you teach the first informative report, such as a demonstration report, explain to the class how to do the self-evaluation by delivering your presentation. Videotape the presentation as you give it. As you execute each step of the procedure, if necessary write on the blackboard abbreviated instructions to reinforce or clarify your actions in executing the mail merge.
2. Ask the students each to bring a disk to the next class meeting. Make a copy of the self-evaluation database for each student.

Later Sessions

1. Make sure the students do the self-evaluation mail merge after every oral presentation. Remember to prepare your own evaluation of each student presentation as well.

2. Schedule a postpresentation conference with the students in groups. Avoid individual conferences as these may cultivate fear and anxiety.
3. Create, update, and revise the database depending on the type and purpose of the presentations and the students' progress.

Caveats and Options

1. The activities require a beginner's knowledge of a word-processing software and its mail-merge feature.
2. Accompany the demonstration with a written version of the procedure on transparencies or acetates for an efficient and effective model demonstration.
3. If you have no access to a speech laboratory, use the classroom for all the presentations and have the students do their self-evaluations at home or in the computer lab of your school.

References and Further Reading

Culiat-Sadorra, M. L. (1990). Using the computer to evaluate and monitor oral performances. *Teaching English for Specific Purposes, 9,* 83–95.

Ellis, K. (1995). Apprehension, self-perceived competency, and teacher immediacy in the laboratory-supported public speaking course: trends and relationships. *Communication Education, 44,* 64–78.

Contributor

Luisa Culiat-Sadorra is an assistant professor and the chair of the Oral Communication Course committee in the English Language Department of De La Salle University, in the Philippines (e-mail: CLAMLCS@mail .dlsu.edu.ph).

Student-Generated Motivation: HyperCard in the ESOL Classroom

Levels
False beginning +;
middle school +

Aims
Activate passive
knowledge of language
Develop critical
thinking and computer
skills

Class Time
About 5 hours

Preparation Time
1–2 hours

Resources
Macintosh computer for
every two students
HyperCard
Copies of model stack
Printer
Handouts

Long-term projects in the ESOL classroom often start with a high degree of motivation that tends to decrease after a few days. In this activity, students' motivation increases as they see their ideas come alive on the computer screen. This task-based project has students working in pairs to create a multimedia garage sale that incorporates text, graphics, and sound. The result is student-generated material offering a variety of follow-up activities to use not only in the class that created it but in other classes as well.

Procedure

Before Class

1. In HyperCard, choose *New Stack* from the *HyperCard File* menu. Click the button labeled *Save*.
2. Make the cover page or card: Cut and paste graphics to create an attractive introduction to the garage sale. Choose the text tool from the *Tools* menu to type a title and any information you want on this card. Double-click the *A* to choose a font and style.
3. Make the advertisement page: Choose *New Card* from the *Edit* menu. Choose *Background* from the Edit menu. Whatever you put here will appear on this card and all subsequent ones. Move between the background (B) and foreground (F) using the same method. You will know you are in the background because of the hash marks that appear in the menu bar.
4. Cut and paste a graphic depicting a typical garage sale item (e.g., a baseball glove, a guitar). Choose the rectangle tool from the tools menu to draw a frame around it (B).

5. Choose *New Field* from the *Objects* menu to make two new text fields (B). Click and drag the bottom right-hand corner to change their size. Click and drag the middle to move them. Double-click the fields to choose a font and style (click the button labeled *Text Style*). Move one field to the right of the graphic, and move the other below it.

6. Choose the browser tool from the *Tools* menu. Type the name of the item you chose (F) in one text field, and type a brief description of its finer points and its cost in the other.

7. Choose *New Button* from the *Objects* menu to make a button to move between this and your cover page (B). Double-click the button. Name the button *Return to Menu*. Click the button labeled *LinkTo ...*, use the arrow keys to return to the menu page, and click the button labeled *This Card*.

8. Do the same on the cover page, creating a button labeled *the name of your item* that takes you to that card (F). Move, reshape, and restyle the buttons the same way you did the text fields.

9. Choose *Audio* from the *Edit* menu to make a button on your advertisement page that plays an advertisement for the item you chose. Click the button labeled *Edit* to edit the sound by clicking, dragging, and deleting.

10. Make a new card (or two if the students are working in pairs) for the students to work on. Put a copy of this stack on each of the computers the students will be working on.

11. Prepare a set of handouts consisting of a copy of the cover page, a sample advertisement page, a blank card on which the students will write about their object, and a worksheet (see the Appendix).

Session 1

1. Ask the students to think of something they own that they used to love but don't use any more and wouldn't mind selling. Have them share their ideas in pairs.

2. As a class, look at the stack on the computer. Give any necessary instructions, based on the computer skills of the class. Point out the basics of the stack, then let the students browse. Point out things

that the students do not notice (e.g., sound buttons, empty cards that they will use).

3. Distribute the handouts. Have the students do the worksheet individually and share their ideas in pairs. Ask the students to individually design their cards on the paper forms in preparation for working on the computer.

Subsequent Sessions

1. As the students progress in creating their cards, demonstrate on the computer how to choose graphics, cut and paste, enter text, and record a "message." Have the students who finish their first card work on a second on their own (choose *New Card* from the Edit menu).

Follow-up

1. Compile the cards into one stack by copying one card at a time and pasting it into a master stack (choose *Copy* and *Paste Card* from the Edit menu). Make buttons for each item on the cover page. Use the *Resource Mover* in *Power Tools*, found in the *Home Stack*, to move the students' sounds into the master stack.

2. Have the students do any or all of these activities:
   - gift search: Have the students look through the stack to find the perfect gift for everyone in their family or in the class and tell why it is perfect.
   - stack correction: Have the students in pairs note all the errors in the stack, then take turns writing them one at a time on the blackboard. The first team that can correct the error gets a point. Afterward, give the students a set amount of time to correct their cards. (If you plan to use this activity with more than one class, save a copy of the original, uncorrected stack to use.)

Caveats and Options

1. If the students have the computer skills, have them each design their own cards using the directions above.

2. Because HyperCard is an English application, the students tend to speak to each other in English during the creation stage. Encourage this phenomenon!
3. Most task-based activities can be translated into a multimedia version using HyperCard. (See Rooks, 1988, 1990, for ideas.)

References and Further Reading

HyperCard (Version 2.3) [Computer software]. (1995). Cupertino, CA: Apple Computer.

Rooks, G. (1988). *The non-stop discussion workbook* (2nd ed.). Boston: Heinle & Heinle.

Rooks, G. (1990). *Can't stop talking* (2nd ed.). Boston: Heinle & Heinle.

Appendix: Worksheet

In planning your Garage Sale, consider the following:

1. What is something you no longer need and would like to sell (e.g., a baseball glove, a guitar). It's an important choice, so decide carefully!

2. What should people know about it? How much will you sell it for?

3. What graphic would you like to use?

4. What will your button "say"? What is the most important thing customers need to know?

Contributor

Scott H. Rule is a faculty member at Aichi Gakuin University in Nagoya, Japan (e-mail: rule@gol.com).

Hyped Communication About Modern Art

Levels
Low intermediate +

Aims
Write and speak
communicatively
Learn about and
interpret modern art

Class Time
1 hour

Preparation Time
30 minutes

Resources
Macintosh computer for
every one to two
students
HyperCard
Diskettes with
backed-up HyperCard
program files

This activity is designed to stimulate communication in English by introducing students to the mysteries of modern abstract art. Abstract art is encountered not only in museums but also in street fairs, on television, and even in advertising campaigns. Because the visual principles underlying abstract art are unfamiliar to many ESL students, they are puzzled by its rationale and the messages. This exercise clarifies some of the abstract visual stimuli to which the ESL student will be exposed. The students look at art, take part in discussions with classmates, write reactions onto the computer, exchange written commentaries, and finally generate and interpret their own creations.

Procedure

1. Install the HyperCard stack shown in the Appendix into the Macintosh.
2. Choose the modern painting that will serve as the stimulus.
3. Show the class the painting and discuss various aspects, such as its name, the color symbolism, and reasons for placement of the diverse elements that make up the painting.
4. Ask the students to type their own reactions on the appropriate card on the computer.
5. Have the students print out their reactions and exchange them.
6. Ask the students to share with the whole class the reactions they found particularly insightful.
7. Have the students use the computer to create their own abstract HyperCard design.
8. Ask the students to interpret their own designs.

Caveats and Options

1. For this activity we used a linear abstract painting by Sean Scully, born in Ireland in 1945, who has lived in the United States since 1975. Theoretically any modern painting can be chosen, but we selected this painting for two reasons:
   - It was easy for the students to generate something similar on the computer using HyperCard. Because the students' creation of an abstract design is an integral part of this exercise, paintings with a simple composition that can be emulated on the computer are more suitable.
   - Because the class took place in a university situated in the United States, we used a painting by a U.S. artist so we could address typical U.S. symbolism.
2. Ask the students to explain their own designs either as a written assignment or orally. If the oral mode is chosen, request input from the whole class and ask the students to defend their own interpretation.

References and Further Reading

Hofmeister, J., & Rudowski, J. (1992). *Learning with HyperCard.* Cincinnati, OH: South Western.

HyperCard (Version 2.3) [Computer software]. (1995). Cupertino, CA: Apple Computer.

Scully, S. (1993). The Catherine paintings. In *Modern Art Museum of Fort Worth calendar,* pp. 1–6.

Appendix: HyperCard Program

The program consists of five cards linked together through buttons that are part of the programming language HyperTalk.

Card 1 introduces ESL students to the activity and provides initial directions on moving to the next card.

Welcome to
"Hyped Communication
about Modern Art "

To continue please "click" the button!

[Click !]

Card 2 describes several icon images the students will encounter while using the program.

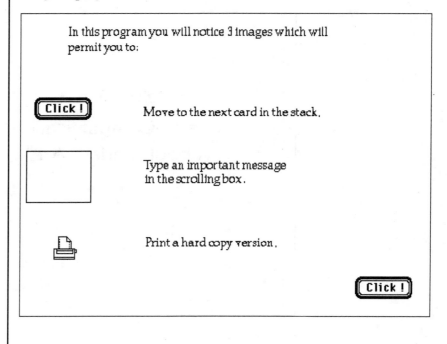

In this program you will notice 3 images which will permit you to:

Click !   Move to the next card in the stack.

Type an important message in the scrolling box.

Print a hard copy version.

Click !

Once the students have observed the painting, they discuss its meaning and write a brief summary inside the field in Card 3.

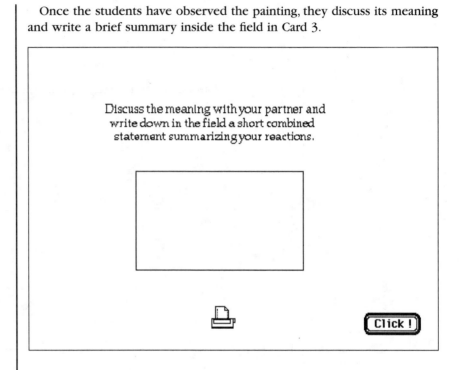

On Card 4, the students design their own abstract art using the available tools from the tools menu.

With your partner create an abstract design.

Click !

Card 5 concludes the activity and returns the student to the beginning of the stack.

We hope you enjoyed
this activity!

See you again !

"Click" the button and return to the beginning!

Click !

Contributors

Susanne Lapp is an assistant professor at the University of Texas–Pan American, and Dorothy Solé teaches ESL at Miami-Dade Community College in Florida, both in the United States.

Sounds Like Fun!

Levels
Any

Aims
Understand the words
in a song
Figure out the correct
spelling for a sound

Class Time
50 minutes (computer
work)
50 minutes
(postcomputer work)

Preparation Time
1 hour

Resources
Computer for each
student
Text reconstruction
program
Cassette players with
earphones
Song on cassettes

In this activity, students listen to a song and reconstruct its words by using text reconstruction software, working at their own pace by means of individual cassette players with earphones. Students are encouraged to rewind the cassette and listen to the song as many times as they want. Some work on sounds and spelling follows this computer work.

Procedure

Before Class

1. Choose a song by one of your students' favorite singers or bands (to motivate the students to carry out the activity) that is appropriate for the level you are teaching, preferably one with vocabulary or grammar points you have been working on.
2. Make as many cassette copies of the song as you need (one for each cassette player).
3. Type the words of the song using a text reconstruction program (e.g., Eclipse; see References and Further Reading).

Session 1: Computer Lab

1. Give examples of different spellings for the same sound.
2. Tell your students how to start the text reconstruction software and play the cassette. Tell them to feel free to stop the cassette and rewind it as many times as necessary for them to understand the words.
3. Ask the students to rebuild the song on screen as they listen to it.
4. Encourage the students to try spelling words they don't know. This will make them realize that similar sounds can be spelled differently.

Session 2: In Class

1. Go over the song. Discuss new vocabulary and recycle grammar points.
2. Place the students in small groups. Make each group responsible for one or two different sounds.
3. Ask the students to list the different ways in which those sounds can be spelled and to select words from the song that exemplify those ways.
4. Give each group a dictionary, and dictate a few words that they probably do not know. Ask them to transcribe the sounds and locate the words in the dictionary.

Caveats and Options

1. If you do not have a cassette player and an earphone for each computer, play the song for all the students on a single cassette player. Monitor the playback and rewind features yourself.
2. Instead of dictating the words yourself, ask one group of students to dictate new words to another. If you wish, do this as a competition among groups.

References and Further Reading

Eclipse [Computer software]. (n.d.) Available: ftp.latrobe.edu.au Directory: pub/CELIA/english/dos/cloze File: eclipse1.exe; gopher://gopher.latrobe.edu.au/Information Technology Services/La Trobe Archive/pub/CELIA/english/dos/cloze/eclipse1.exe

Contributor

José Pedro Fantin is an EFL teacher, a computer science student, and a teacher trainer/technology coordinator in Porto Alegre, Brazil (e-mail: jpfantin@pro.via-rs.com.br).

Campus Quiz

Levels
Low intermediate +

Aims
Develop reference skills
Practice question forms
Find useful information

Class Time
2–3 class sessions

Preparation Time
15 minutes before
Session 1
60 minutes before final
session

Resources
Computer for every
three to five students
Reference material on
your institution
Authoring software

In this activity students use a range of readily available authentic reference sources to create their own computer-based quiz. In the process of preparing their own quizzes and answering those prepared by other groups, the students acquire new information about the environment in which they are studying (or are about to study). The teacher has opportunities to observe their language shortfalls both in the preparation phase and while editing the quizzes before the final session. Final versions of the quizzes can be stored for reuse, possibly as self-access material.

Procedure

1. Assemble a range of texts (e.g., maps, calendars, timetables, prospectuses, student guides, library guides, advertising literature, internal telephone directories, photographs, reports) relating to the relevant institution(s) where the students are studying (or are about to study). Include a variety of information sources and enough copies for every group to have access to several different types of text.
2. Author a very short and simple quiz, using question-and-answer authoring software (see References and Further Reading). In the quiz, demonstrate a variety of question types, and relate them to the institution. Make copies of the quiz for each group of students.

Session 1

1. Ask the students what they will need to know when they start studying at a new institution. Write some of their suggestions on the blackboard. (The questions they suggest may even match some of your own quiz questions.)

2. Group the students at the computers. Ask them to take the quiz you have prepared, using the software. Visit each group to ensure that the students understand how to use the software.
3. Distribute the reference sources to the groups of students.
4. Direct the students to prepare, in groups, a 10-question quiz to help new students get to know their learning environment. Visit the groups to comment and advise.
5. After Session 1, edit the students' quizzes on disk. If you wish, merge some of the quizzes so that each quiz has 20 or 30 items rather than 10. Make sure (if you can) that the questions and answers are correct, and delete any questions that are asked more than once. Make a note of any frequently occurring language errors, particularly those relating to question forms. Copy the quizzes onto disks.

Session 2

1. Distribute the quizzes on disk, and have the students answer quizzes produced by other groups. Allow access to the original sources so that the students can check their answers.
2. At the end of the session, allow a few minutes for class discussion. The students may want to vote for the best quiz or discuss the answers to some of the questions. If you wish, comment on some of the language errors you noticed when you were editing the quizzes

Caveats and Options

1. The type of authoring software recommended for this activity is very easy to use, but students with no previous experience with the software may need a second session to prepare their quizzes on disk.
2. Advanced classes may be able to prepare and author their quizzes in Session 1. Lower level classes may need a second preparation session before they exchange their final product with other groups.
3. In a mixed-ability class, give weaker students less linguistically demanding texts, such as timetables, calendars, or maps.
4. Give each group a different theme for the quiz (e.g., finding your way around campus, university staff, university departments).
5. Save the final quizzes for reuse on a self-access basis.

References and Further Reading

Choicemaster [Computer software]. (n.d.). London: Wida Software/Eurocentres.

Prompt [Computer software]. (n.d.). New York: Gessler Educational Software.

Q and A Plus [Computer software]. (n.d.). New Alyth, Australia: Lochee.

Question Mark [Computer software]. (n.d.). London: Question Mark Computing.

Testmaster [Computer software]. (n.d.). London: Wida Software/Eurocentres.

Contributor

Hilary Nesi is a lecturer in the Centre for English Language Teacher Education at the University of Warwick, England. Her research interests include computer-assisted language learning and English for academic purposes materials development (e-mail: elraf@snow.csv.warwick.ac.uk).

Interpreting Data

Levels
High intermediate +

Aims
Gather information
about personal habits/
routines
Transfer information
into graphs/tables and
write about it

Class Time
1–2 hours

Preparation Time
15 minutes

Resources
Computer for every two
students
Word-processing
software
Spreadsheet software
Printer

As part of the International English Language Test, students are required to study a graph, table, or diagram and write 150 words about the information presented. Teachers with intermediate to advanced students focus on this area as part of their overall writing program. This activity is useful as an introduction to interpreting data. The students work together on an interview schedule and transfer information obtained into numerical form in a table or graph. Students then write about the information gathered by other groups. The teacher collects a writing sample from students, and students are exposed to other class members' writing.

Procedure

1. Arrange the students in pairs and ask them to decide on a habit about which they could question people (e.g., how many hours they sleep each night).
2. Allow the students 15–20 minutes to question native and nonnative speakers (or different nationality or age groups) and ask them to collate their responses.
3. In the computer class, instruct the students to enter the data they have collected and compose a graph using the spreadsheet software. Have them print the graph and save the file. Circulate, comment, and assist with the graphs.
4. Direct the students to swap disks or computers and compose a short text on the data in the graph. Circulate, comment, and give advice on the writing.
5. Tell the students to save the written text and print it. Give the printout to the students who created the graph.
6. Direct the students to correct the writing, and lead a discussion on what to write about when interpreting data in graphs and tables.

Caveats and Options

1. Before doing this activity, the students need basic skills in developing spreadsheets and basic word-processing skills.
2. If you wish, develop a worksheet with instructions for the students.
3. This lesson can serve as an introduction to computer-assisted writing. Students who are already skilled in these areas can enhance their work by changing fonts, point sizes, and other word-processing features.
4. For a follow-up oral information-gap exercise, tell the students to leave their names off the graphs and the written texts and to print them on separate pages. Distribute the graphs and the written texts, and instruct the students to circulate and ask questions about the graphs and texts in order to match them.
5. Copy each graph or table onto an overhead transparency, and have the students read the text to match the graph. Elicit alterations and additions to the written text.
6. Give the students one of the written texts, and ask them to present it in a different graphic or tabular form.

Contributor

Gayle Coleman has a graduate diploma and an MA in applied linguistics and is a language instructor in the TESOL Programs, University of Queensland, Australia.

Let's Talk!

Levels
Low intermediate +

Aims
Practice speaking and
listening
Learn cooperatively
Learn classmates'
cultural background

Class Time
1 hour +

Preparation Time
15 minutes +

Resources
Computer for each
student
Earphones or
headphones for each
student (optional)

Many computer activities attempting to make students speak use discussion techniques based on what the computer presents. The drawback is that some students do not participate, and stronger ones can often monopolize the situation. Alternatively, shy groups and low-level students may not talk at all. In Let's Talk!, on the other hand, the program is split into two parts, and only one part is given to each student. The students can resolve the resulting information gap only by asking each other questions and answering them. The collaboration encouraged can be combined with competition between groups to produce a potentially very lively and motivating speaking class. The program, which is based upon a family, is presented as a genealogical data file; the hope is that the topic will stimulate interest, as people like talking about people.

Procedure

Before Class

1. Send e-mail to Paul Lewis (pndl@gol.com) for details on how to get the special software for this activity, which is available as shareware from the author and is currently limited to Macintosh-based systems. The program's starting point is a family tree; clicking on any of the members takes the student to that person's data file, from which the information can be accessed in a variety of forms, including pictures, text, and sounds. A built-in reference file provides help, particularly with world knowledge. A worksheet of tasks relating to the information within the program is available with the program itself. The worksheet can be amended as necessary.

2. Look through the program and the tasks that accompany it, and decide whether the tasks are appropriate for the class. If not, rewrite them. Photocopy the task sheets (one for each student) or write the questions on a black- or white board.
3. Copy the program onto each computer's hard drive, or give the students a disk and let them install it.

In Class

1. Put the students into pairs (A and B). Make sure A's and B's screens are turned away from each other.
2. Give out the task sheet and explain the activity. Stress the following points:
   - The students must not look at each other's screens.
   - They should work together to complete the questions. All the information can be found somewhere in the program.
   - All the discussion should be in English (unless you specify otherwise).
3. Launch the program. Make sure that in each pair one student is using Part A and the other, Part B.
4. Let the students discover the program on their own. They will be able to discover most of its facets easily by clicking on the buttons. If a student gets very lost at the beginning, give a few pointers on navigating the stack.
5. While the activity is going on, circulate, helping students with problems and encouraging plenty of interaction in English.
6. As a follow-up activity, have the students enter their own data file and print it out. Alternatively, have them do a project on family trees and related history.

Caveats and Options

1. Have the pairs compete to see which can complete the task sheet first.
2. To halve the number of computers needed, have two students share an A computer and two others share a B.

3. Have the students do the activity in groups of three or four (A, B, C, and D). It is hoped that this option will be built into the shareware program (see the read-me file for details).
4. Put your own customized data files (e.g., biography, work history) into the program (see the read-me file for details).

References and Further Reading

Lewis, P. (1994). *Interaction patterns within the CALL environment: From psycholinguistics to programs.* Unpublished master's dissertation, University of Brighton, England.

Contributor

Paul Lewis teaches at Kinjogakuin University and Aichi-Shukutoku Junior College, in Nagoya, Japan. The activity above formed part of his master's dissertation (Brighton University, England) (e-mail: pndl@gol .com).